Backpack to Rucksack

Insight Into Leadership & Resilience From Military Experts

Daniel Zia Joseph
M.S. Organizational Psychology

Independently Published

3960 W Point Loma Blvd
Suite H80
San Diego, CA 92110
combatpsych.com

BACKPACK TO RUCKSACK

Also Available

For Professionals

Workbook: Cognitive Tools for Leaders
Daniel Zia Joseph

Backpack To Rucksack

Insight Into Leadership & Resilience By Military Experts

Daniel Zia Joseph
M.S. Organizational Psychology

Published independently
3960 W Point Loma Blvd, Suite H80, San Diego, CA 92110
www.combatpsych.com

Paperback ISBN: 9798840161647
Hardcover ISBN: 9798371363923

Library of Congress Control Number: 2022915343

First paperback edition: January 2023

Edited by: Curren Unruh
Cover art by: Daniel Zia Joseph
Layout by: Daniel Zia Joseph
Photographs by: Daniel Zia Joseph

This manuscript has been officially cleared for public release by

DEPARTMENT OF DEFENSE
DEFENSE OFFICE OF PREPUBLICATION AND SECURITY REVIEW
1155 DEFENSE PENTAGON
WASHINGTON, DC 20301-1155

DEDICATION

To every Veteran & military mentor in this book, thank you.

CONTENTS

DEDICATION

ACKNOWLEDGEMENTS

FOREWARD

PREFACE

INTRODUCTION

GLOSSARY

1 - MILITARY & ME 1

2 - ATTRITION, HUMILITY & CALM 20

3 - HYPE & STEREOTYPES 42

4 - COMMAND CLIMATE IS MAKE OR BREAK 63

5 - TRUE IDENTITY 89

6- COURAGE TO STAY AUTHENTIC 113

7- SOMEONE BIGGER, BETTER, & STRONGER 133

8 - KINDNESS IS STRENGTH 152

9 - DO IT OR SHUT UP 172

10 - TAKE THE CAPE OFF 188

11 - AGE IS AN ASSET 208

12 - PAY ATTENTION TO PACE 229

13 - YOU'RE WELCOME HERE 249

14 - PEOPLE OVER POLITICS 264
15 - FAMILY FAR FROM HOME 280
16 - RELATIONSHIP MANAGEMENT 295
17 - GARRISON, FIELD, & YOU 311
18 - DON'T FEAR TYRANTS 326
About The Author 341

ACKNOWLEDGEMENTS

Sitting at a table drinking whiskey with a combat Veteran I was describing my anxiety response to sparring on the mats in Jiu-Jitsu.

"My heart rate increases, vision narrows, and body becomes rigid. Chest constriction. I feel a heavy weight crushing my stomach. Time slows. I lose the ability to speak. I flash back into a dark empty place that just has no words, but a lot of raw feelings, trapped between flight and freeze. People notice and it's awkward so I isolate. Later, when I finally get away to regain my breath that's when my mind begins racing. My situational awareness spikes off the charts and seeps into every crevice of the room, detecting threats. I feel like I'm being chased by an invisible monster. Sometimes I can get stuck there for days. Exhausting. That's when I want to be dead, to not live on in the dark misery of it all."

Looking up, I saw tears welling in Chris' eyes. "You just described everything I feel about combat in Iraq." Damn.

Long pause. We understood each other. We both did our best not to cry. So, there it is. Soldiers like him are my why. Chris and the Soldiers I know who grapple with suicide are why I wrote this book.

FOREWARD

Twelve service members I served with killed themselves. Eleven Marines and one Soldier. Nine were Marines who deployed with me. This is a Cancer that needs to be cut out by addressing it. The solution is not tossing them aside. Some commands have done that before due to an arrogant or lazy nature driven by fear of a tarnished image from political weakness. Personally, as a leader, I do not wish to be led by anyone who is arrogant or who is not invested in my successfully protecting those to my left and right against all enemies, physical or mental. Repeated failures in leadership cause some of the finest men and women in the world to suffer in silence.

Leaders are not perfect humans. Whether in the military or civil service, they are everyday men and women desiring to lead others through life and death-scenarios, affecting lives and world outcomes on a deep level. Leaders must be willing to define EVERY piece of themselves and question themselves from the perspective of a scientific/ spiritual process that will drive perfection.

This book is not meant to be a perfect answer to leadership problems and failure, but a tool for enhancing perspective and a hell of a piece to consider. Our nation's success increases when you enable those serving with you to harness their absolute max capability. This book is full of lessons learned from multiple perspectives. It also involves prestigious warriors who accomplished far more than me. They stand on what I would call the Highest Mountain, the base of which all should strive to achieve.

My modus operandi is that to place the mission first, you must with the utmost of your ability, place your troops above yourself and your mission. You heard right. Slow down leaders before you lose your minds! Company-grade leaders and lower-rank subordinates both hold the keys to influence those above them and impact training for the better. There is a point to this that the leading community has forgotten.

Enlisted and Officer Experience:

I spent nine years with the U.S. Marines as a 6312(Avionics–Comm/NAV/Weapons) and an 0331 (Machine Gunner-Section Leader) as well as six years in the ARNG (Army National Guard) with four of those as a Commissioned Officer–12A in a Combat Engineer for a BEB.

My civilian career includes Professional Firefighting, Paramedic, and a TAC-P (Tactical Paramedic) for multiple SWAT teams serving as an Officer 1st, Medic 2nd. I've been asked, "What's your political angle?" My truthful response is that I have NO angle. My goal is simple: Defend those who cannot defend themselves, uphold the laws as they are, keep evil from expanding, and be present medically/

mentally for those said to be having the "worst day of their life."

What Combat Taught Me About Leadership:

Combat deployments taught me that leaders are not those who boast about themselves or yell "follow me" in the heat of combat. They don't always have identifying rank. Some are subordinates, junior within the ranks. In my case, a Private First Class (E-3) was one of the best leaders I have met to date. This is important. Leaders must identify individuals in our organizations who can drive mission success, enhancing our abilities by utilizing their own.

The combat environment also taught me how to completely rely on men and women I hardly knew. Some of them mentally sharp. Others not so much, but when it came time to get to work, they were complete animals. If we as leaders will humble ourselves, we can relate to these Patriots on a personal level. I am not saying put yourself in a position of fraternization. In war, personal relationships are vital for crushing the enemy. Some of my own leaders demonstrated this before I started leading. We would have walked through Hell with them without question.

I want hard Warriors around, not soft Soldiers. Part of this is being able to turn a switch on and off for the appropriate environment. We need tools to fight mentally. A "good" military leader is firm and fair, but a "great" leader invests every opportunity to sharpen the minds and hearts of those he is appointed to lead. This is not a game of, "Do it because I said." Give the WHY. Provide subordinates with what they need to be absolutely violent and successful and do not forget to address the "Elephant in the Room" – Mental Health. Not only for follow on tasks, but also for times of isolation or when reintegrating into society.

Before the next war, I would demand that we strengthen our bodies and our minds to both be resilient. Warriors that never waiver, hungry to decisively prepare themselves mentally, physically, and emotionally to decimate anyone or anything of this natural earth that dares to infringe our flag. Many leaders have forgotten what it means to be a vicious killer for their country while having restraint where necessary. In war or common life, having an emotional connection to the "killer" mindset for the defense of someone else or yourself does not make one weak. Rather, it makes one more effective in decision-making and more violent when that decision is made, whether hasty or deliberate.

Once again, I want smart Warriors that are well-trained, have their own minds, able to aggressively and meticulously carry out my intent with or without me present. Having just a "Soldier" mentality will leave us with higher casualty rates, unstable mental health, and reckless mistakes. This happens when subordinates are unable to think for themselves and are told to only follow orders (even unlawful ones).

To Past, Present, and Future Leaders

Dan asked if he could put a bit about me in his book. At first, I wondered what made me a good fit. I trusted him to write a small piece of my story to add to the dynamic of what he was trying to convey. At the time I am writing this, I have known him for several years. From time to time, we have deep discussions from a place of bettering our minds and gaining perspective. We discuss leadership principles (educational vs. reality), and dynamics of basic human psychology regarding both subordinates and leaders. The point of our conversations is to understand what is required to gain mission success given the diverse backgrounds of the Warriors serving WITH us as leaders.

Mistakes are part of the journey. Dan has many times discussed with me his failures, wayward past, and how he "used to be." My response is: it does not matter what you have done. I know who you are today, and who you are today is why I trust you and call you a brother. He is a believer like me and has the heart of a Warrior. He is trustworthy, and forthcoming, loves his troops, and would do anything under the sun to make them successful in any environment. By telling his story, he might lift the weight off of someone else like him within the ranks. Helping them realize that it is not the past that defines a Warrior, but rather what they have become and what they are willing to do.

My desire is for all of you to read this book in its entirety with a humble perspective to be a better leader (current or future) and the intent to increase the effectiveness of your capabilities.

Austin,
Firefighter-Paramedic
TAC-P (SWAT)Sheriff Deputy
USMC 6312/0331(Prior Enlisted)
12A US Army Commissioned Officer

PREFACE

Each chapter, excluding chapter 1, begins with terms and definitions related to leadership psychology and are built into four sections:

SECTION 1: INTRODUCTION TO THE TOPIC
Particular growth opportunity involving wisdom shared by my military friend

SECTION 2: A GOOD MILITARY LEADER
Introducing the main character and inspiration of the chapter

SECTION 3: PSYCHOLOGICAL APPLICATION
Citing relevant contemporary research involving organizational psychology and human neurobiology

SECTION 4: LEADERSHIP ADVICE
Specific quote(s) of advice and how they influenced me

INTRODUCTION

Message from my Soldier who is a suicide attempt survivor:

I spent five years in the Army as an Enlisted Soldier. I've experienced so much in those years. From the ups and downs of everyday life to the Army life. I've spent time stationed around the world and learned so much from all that served alongside me, from the lowest Soldier to the officers. Those five years haven't been so kind. Depression crept up as a result of being away from family, on isolated bases, lacking healthy outlets, and being around others having issues with depression/suicide. On top of all this was a stigma about coming forward to get help.

During my time, I have gone from having friends to being alone and on my own, struggling to cope with my issues thus causing my depression to get worse. I felt I had to keep it a secret and never say anything, which isn't the case. You gotta speak up before it's too late and you go from depressed to attempting to take your own life: SUICIDE IS NOT THE ANSWER. Believe me, I tried it and woke up on the other side with a second chance.

To Those Struggling:

I wanted to reach out and say you're not alone. Yes, there actually are others like you all out here in the world. It's a sign of true strength for you to admit you need help. Don't listen to those that say it's weakness; they don't know the weight that it puts on one's shoulders. Find a leader who will listen to you, I don't care how high up the chain of command you have to go. I talked to my LT, the guy writing this book, and he cared!

To Leaders:

I'd just ask those leaders out there that you take a step off your perch and come down to your Junior Enlisted Soldiers. Truly ask how they're all doing because just one small effort could change anyone's mood and day. Leadership needs to stop worrying about their unit's image and reputation and actually take the time to learn something from those under them.

Doing this, I feel, would truly lower the number of suicides in the military tenfold. Leaders, don't wait till it's too late to speak up. Trust me, you'll be amazed at the difference it makes. When leaders truly care, it feels like being free as a huge weight is lifted.

How I Turned My Life Around

After leaving the Army I turned to what I knew best: horses and the country. I got a job at a resort/dude ranch giving guests trail rides where I'm still trying to take it day by day throughout the struggle

AGAIN, TO THOSE STRUGGLING ALONE, KEEP ON FIGHTING. YOU ARE ALL SO WORTH IT.

Cody
Wrangler @ Alisal Guest Ranch and Resort
former Enlisted 12B (Combat Engineer)
Retired SGT 12B (Combat Engineer)

GLOSSARY

9-Line: emergency medical evacuation request procedure

AO: Area of Operations

Assault Force: friendly element maneuvering towards the enemy

BAH: Basic Allowance for Housing

BCT: Basic Combat Training (i.e., "Boot camp")

BOLC: Basic Officer Leader Course

C4: Composition C-4, plastic explosive primarily made from RDX

CASEVAC: Casualty evacuation

Concertina wire: large coil razor wire, antivehicle obstacle

C-RAM: Counter-Rocket, Artillery, Mortar weapon system

CQC: Close-quarters Combat

DA: Direct Action

EA: Engagement Area

EBOLC: Engineer Basic Officer Leadership Course

ENDEX: End of Exercise

FTX: Field Training Exercise

Ghillie suit: full body camouflage mimicking surrounding foliage

Green Berets: United States Army Special Forces

HVT: High-Value Targets

JB: Joint Base

JBC-P: Join Battle Command Platform, vehicle mounted computer

KT: Key Terrain (Major or Minor elements)

LOA: Limit of Advance

Major Terrain Features (5) : Hill, Ridge, Valley, Saddle, Depression

Minor Terrain Features (3): Draw, Spur, Cliff

M4: 5.56mm Carbine (compact rifle)

M240B: 7.62mm medium machine gun

M249 (SAW): 5.56mm light machine gun (Squad Automatic Weapon)

MEPS: Military Entrance Processing Stations

MARSOC: United States Marine Forces Special Operations Command

NCO: Non-Commissioned Officer

NOD: night optic device

NVG: night vision goggle

OCS: Officer Candidate School

OIC: Officer in Charge

OML: Order of Merit List

OER: Officer Evaluation Reports

OPFOR: Opposing Force

PACE Plan: Primary, Alternate, Contingency, Emergency

PCS: Permanent Change of Station

Priming charge: primary detonation device used to initiate explosion

RFI: request for information

ROE: Rules of Engagement

RTO: Radio telephone operator

Sapper: military combat engineer (French for "spadework/trench")

SBF: support by fire, element suppressing enemy, enable assault force

SEAL: United States Navy Sea, Air, and Land (SEAL) Teams

SF: Special Forces

SFAS: Special Forces Assessment and Selection

Sitrep: situation report

SME: Subject Matter Expert

SoF: Special Operations Forces

SO: Special Operations

TDY: Temporary Duty

TRP: Target Reference Point

XO: Executive Officer

BACKPACK TO RUCKSACK

1 - MILITARY & ME

"His object should be, to gain the love of his men, by treating them with every possible kindness and humanity, enquiring into their complaints, and when well founded, seeing them redressed."

\- **BARON VON STEUBEN** *(1794)*

Volunteered to help George Washington found the Continental Army

Let me be the first to admit I actively wrestle with the astounding complexity of leadership. It's unpredictable. People are messy. Constellations of variables exist. I wish every leadership decision came with a clear right-or-wrong response just like an academic test so I could know exactly what to do next time. *Nope!* Rarely is there a perfect answer when it comes to managing human beings and all the emotions we bring to the table. All I can say is that the clearer a leader's mind is, the better decisions they will make. Simple problem sets in the workplace can quickly be compounded in difficulty by distressed psychological states of decision-makers. Military personnel know this all too well.

Hurry up and wait. Urgency can make everything an emergency. Stress is programmed into our combat training which increases the intensity of life both at work and at home. It's hard knowing how to rest. Before we know it, we take out our frustration on others. We must learn how to counteract prolonged stress states with science-based psychological tools and mental resilience. Self-regulation prevents self-medication. This is arguably more important than knowing how to fire a rifle. Post 9/11, more veterans died by suicide than in combat by about 4:1. We owe it to them to deepen our awareness.

My goal with this book is to be a guide in navigating through psychological principles related to leadership. Having never been deployed to a combat zone, I hesitate to claim the role of military leadership subject matter expert. Instead, I see myself as an observer who listens and takes notes. Working alongside service members having multiple combat tours deepened my perspective. A few gave me permission to share their stories which I'm humbled by. Brutality of war seems impossible to convey in words. Many times, when my friends and mentors spoke about their past deployments, I found my jaw hanging. They shared things I could never imagine telling others, and it burns me to think how hellish this makes their inner world.

Even without deploying overseas, the amount of chaos we must manage is incredible. War throws gas on that fire. Leaders in the military must take into consideration the unspoken weight carried by so many of our peers and subordinates because of the battles they have experienced. I'm forever impacted by this. For anyone in the military, it's important to have a healthy mind ready to absorb constant shock, just like the suspension of a vehicle built to take on rough terrain.

This isn't just for us. Everyone can grow their mindset. Knowledge about managing our brains offers universal benefits. I invite those outside the military to learn as well. Leaders of any organization will benefit from these cross-disciplinary skill sets regarding self-control and professional human relationships.

Curating leadership advice, I wrote this book to focus on positive characteristics I admire in several amazing military service members. They helped shape me before and during my time of service. A few cherished moments with them outweigh all the hard times. Writing their words on these pages while I reflected on our time together somehow helped me feel like I was sitting alongside them. Their warm smiles eclipse any harsh scowls I have come across. They have taught me to focus on the wins in life no matter how small.

Gratitude reminds me to spotlight the good while acknowledging that any bad situations serve the purpose of providing contrast. Like any human, I have my biases, so it's important to admit subjectivity when I define something as "good" or "bad". Grad school hammered this point home! Quoting scientific research publications throughout this book is my way of trying to stay balanced. I hope you find objective truth and substance without any of my personal agenda clouding the message.

My contract in the military spans a total of 1,344 days starting January 2019 and ending September 2022. I was 32 years old when I joined, having spent several years running my own business. My path in the Army involved Basic Training (BCT), Officer Candidate School (OCS), Engineer Basic Officer Leadership Course (EBOLC), and Combat Engineer (Sapper) Platoon Leadership.

Once I decided to join the military and before I shipped out for training I sold my car, gave away my possessions, and moved out of my apartment. I went on a nomadic journey that involved crashing on friends' couches, floors, and sometimes secretly in church basements. (See *Six Figure Couch Surfer).*

My military journey was nothing as expected. Basic Training was delayed by almost a year due to MEPS having to clear me after shoulder and knee surgeries. Once I graduated from BCT I failed land navigation in OCS and recycled from Alpha Company back to day 1 with Bravo Company delaying my commission 30 days later than anticipated. A few days before the branching ceremony in OCS, whereby we discover what jobs we will have in the military, I decided at the last minute to select the Corps of Engineers to pursue a career as an Army diver. However, the global COVID pandemic shut down our school options and altered our career trajectories due to lockdowns and stop-movement orders. Dive school was off the table, and I was due to ship out for my first duty station for an unknown job: OPFOR (Opposing Force) Sapper platoon leader.

The list continues. I thought deploying was a sure thing. I joined the Army to leave my home state of California and see the world abroad. However, my orders sent me right back to California where I had no idea Army bases existed. On top of that, I didn't know there was such a thing as non-deployable units. I went to such a unit and never once deployed overseas. More unexpected changes were to come. Just before the last year of my contract, my father died of heart disease on the 4th of July 2021. The American Red Cross helped ensure I was by his side when he passed, but many service members sacrificed such things in the name of duty. Three months later I was rear-ended in a hit-and-run collision that totaled my vehicle and aggravated a neck injury that occurred in training. Due to the injury, I was on a medical profile that limited me from being in the field my last year. None of this was part of the plan, but I needed to accept reality and move forward. Mindset was everything.

Expect flux. Uncertainty and change were constant during my time in the military. Mission planning never perfectly aligns with real word scenarios, and constant last-minute changes require flexibility and quick adaptation. I had experienced this same phenomenon in entrepreneurial startups. Ideas are great on a sterile whiteboard, but in the field, numerous unforeseen issues arise. It keeps things interesting. Some solutions are immediate while others take a long time to implement. Some solutions don't work at all. That's ok. Failure is a part of the growth journey for any leader, but so is getting back up and learning from mistakes.

Consider my time in OCS. During land navigation through the dense forest of Georgia, I'd be in a frantic run towards my intended destination while trying to read my map and compass only to trip over a log and end up with a mouthful of dirt and moss. *Ooof!* I had to gather everything up, establish my direction, and pick up again. No matter what happened or how hard I fell, the map and compass were true and reliable resources. Good advice is the same way. Being able to fall back on sound wisdom from my friends and mentors helped me reorient myself and head back in the right direction. No matter how many mistakes I made, and I know I made many, I could always regain my bearing and try again.

As a junior officer, I accepted that most things were out of my control, except for my attitude. I could always work on that. New officers require mentoring and training to understand how their specific military unit functions. It takes time. Initially, my positional authority was low. Many people and scenarios I wanted to change were beyond my level of influence. There was no point in fighting reality. I mastered the art of keeping my mouth shut unless I could affect change. *Carry on!*

Whenever else possible, I took ownership of any variable I could control no matter how small. It's the little things. Enabling myself to optimize these few areas in my life gave me newfound confidence and a sense of discipline. My leadership style, finances, physical fitness, and education all incrementally improved. Every step counted. Resilience, creativity, and self-efficacy absolutely took off as I sought constant improvement. Though I must admit the pain and discomfort of Army life rocked my world, the toughest parts of the military brought about the most growth. Looking back now I needed all the good and bad to evolve. I especially needed the right people around me to provide encouragement and support.

Relationships helped pull me through the hard times. I couldn't do it alone. The biggest truth the military taught me is that the most valuable asset of any organization is its people. Organizations and policies are inherently lifeless. Without anyone willing to follow, a leader walks alone. We don't often discuss compassion, empathy, and love in the military, but that is exactly what it takes to keep from falling apart. I've seen strong people crash into a wall mentally and emotionally because they lacked sincere connection. I almost lost several colleagues to this personally, and it's for them I write this book. How can I say that I want to help support veterans struggling with PTSD, depression, or suicide if I don't apply this to leadership on the active-duty side?

Shared struggles are powerful motivators. Hardships can galvanize the military community. Shared suffering bonded us beyond what I anticipated. Several of these relationships I made will certainly last a lifetime. Military brothers and sisters helped me keep hope through difficult times. I leaned on them for advice, encouragement, and connection when far from home. Whenever I felt alone or stuck, I called on them for heartfelt guidance. Many encouraged me to write this book because of how deeply my experiences resonate with theirs. I am grateful for their love and support. This book is as much their story as it is mine.

Thank you to every service member in this book. You are all encouraging examples to me and to countless others, I pray. As I write these words, I happily reflect on just how much you shaped my life. Many deficits in my character and mindset were filled because you lived out lives of discipline, adventure, and assertion. Thanks for being my first battle buddies.

Most of all, on behalf of my father (from Kirkuk) and mother (from Habbaniyah), as well as my entire family, thank you to all who fought for freedom in Iraq during the Global War on Terror. As the child of Iraqi immigrants seeking refuge from violence and oppression, I feel I owe you a debt. All I can think to do is try and strengthen our armed forces by encouraging holistic leadership through book writing. I hope to do more. Freedom here in the USA is worlds away from what my parents told me they experienced growing up. You helped pay that price. We are forever grateful to call America our home where we are afforded liberties we otherwise would not have. This truly is the greatest nation in the world.

Now, remember to fight the war within.

MY LIFE BEFORE THE MILITARY

I lived in San Diego, CA, on the sunny harbor overlooking the downtown skyline next door to my favorite cafe. With a nice Mediterranean climate, the ocean breeze brought in the smell of saltwater through the bright, open windows. Sunshine flooded my living room, along with the sounds of birds singing. Sailboats decorated the cool blue harbor, and palm trees swayed in relaxation. From this updated luxury apartment with white kitchen cabinets, beautiful dark wood floors, and in-unit laundry, I lived the life I wanted, or so I thought, making a comfortable six-figure salary. Life was amazing, at least on the surface.

I pursued authentic interests and avoided busy work. Relationships inspired my business development;

I enjoyed my clients. I didn't aim to please any authority figure and my life was fully in my control. There was no rush to meet deadlines, so I could conduct my business with courtesy. Money was just a byproduct of my passion.

My income was generated around remote, freelance work. My industry of choice was the intersection of the genetic research industry and software engineering. They call this industry bioinformatics. Software coders create machine learning algorithms edging towards AI to predictively identify and cure disease. I loved these scientists. They were introverts like me and made me feel accepted as a fellow nerd. We were supportive of each other. We hated the idea of selling out to investors to be considered valuable. Passion for science drove us.

One company I worked with had the power to tell a barely pregnant woman all the diseases the child carried that would manifest decades down the road in adulthood. These companies have the potential to use gene editing tools based on both software and biological molecules to snip out bad genes and replace them with optimal genes. Imagine manufacturing human embryos genetically screened for disease and selected for optimal performance.

For now, the law is that scientists can't edit a human and have a woman give birth to the altered code. The modified embryo must be incinerated within 14 days of creation. Despite this law, there is at least one known case in which two genetically modified humans were born. The human arms race is just beginning.

While these clients of mine sought to change the trajectory of humanity, I wanted to find successful companies to work with. Work for me was cerebrally stimulating, rewarding, and fun. During my workdays, I had plenty of time for Jiu-Jitsu, where I could hang with world-famous black belts. Even though I was around them daily, I could barely mitigate butterflies in my stomach whenever I crossed paths with these legends. Every training session was epic.

On a deeply personal note, about Jiu-Jitsu, it reconnected me with my body. I noticed my breath, muscle tension, and anxiety. After years of disassociation, I felt present again. Scary things started coming back up. Something from the past felt stuck, frozen in time. Coaches unknowingly guided me towards having to face this inner darkness. Many of my mentors on the mat were in the military and I trusted them. My heart was pounding out of my chest, and I wanted to run away. I'd go home with thoughts of being inadequate, a failure, and unwanted. Dark feelings set in. Thoughts in my head told me to stop trying to learn how to fight. Instead, I kept coming back to the mats.

Earlier in this book, I mentioned my struggle with self-medication through excessive alcohol consumption, parties, and social distractions, including friends who made poor life decisions involving illicit drug use. There was a powerful reason I sought escapism. At a young age I experienced repeated physical abuse and after that sexual assault. Shame crushed me.

Physical abuse during childhood trained me to not defend myself. It off lined my motor response to fighting off a threat. Easy target. This made me vulnerable for abuses I experienced later in life. These experiences put my brain in overdrive. I suppressed it all as deeply as possible. I didn't want to face it. I couldn't. This took its toll on my body and mind. Anxiety was always high, so I needed to find ways to override the signal. The noise was the only way I knew how. I sought as much chaos as possible to drown my pain. Unfortunately, my newfound medicine now slowly began to poison me.

After years of battling hangovers and waking up to horrible life decisions, I began to make my way back to faith and spirituality. Reading hundreds of self-help books, I became obsessed with psychology. Meditation helped me delve deeper into past trauma and the darkness within. Breath control was a powerful new tool I used to guide my mind through tension. Jiu-Jitsu helped me heal, but the cost was that it brought about flashbacks from hidden memories of physical abuse. Experiencing the flight and freeze response in front of my coaches and sparring partners was heavy.

Despite this weightiness, my coaches helped me stick with it and not give up. True warriors never made me feel weak. Instead, they imparted their strength. They told me not to quit. This was a spiritual and physical journey. Faith helped. I believed in a restored version of myself. I didn't have to apologize for my existence anymore. I left the party scene and slowly broke addictive cycles. Next, I was sweating out my stress on the mats while bonding with healthy military friends. They encouraged me. I needed encouragement because this is a long, messy process. Fear never stopped calling my name. I constantly wrestled against anxiety every time I parked my car and walked into the gym. Getting beat up on the mats made me feel like a victim again. It tore me up. Memories echoed. However, as scared as I was of facing my weakness, there was nowhere else to go.

Past memories get heavy. This was a painful, bloody fight that took me down to depths within myself I thought would end my life altogether. Repressed emotions felt like heavy chains wrapped around my stomach with a sinking anchor pulling me down through the floor into a hellish black abyss. Breathing was difficult under all the weight. I wanted to die. But I wanted to live more.

Every training session is a small win. Growth is still happening. I'm not done healing from anxieties of the past and probably never will be. I long to escape despair. I still fall on my face. I want to numb out from the revving thoughts and hypervigilance. But despite the odds, I'll never stop fighting. Even when I get laid out, I know to always get back up. After all, I didn't die in that low place. Coaches, mentors, and friends supported me. After surviving this dark chapter of facing my past wounds, I learned there was more life experience I wanted. This time I wanted to be present for it. I sought a new purpose beyond myself. Time for a new foundation. Which path to take was the question.

MY "WHY"

So why leave all the good stuff in life for the Army at 32? Well, I asked myself this question a lot over the past thousand days. One day before I joined, while invoicing my six figures from the beach, I got a call from a military friend who wanted to catch up. He was a Special Operations Forces Platoon Leader at the time and was in town between deployments to the Middle East.

War was brewing hot at this time in both Syria and Iraq. News media streamed videos of ISIS massacring men, women, and children around the clock. My friend was part of a community of warriors facing this evil and killing the enemy. Here I was enjoying the sunshine at the beach every day while he was fighting in battles across the world to liberate victims of tyranny. My parents are from Iraq. American service members I knew had fought to free the towns and villages my family originated from. This was the biggest reason I joined the military.

My parents barely escaped Baghdad with their lives in the 1970s when Saddam rose to power. Life was hell there. As children, they routinely lined up to applaud the public execution of political dissidents. Threats of death loomed constantly. Females especially had it bad. My mother's best friend was kidnapped by political officials as a young girl, never to be found again. The same evil men almost captured my own mother as they came knocking on her door in the middle of the night to drag her out of bed when she was around 16 years old. Men were regularly forced as conscripts into the military without proper clothing or weapons to fight with rifles pointed at their backs. Life in Iraq entailed constant violence, threats of sexual assault, and government surveillance. This was almost my fate.

Luckily, I was born in America about ten years after my parents escaped. It wasn't easy for them because their family members had to split up and find various routes out. Some were killed. I was raised to appreciate freedom. Being here in the states is no small thing. Friends I made in the military were all contributing to the cause of liberty and justice. My brother deployed as a Marine, as well, to do his part.

Evil exists beyond our comprehension in some places in the world. Hell on earth. What if I lived this daily? Dictatorship could have imprisoned my potential. My God-given freedom could have been subject to government control or entirely snuffed out. Only America would fight this. I admire anyone stepping into such darkness to fight terror. Heroes. They'd never call themselves that, but I do. I dig being friends with such awesome warriors. Again, this buddy of mine was on secret missions around the world fighting without any recognition. He didn't want it.

Many battles obscurely mentioned in the news where enemies were killed and hostages rescued were, in fact, operations involving elite units the public would never know to thank. My friends were there. They didn't say much about missions, yet they came back from multiple deployments having an ever-growing intensity for patriotic duty. Their energy was electric. Their eyes reflected weighty victories won in intense combat. They were constantly seeing death and killing enemies in dark corners of the world while I was living in a safe, small bubble kept safe by their sacrifice. I told myself I had to give back in some way and be even just a small, distant part of the global military family.

Outside of combat, these service members had discipline, big hearts, and a taste for adventure. Their presence in my life inspired me to be a better man. Every time we hung out, I had a mini existential crisis, wondering if I had what it took to be like them. Waking up at 4 am to train was routine for them. I longed for such motivation. Traveling the world to experience new cultures and lands grew their knowledge of our global ecosystem while I stayed put in one city. Learning new skills from tying knots to operating weapon systems and shaping explosive charges made my skills related to sending emails feel insubstantial. I wanted to get my hands dirty too while learning new things.

Physical fitness was also a powerful attractor. A casual workout or trail run with these friends left me keeled over and vomiting. Normal mornings for them involved waking up before sunrise to mountain bike in darkness with a headlamp or free dive in the ocean, all before sunrise. This was only the first workout of the day. The rest of the day could include skydiving, trail running, or surfing before capping off the night with a good beer. With a smile on their faces, they endured hours of physical exertion because they knew how precious every minute of free time was. After all, in their line of work, death is a normal risk. Living life to the fullest is their way of remaining brave despite what could loom ahead. I wanted to live life with the same open sense of freedom. I felt like I needed more pain and less comfort in my life. I needed to stop seeking leisurely exercise and develop a powerful new version of myself built on a significant mindset shift.

Fear gripped me whenever I contemplated leaving my predictable life routine. I felt compelled to break out of my bubble, yet I felt helplessly trapped within it. Vicariously I attempted to live through military friends, but that only goes a short distance. An ache grew within me to put on a uniform and train alongside them. But what about all this fear inside me? These friends were versions of myself I wished I could be but was too scared to attempt. I feared potential, and they wielded it like a broad sword. Every time we hung out, I leaned a little more towards joining the military.

I wasn't satisfied with who I was in the business world because I had a deep, primal urge to learn what it means to fight. This sort of raw energy remains painfully caged up as it growls and roars to be released. Day and night, it paces the cage inside like a lion pining for open terrain to sprint and roam free. Sitting at my desk seemed wrong. While I could absolutely accomplish the goals set before me, the reward was nominal.

Experiencing truly terrifying risks is what I wanted, not a contract negotiation on unvested equity. I turned away a potential $1.5 million gig to help a startup company grow from scratch because I didn't want to settle down and grow roots that locked me into a role revolving around my computer. At this point, I knew that no dollar amount could pay me to stay put. Money with startups is never guaranteed anyway. I wanted to step into what truly made me afraid. It wasn't business development or startup risks.

Most men and women in my career field either found a way to release it or simply drown the animal out with drugs and alcohol. Jiu-Jitsu helped me free the beast a little, but I wanted to build my life around learning the tough skills of self-mastery. Military friends demonstrated the stark contrast between being a civilian and becoming a trained warrior. Many were battle-hardened, and I was corporate soft.

After years of back and forth, I was about to age out of the military recruiting window. Wrestling with the freedom and income I had was wearing on me. Yet I knew there would always be an opportunity in the future to restart my business hustle. Hungry for challenges and inspired by these friends, I decided to finally make the jump. I signed the contract in 2018 after a few sports' injury-related surgeries and began my process of getting medically cleared to join.

AFTER MY DECISION

I doubted my own strength throughout life because I was convinced I was weak. Once I realized nobody was holding me back except myself, I knew it was time to make big changes. Joining the military was a powerful, positive decision and the hardest thing I have ever done. It was time to choose the path of suffering to personally experience my own resilience. I had no idea what was ahead which added to the exhilaration. Embracing uncertainty was already a newfound strength that I found pleasantly surprising. What was I getting myself into? Definitely some tough situations.

Enduring pandemic lockdowns on remote, desert Army bases is no easy feat. I had to quickly find my own solutions to emotional distress. How could I feel like I was growing when I felt isolated and stuck? I invested in my mindset. Obtaining my master's degree in Organizational Psychology allowed me to pay careful attention to mental health, job satisfaction, and morale throughout the organization. Applying what my military friends taught me before I joined helped me listen to the stories and lives around me. I learned that people are the most important part of an organization though many leaders overlook this as they focus on policies and systems.

Often, I caught myself regretting that I hadn't

joined earlier in life, but I remembered to stop comparing myself to others. Had I joined earlier, there was no way I could bring the knowledge I had at 32 years old. So rather than looking at what could have been, I chose gratitude for the path I took and the people I met. These brothers and sisters in the military will be like family to me for the rest of my life.

No two paths are ever the same. Being in the military has inherent risks that are subject to sudden change based on global events. I would never have expected a global pandemic to start during my time in training. I also didn't know there were nondeployable units in the military. Nothing about my military journey went the way I expected. Knowing I grew in the midst of such uncertainty has bolstered my resolve to meet and defeat upcoming difficulties in life.

Difficulties allow strength to manifest. Darkness serves to demonstrate the impact of having even a little light. Pain seasons the tasteful joys of pleasure. The littlest things mean the most. Suffering alongside others creates a bond unlike any other. All of this comes with a cost. Freedom, autonomy, and comfort are jettisoned once that contract is signed, but great things lie ahead. It’s a challenge most understandably don’t take.

The regret of not having done it would personally bother me for the rest of my life. My heart told me to join, and I was scared the whole time. Looking back now, I see more growth than I felt during the journey. Writing this book was my way of processing the past several years. Hope it helps.

LT DANIEL Z JOSEPH

1ST PLATOON

References:

United States. Army. & Steuben, Friedrich Wilhelm Ludolf Gerhard Augustin. & Doolittle, Amos. & Massachusetts. Militia. & United States. (1794). Regulations for the order and discipline of the troops of the United States To which is added, an appendix, containing the United States' Militia Act, passed in Congress, May, 1792. Printed at Exeter [N.H.] : by Henry Ranlet, for Thomas & Andrews, Faust's Statue, no. 46, Newbury-Street, Boston, MDCCXCIV. [1794]

2 - ATTRITION, HUMILITY & CALM

"People assume everyone in Special Forces looks huge. If you want to see which guy is SF, look for the lean guy who looks like he's been starved. We are endurance athletes. That's how we train for most of our pipeline."

- ***GREG*** *[Army Green Beret Officer]*

Attrition: reducing members of a group by prolonged stress or pressure

Equanimity: maintaining a calm, level-head during chaotic situations

Grit: persistent resilience and perseverance

SECTION 1: INTRODUCTION TO THE TOPIC

I'm at a beach house party in Santa Barbara with the wealthiest kids I have ever met. Some of my college classmates invited me to come hang out. Children of professional athletes, movie producers, and Hollywood actors are out and about. World-famous pro surfers, Olympic athletes, and movie stars come and go. Some students are famous entertainers and reality television stars. It's common to see characters from recent blockbuster movies and reality shows walking around in the flesh. A few have a knack for wearing sunglasses indoors. People riding by on beach cruisers shout and wave whenever they spot someone famous standing in the front yard. Though I feel invisible, I desperately want to belong. This is it. College life is my chance to make up for being uncool in high school.

Socioeconomically, this Southern California college world is foreign to me. Growing up, a lot of my peers attended academies and preparatory schools costing tens of thousands per year. Royalty. Many grew up living lives I only saw in movies. While in prep school, they learned to throw epic parties whenever parents were jet-setting around the globe. Driving Italian sports cars and swapping prescription pills like trading cards were normal activities. One model told me her dad has a "cocaine lawyer" on retainer in San Francisco for whenever drug possession charges needed to be reduced or dismissed. Wow. While some of these trust fund babies are raised to work hard, they definitely partied harder. Some were gifted houses and real estate properties in trusts the day they were born. Others received early shares of billion-dollar companies in Silicon Valley. Born into greatness seemed so surreal to me.

My nerves were always tense just driving to these neighborhoods. Super fancy homes. In areas like these, I'm always sure to park my beater several blocks away to keep from flagging myself as the poorest one around. What would everyone else think if they saw my dented car? I want to avoid the truth as long as possible. I walk through the neighborhood like a tourist. As soon as I step into the house, I pan the room to ensure my clothes match the local populace. The brands match, but the person they cover does not. Outsider. My face shows I'm nervous, I don't belong here, and everyone else knows it. They are carefree, and I care way too much. No one at their level is concerned with anything but enjoying their elite status. *Ha!* Oh, how mistaken I am, but it'll be years until I understand. Stepping wide-eyed into the smoke and booze, I search for my classmates.

As a 17-year-old college freshman, I'd never had alcohol before. Before this, I was studious and avoided going to wild parties. Growing up strait-laced kept me out of trouble. Playing alone was my thing. Consequently, I also missed out on having the usual adventures. Wanting to explore my potential while feeling directionless led me down some bad paths. My academics suffer. I was introduced to a world of chaotic pleasure. No rules exist in this space, except to have fun. It's restless. Hedonism comes with constant noise and commotion which I don't care for, but what I want is to fit in with an exclusive group. I'm seeking validation and it'll cost me pieces of my soul, plus my money.

Unlike everyone else at these parties, I'm always broke. Going out adds thousands in credit card debt. I spent $100 on one shirt plus $280 on pants so I could try to blend in. A friend told me that once I put on jeans like his, I'd never wear ordinary denim again. He was right, I never knew the fabric could be this stretchy. He encouraged me to spend money to look the part. Maxing out credit lines was a regular occurrence. Necessary. Name-brand polos and designer jeans served as camouflage at this time in my life. I'm scared of being different, but no matter what I do it's obvious I am. My awkwardness and interest rates keep compounding.

Party conversations are strange social exercises. Lots of peacocking. Teenagers around me talk about stock investments, real estate purchases, and family ties to politicians. Many discuss running family businesses while others describe working with actors, directors, music executives, and various celebrities. Name dropping establishes relevance. Commanding the room with loud conversations is a way to compete for audience approval. Attention is currency. Family pedigree establishes dominance in the social hierarchy. With every new guest arriving more drinks are poured, the music volume increases, and chaos takes over life. The longer it keeps taking me to find anyone I know, the more I stand alone sweating.

How do I talk to anyone here? I'm nobody. What do I possibly have to brag about? Pressure builds in my chest and my heart rate spikes. I put my hand on someone's shoulder to try and swim through the crowd. They turn around, and seeing I'm a stranger, look down at me with disgust. Panic. I'm caught under a deep wave of social anxiety. My heart races, and I can feel my chest thumping. Time for a drink. Where is the keg? I'm way out of my league here. I need to get wasted.

I stayed wasted for years until I realized my identity was empty. Even my friends couldn't fill the ravenous void. My life was based on the judgment of others and the irony was that many of them were lost too. In the next few years there would be DUIs, overdoses, breakups, divorces, and jail time for many of them. I was alongside them running from a powerful, deeply isolating existential question: Who am I? I could never find the answer without leaving everything I knew behind.

Social reset. Ten years later in life, I met friends of a whole new type who were extraordinarily elite in a very special way. A class of rare warriors. Success wasn't handed to them. It was earned by their own personal suffering and deep sacrifice.

SECTION 2: A GOOD MILITARY LEADER

On Thanksgiving 2017, I was invited to a friend's house for food with his family. I rode my bicycle 40 miles that day and arrived sweaty, exhausted, and hungry. Wearing a large, heavy daypack while pedaling uphill made the trip even more of a fun challenge. My butt ached. Hopping off my bike, I shook out my legs and tried waking up tingling body parts that had lost blood flow. Waddling sorely to the door, I barely knocked before it swung open.

I was quickly introduced to several relatives and family friends who were all smiles. Guests there included a Navy pilot, an EOD tech, and a quiet guy from the Army named Greg. To my surprise, he wasn't a civilian. He was the first Green Beret officer I had ever met. He had an unassuming manner of conducting himself given his everyman vibe. Physically, he was wiry. His build was optimal for sustained periods of endurance that required great stamina. He was calm, friendly, and approachable. We hit it off immediately. I enjoyed his sharp wit. Greg and I stayed in the kitchen drinking beer when everyone went to sleep that night. We discussed military leadership and global affairs. He tested my knowledge.

Up to this point in life, I had only met one other Soldier before. All my military friends were in the Navy or Marines. We didn't have many Army bases around. Greg immediately made me rethink my previous assumptions about his branch. I thought Soldiers would be robotic and show no personality compared to beach-dwelling Sailors and Marines. I couldn't have been more wrong. He demonstrated how Soldiers could be gregarious, educated self-starters motivated to lead with emotional intelligence. His perception was keen. He possessed a powerful ability to read people and accurately assess them, whether friend or foe. His military training made him a well-rounded warrior.

I admired several of his personality traits, especially his drive. Overcoming tough challenges made his resolve unshakable because he had suffered through training, and now fear had no hold on him. He learned how to stay objective and control emotion. His level head allowed him to downplay the dramatic intensity others used to seem intimidating. Pain didn't scare him. The way he cut down to the reality of a situation made him a reliable source of guidance. Overall, I appreciated the calm nature with which he approached life issues. He excelled in the Army as a result. His take on the difficulties others complain about gave a reasonable, friendly perspective on what it means to pursue greatness. Tough times build strength. Motivation brings success. Work ethic and integrity were key elements of his steady approach. He dropped wisdom on me.

Greg fully understood the games people play to elevate themselves. He had seen guys try to look better than others and spotlight themselves, especially when working towards Special Forces. Those dudes failed out. Their willingness to step on others didn't stop him from relying on personal convictions to do the right thing. He ignored the noise around him and zeroed in on the goals he wanted to achieve. We spoke candidly about the psychological component of competition inside and outside the military. He quickly noticed my high-energy drive for embracing uncertainty and told me to consider joining the Army. I had never contemplated it before. *Hmmm.* I was humbled to be encouraged to join by a proven warrior like him. I knew to not take his invitation lightly. My wheels turned. Eventually, when I finally signed a contract with the Army, he had everything to do with that choice.

During our conversations, I found that Greg preferred pursuing specific paths in life that others feared. He found comfort in the distillation process that occurs when people quit and drop out of a race. It's cleansing. Selection processes using hardship to wean away the weak create a close-knit clan that shares a common perspective. Suffering helps uncover strength. It holds, whether applied to civilian life as an individual facing great challenges, or military training pipelines. Grit is discovered only by the fire of trial.

Months later, I shared I was torn about which military career or branch to consider. He told me to not feel pressured. Instead, he encouraged me to focus on maintaining resolve to crush whatever path I choose, military or not. He was not critical or judgmental, and he perceived strength as having many variations. "Military life is not for everyone," he said. "Some seek to prove themselves through entrepreneurial ventures while others seek it in the military." In either case, whether I continued running my business or signed a military contract, he let me know I could always find a way to support troops. The way he removed pressure from joining the military only made me burn with a deeper desire to don the uniform.

When he asked me what I thought about Special Forces, I told him I was way too much of a geek to ever fit in with that crowd. He smiled and told me that I was wrong. He said every teammate he worked with was geeky in at least one area of life. They could be into electronics, comics, books, fitness, or anything else, but they were absolutely nerds regarding one specific thing. Most people would never expect that. He talked about the incredible level of intelligence almost every team guy possesses and how the movies commonly get them wrong.

Team guys don't walk around with bulging muscles, especially the ones recently coming out of training pipelines. They are lean and trained to cover long distances with little food or rest. He spoke about how many outsiders make assumptions that are usually incorrect because they read about one or two things online. I admired his ability to laser through all the nonsense most people swear by. I was shocked to see how similar he was to the SEALs and MARSOC operators I know. Very chill. Once again, here was a team guy with a good heart and a solid head on his shoulders. He gives the military a very good name. We kept in touch, and he guided me in preparing for my role as a future platoon leader in the Army.

SECTION 3: PSYCHOLOGICAL APPLICATION

Attrition is a powerful tool when it comes

to shaping the strength of a military department or program. It highlights mental toughness. Greg acknowledged that this process enticed him to pursue exclusive military communities. The biggest eliminating factor by far is psychological weakness even more than physical demands. The fear of pain alone is enough to make people quit. One research project conducted by the USMC on 3,438 Recon trainees found that individuals who decide to quit "most commonly cited mental stress...less commonly cited reasons were physical" (Barrett et al., 2021). Handling such stress requires a mindset that can see the big picture while breaking down the overwhelming challenges into small, manageable pieces.

Steadfast mindset is key to sustaining difficult training. Soldiers in Army SFAS (Special Forces Assessment and Selection) fail when they mentally dissociate or detach during stressful circumstances, causing them to lose the ability to stay present in the situation (Morgan et al., (2008). Being present hurts. Dissociation is a psychological defense mechanism that helps someone disconnect from their body to avoid feeling overwhelming pain. This is especially relevant when someone feels overwhelmed by a situation with no anticipated end in sight. Minimizing emotional overwhelm by remaining calm during military training is important. It's common for successful service members to focus on making it one meal at a time until they graduate.

Greg passed Special Forces selection because of the calmness and humility he exudes. I later found how impactful these qualities are to military success when I came across like-minded Soldiers. It's comforting.

Such qualities enable leaders to be open and honest with teammates while simultaneously withstanding the desire to run from difficulty. Leaders like Greg keep stress levels manageable for everyone else and provide guidance toward solutions.

Military training has a way of breaking the ego. Pride gets bruised. Humility, on the other hand, is associated with less anxiety, psychological well-being, and heightened self-efficacy (Ross & Wright, 2021). Enduring suffering is more tolerable for those able to manage their pride. By accepting discomfort, they don't allow difficult situations to cause emotional distress. They know their limits and understand what they can handle. Humble leaders can process discomfort with openness thereby allowing increased resilience. Humility helps minimize denial and illusions evoked by pride (Kesebir, 2014). Leaders with this quality are willing to face uncomfortable realities because they don't try to resist pain out of fear. They can relinquish any personal agenda to accept reality.

Humility also benefits leaders who are willing to keep an open mind. Flexibility is key. In the military, change is abrupt. Battle plans, for instance, can completely change once execution begins. Whether equipment malfunctions, supply lines break, or the enemy alters their expected trajectory, no plan can ever be perfect. Good leaders keep a finger on the pulse by listening to feedback from those on the ground. With bad leaders, pride kills receptivity to change, and people suffer as a result.

Being able to listen to one's colleagues and make changes means having the humility to relinquish control. Adapting plans may hurt the ego and admitting erroneous judgment can be difficult because of pride. No human is perfect, yet some leaders are too stubborn to admit errors. It's easy to excuse arrogance as tenacity but, over time, it wears down the team. Leaders who aim to serve others rather than demand blind obedience avoid this pitfall. They seek out correction whenever their directives misalign with intended goals.

Openness and transparency are other marks of humility within a leader. These acts demonstrate a willingness to be held accountable for critical decisions. Leaders with these traits encourage dialogue to ensure their decisions are helpful. They want others to know what to expect when changes must be made. Knowing what to expect helps alleviate stress in an organization. Such treatment always conveys respect towards subordinates. Treating service members in the military as intelligent adults is important. Leaders do this by providing reasoning to back specific orders and directives. Maintaining clear, respectful dialogue boosts morale and trust in a leader. Nothing will destroy a leader's relevance quicker than speaking to people like they are stupid.

Calm is tied to humility and provides countless benefits. Calm, non-impulsive leaders bring about positive reactions in their followers because they reduce stress, even during high-intensity situations (Arendt et al., 2019). Simply observing their demeanor helps ease tension and invokes strength. As leaders exude desirable behaviors in the workplace, "employees develop trust, respect, and positive attitudes, not only toward the leader but also to the organization or occupation" (Kim & Cruz, 2022). Military leaders, therefore, strengthen the entire branch they work in by demonstrating good qualities.

Calm leaders are also able to make thoughtful judgments because they aren't distracted by their impulses. A calm mind inhibits impulsive reactivity or emotional overreaction. By staying in control psychologically, such leaders can endure difficult situations with increased resilience. They withstand the pain and achieve their goals. Studies are examining how "inhibitory control (IC), the executive control function which supports our goal-directed behavior and regulates our emotional response, may underlie resilience" (Afek, 2021). Inhibition keeps one from burning fuel on wasted efforts and instead channels energy into the pursuit of meaningful goals.

Leaders who manage their emotions maintain awareness of strengths, weaknesses, and errors. Their attitudes influence others to "calm a chaotic environment" (Bunin et al., 2021). In organizations built on uncertainty, calm leaders provide a buffer to absorb the impact of sudden change. When a plan falls apart, or an obstacle appears out of the darkness, taking things slow and steady is critical. Even if a situation can't be controlled, one's thoughts can always be slowed through deep breaths and focus. Staying calm allows a leader to formulate strategic responses to any event or person who threatens destruction.

When it comes to studying the managerial impact of calm and humility, one publication on military leadership emphasizes three powerful results:

1) adaptability to change
2) caring for subordinates
3) open communication

Even in lethal situations these qualities "result in optimized performance at multiple levels when crisis conditions are encountered" (Bunin et al., 2021). Again, I see how all three of these aspects are handled through calm leaders who take a humble approach. Greg inherently exhibits all of these through his leadership style on the teams.

During our several discussions before I joined the Army, Greg continually shared several impactful statements. He let me know what books and resources he used to grow his knowledge. Leaders are readers. Anytime he mentioned a book on military leadership, I made sure to write the title down and get a copy for myself. I was hungry to learn as much as possible from him. He made his way through the "big Army" and onto the teams, allowing him to gain tremendous insight. I valued every minute we spoke. Writing his words in this book serves as my attempt to give back so others can benefit as well.

Some critics say that the leadership principles used in elite Special Forces communities don't apply to the conventional military, but I disagree. Everyone in the military is an adult. We can choose to grow our people rather than control them. Teach them to think for themselves. While I understand autonomy must be earned, there are principles that apply to the general population. Teams encourage respectful treatment across ranks while promoting autonomy and innovative thought. I understand these to be universally desirable qualities inside and outside the military. Any leadership principles that friends in elite military units give me are worth applying anywhere else. Their ideas are founded upon well-established research.

Here are three powerful pieces of advice Greg offered me before I joined the Army:

SECTION 4: LEADERSHIP ADVICE

> *"Choose hard paths others complain about; they work as a filter. Just be patient for the process to work, and in time, you'll find the brotherhood you want." (Pursue Attrition)*

> *"You'll eventually see the same people again, so don't burn bridges. Even if someone is a bad person and they try to start trouble, be the bigger person by showing them respect. They'll ruin their reputation while you preserve yours." (Stay Calm)*

> *"Keep your mouth shut and never tell people how great you are at anything. Simply show them through your work ethic. Before you know it, you'll find yourself rubbing elbows alongside like-minded brothers. Stay humble and focus on putting out as hard as you can. Success will come eventually." (Be humble)*

From the minute I shipped out for BCT at Fort Jackson, these truths were powerful tools for me to keep in mind. They guided me whenever I navigated egos and personality conflicts. As a result, I was able to focus attention on the good people around me and block out the bad. There was plenty of distracting negativity to go around, but my mind didn't have to wander. I never needed to engage in frivolous arguments or prove any point. Silence was finally ok. *Growth!*

Advice from Greg works inside and outside the military. Thanks to him, I learned to accurately read people and assess the level of engagement I'd be willing to offer them based on what they brought to the table, positivity, or negativity. Respectfully, I minimized exposure to anyone seeking to increase tension in the workplace. No unnecessary negativity or complaining. My energy was reserved for setting and achieving goals. I invested in stable friendships and became intentionally selective about who I allowed to speak into my life. If someone caused rifts and fights among peers, I knew to disengage and walk away. With less tension in my life, I could lead with a calm state of mind.

In the past I was starved for relevance, my mind in restless pursuit of validation. Now I felt compelled to work hard without self-promotion and believed it would eventually pay off. Some leaders tried egging on competitions between peers even to the point of creating conflicts, but I saw that as detrimental to stability in the organization. Bragging about success or dominance was a waste of time and attracted the wrong people. Competing for social relevance consumes valuable energy. Instead, I sought to push myself privately and connect with like-minded friends. No time for drama. Even if someone pushed my buttons, I accepted that it was my job to control myself, not others. It paid off.

One specific example occurred in OCS when we were learning what kind of leaders we would be. During a workout competition, a class peer tried to trip me and then shove me to the ground. We were running metal bleachers and the fall would've been ugly. He was also cutting corners throughout the race. Cheater. My adrenaline spiked and all I could think of was how disrespectful and dangerous he was. I saw red. Initially, my fear of inadequacy prompted me to retaliate. After shoulder-checking him, he responded in kind which really set me off, but I knew I had a decision to make. I paused.

I wanted to smash him and force him to admit how wrong he was. I wanted to tell him I was faster than him. I wanted him to apologize. But I remembered Greg's words about staying calm and never burning bridges. Deep breath. I let him finish the race by cutting corners. Had I started a fight it would have resulted in mass punishment from our instructors and ruined the day for all my peers. I needed to control my emotional reaction for their sake. Towards the end of the race, our instructor caught him cheating and he was handled; it was good that I focused on controlling myself.

Before joining the military, I was painfully insecure and defensive. A small slight could keep me reeling in rumination for days. Back in my party days, I was encouraged to show off to gain relevance. When someone made an abrasive remark, I learned to run my mouth. Talk was all I had. No Jiu-Jitsu at that stage in life. God knows how badly I needed to be choked out and pummeled on the mats, but that comes later. Knowing I couldn't physically back up my tough act, I kept a loud bark. I was scared. Remaining quiet felt like a liability. But in the military, things changed. My phase of desiring social relevance ended. Squabbling felt nauseatingly childish, and I expected people around me to act like adults. So, I avoided fights, negativity, and gossip as much as possible, especially because the military is a small community.

Remaining stoic, I eventually understood helped to preserve mental energy and thus my sanity. Leaders who let emotions control them created terribly exhausting work environments. As students during initial entry training, we were able to put emotional control into practice. Stressful exercises during military training can set a lot of people off. For example, those who can't handle the pressure physically tense up or verbally snap at others. They lose self-control, cheat, or attack peers, sometimes resulting in their dismissal. When a peer lost emotional control it was a red flag, signaling they lacked the ability to lead. Seeing them removed from the class was a relief because it meant people would not have to suffer under the leadership of someone who could not control their emotions. That's attrition at work.

Attrition is a reduction in the number of trainees who graduate from a training program. It's a distillation process. Instructors apply pressure to see who breaks. When someone blatantly commits a serious infraction that gets them kicked out of a military program, we call that self-selecting out. They chose to remove themselves. Most times, they will never admit to wanting out of the program, instead claiming it was an honest mistake. However, when considering consistent behavior patterns, it's clear they never wanted to be there. Self-sabotage occurs. It's common to lose several students per graduating class. Attrition did indeed work its magic as Greg predicted whenever the wrong people left, and the right ones remained. On many occasions, it boiled down to pride.

I wanted to be the leader I wanted to have. Managing my own pride took work. Military life bruised my ego countless times as I attempted to minimize my emotional reactivity to tough people and situations. When under pressure from sleep deprivation, hunger, or exposure to weather, I needed to control my words and behaviors. Remaining calm, assertive, and respectful is no easy task in these conditions. Triple-digit temperatures in a hot, barren desert don't make tactical battle planning and execution easier. Tempers run high. When someone makes a disparaging or condescending comment I want to react, whether they're a leader, peer, or subordinate. However, contemplating destructive fallout makes me carefully reconsider. Do I want the fight to drag on? Do I want to engage with that person if they lack good judgment? What is the best use of my energy? How may I respond without exacerbating the issue?

One of the toughest situations in any working environment is having a colleague who brings bitterness and resentment to work and means to hurt others. It's even worse when they are unable or unwilling to acknowledge their own negative attitude. There is no easy way to respond. Simply reprimanding them doesn't address the underlying issues they have. Worse, they'll simply find others to hurt. Establishing boundaries and guidelines at work is key to protecting people, but that doesn't stop passive aggression. Coworkers like this can sabotage good leaders. What's the answer? Fire them? But then society still carries the problem. Do we treat symptoms, quarantine the disease, or find a cure?

I still don't know the perfect answer to this, but I do know that staying calm and controlling an ego-defensive response mitigates damage. Pride ruins relationships. I worked for someone who was constantly draining the morale of everybody around him. At the end of the day, he was distressed from a lifetime of hurt that bled into his professional life. His marriage was ending, and he wasn't happy with life. On one hand I felt for him, on the other, I was frustrated. As a leader myself, I had to be thoughtful. I made it a point to never use his desire for conflict as a means of testing my own power. What would be the point? He needed help.

When he tried bullying me, I ignored his disrespectful behavior and stayed neutral. Eventually, he found my lack of response unrewarding, and this dissuaded him from further attacks. I felt relieved. Sadly, he did succeed in channeling his pain toward others and caused a great deal of emotional and mental distress. His job performance was good so there wasn't an easy way to flag him until people began speaking up together. When I finally found out what was happening, I did what I could to encourage those he hurt to pursue a professional response. Many were afraid. Silent. It was understandable given his level of authority.

Since he was a key asset to the organization, I wondered if removing him would be harmful or beneficial. Maybe I was being too sensitive. Then again, isn't sensitivity a strength that helps me understand how to best treat others? What made matters worse was this man's belief that subordinates didn't deserve kindness. Some agreed with him, though they disagreed with his approach. With so many opinions and perspectives, who was right? Yep, leadership is messy.

Overall, I tried my best to learn through hardships when it came to managing difficult people. Sometimes creating distance was the only available route to take. It still felt incomplete. I wanted to fix the situation my way, but was that just my pride talking? As a leader, the game can be played many ways. There's even the option of ending the game altogether by pushing over the tables. It really depends on individual personality and beliefs. The biggest takeaway I learned is that just because I can protect myself from somebody toxic, feeling good doesn't necessarily follow. I lose sleep if I know others are still vulnerable to the abuse of a toxic leader.

Life in the military was the most challenging and rewarding time of my life. I constantly needed to remain calm and monitor my attitude. While I am forever grateful for the situations I experienced, there are some I never wish to face again. Death Valley, CA was one. On August 16, 2020, it reached 130 degrees Fahrenheit, one of the hottest recorded temperatures on Earth. While living in metal shipping containers, we wore our full kit (helmet, pants, long-sleeved shirts, and tactical vests). Heat waves emanated from every wall like an oven.

Somehow, I kept calm, even though my body wanted to collapse. Working 24 hours a day in this miserable environment with other exhausted Soldiers is not easy. Staying positive took sincere effort. One trick that helped was to put a handful of ice under your hat for a quick cool down. In tough work environments like that one, relying on strong, positive leaders was vital. I needed to know they cared. Because of them, despite the difficulties of the austere desert, we accomplished the mission while supporting one another.

Thanks to the Army, I can now handle myself in challenging situations better than ever. I learned more about my capabilities, limits, and ego. I know how to make a difficult judgment call and manage complex situations that seem to have no clear end in sight. When chaos increases, I slow my mind, read the problem, keep my mouth closed, and formulate an approach. Calm keeps me in the fight longer and helps me contribute my best to the organization. I used to fear complicated, intense situations. Now, because of the military, I enjoy working through the puzzle before me and the ego within me— a powerful way to grow. I couldn't have done it without the guidance and advice from amazing friends throughout the suck.

Thanks, Greg.

References:

Afek, A., Ben-Avraham, R., Davidov, A., Berezin Cohen, N., Ben Yehuda, A., Gilboa, Y., & Nahum, M. (2021). Psychological Resilience, Mental Health, and Inhibitory Control Among Youth and Young Adults Under Stress. Frontiers in psychiatry, 11, 608588. https://doi.org/10.3389/fpsyt.2020.608588

Arendt, J., Pircher Verdorfer, A., & Kugler, K. G. (2019). Mindfulness and Leadership Communication as a Behavioral Correlate of Leader Mindfulness and Its Effec on Follower Satisfaction. Frontiers in psychology, 10, 667. https://doi.org/10.3389/fpsyg.2019.00667

Bunin, J. L., Chung, K. K., & Mount, C. A. (2021). Ten Leadership Principles from the Military Applied to Critical Care. ATS scholar, 2(3), 317–326. https://doi.org/10.34197/ats-scholar.2020-0170PS

Kesebir P. (2014). A quiet ego quiets death anxiety: humility as an existential anxiety buffer. Journal of personality and social psychology, 106(4), 610–623. https://doi.org/10.1037/a0035814

Kim, H. D., & Cruz, A. B. (2022). Transformational Leadership and Psychological Well-Being of Service-Oriented Staff: Hybrid Data Synthesis Technique. International journal of environmental research and public health, 19(13), 8189. https://doi.org/10.3390/ijerph19138189

Morgan, C. A., Southwick, S. M., Hazliett, G., & Dial-Ward, M. (2008). Baseline dissociation and prospective success in special forces assessment and selection. Psychiatry (Edgmont (Pa. : Township)), 5(7), 53–58.

Ross, L. T., & Wright, J. C. (2021). Humility, Personality, and Psychological Functioning. Psychological reports, 332941211062819. Advance online publication. https://doi.org/10.1177/00332941211062819

Trevor J. Barrett, Mona Sobhani, Glenn R. Fox, Benjamin Files, Nicholas Patitsas, Josiah Duhaime, Rebecca Ebert, Rob Faulk & Leslie Saxon (2022) Diverse predictors of early attrition in an elite Marine training school, Military Psychology, 34:4, 388-397, DOI:10.1080/08995605.2021.1993721

3 - HYPE & STEREOTYPES

"I'm a glorified button pusher flying expensive equipment."
*- **TODD** [USMC F18 Fighter Pilot]*

Objectivity: lear perspective on a situation based on unbiased information

Self-Awareness: understanding one's own abilities, limitations, and desires

Self-Serving Bias: ideas held onto to reinforce preexisting or beliefs

Stereotype: characteristics assumed as normal for a particular group

SECTION 1: INTRODUCTION TO THE TOPIC

Every Saturday morning I'd join a meetup group at South Mission Beach to play volleyball and start the weekend off right. Many of the men in the group I played with were in the Navy. We played in teams of six, so with over 20 of us, we had to rotate people in and out after each point. Soft, warm sand cushioned our bare feet as we played.

South Mission Beach has about a dozen courts.

Next to ours, some Olympic hopefuls were training 2x2. When our ball flew onto their court, I ran to retrieve it. I don't know the name of the female I spoke with, but I remember feeling like I was the size of one of her legs. She was super friendly and invited us to use their court once they finished. I thanked her and jumped back into my game.

As we played, someone pulled up on a motorcycle and everyone abruptly stopped playing and stared toward the parking lot. The people in my group kept saying, "It's her" and "She's on her bike." As I turned my attention to the parking lot, I saw someone removing a full-face helmet to reveal a beautiful woman with light eyes and an athletic physique. A man pulled up next to her on his motorcycle and everyone audibly sighed as if their hearts were breaking. "Who is she?" I asked. Without taking their eyes off her they told me she was a new fighter pilot. Eventually, we got back to our game, but the conversation about her didn't stop. She was a powerful symbol of untouchable beauty and military might.

The popularity of fighter pilots is based on the exclusivity of their club. Their career functions almost as a social class to which outsiders peer in with curiosity and awe. With all the tough training involved, it makes sense they stand out in the military. Commanding such fierce tactical firepower in battle is an incredible asset and symbol of American pride. For each pilot, there is an extensive support team standing behind them, receiving little attention. The spotlight falls on the face of the one in the cockpit. Immediately, it seemed this woman was a paragon of excellence because of her accomplishments as a fighter pilot.

Earning wings as a jet fighter is no easy feat. Fewer than one percent of applicants make it that far since air-to-air combat training requires physical and mental toughness. Stereotypes around this elite class of warriors are well known. They are assumed to walk around with an air of arrogance because they are the best. Sometimes this is true and sometimes it isn't. The same thing can be said about a variety of stereotypes. Whether someone has certain tabs on their shoulders especially feeds into assumptions about them. So does their size, physical fitness, and combat experience. Stereotypes serve the purpose of categorizing people, but they are often wrong, or at best incomplete. Being a female in the military only adds further presumptions.

Female military friends I consider sisters in arms have shared with me the frustration of stereotypes impacting their lives. Through ongoing professionalism, Erin demonstrated that she in no way desired special attention or treatment based on her gender. As a prior enlisted Soldier before becoming an officer, her insight into military leadership dynamics was rich. She maintains authenticity in her leadership style and is comfortable being assertive when necessary.

It's not easy for a woman facing negative biases to carry a rifle and lead a group of men into battle scenarios, but she did so, putting aside any presumptions. One night it was her turn to be evaluated for platoon leadership ability. She made me squad leader on our FTX (field training exercise) required for graduation. We were to secretly recon a concrete bridge to enable a convoy element to cross. Gathering the dimensions of the bridge would allow us to calculate the appropriate size of C4 explosives to demolish it once the convoy had passed. It takes time to determine how and where to place explosive charges when looking to cut through steel structures. We needed to hurry before enemy forces spotted our element. Instructors threw several explosive simulation rounds around the woods to get us riled up. They also set several traps for us in one of the most intense battle scenarios we were going to experience.

Erin ordered me out into the darkness to secure the bridge. Cadre walked behind me to observe. Anticipating danger, I got on all fours, then belly down with my face at their boots. My weapon was slung onto my back as I bear crawled across the bridge to avoid potential enemy fire. I fumbled with my infrared light in a frantic search for potential explosives. Searching for trip wires and IEDs with night vision optics is tough. There are procedures to detect metal wires in the darkness, but I didn't know them yet. Moving slowly, I communicated back to Erin, who waited with the security overwatch element.

Suddenly, explosions started erupting. I had hit a trap. It was a mass casualty exercise where the cadre planned to kill most of us off. This increased pressure on us all and tested Erin's stress management. When opinions piled onto her during an influx of chaos, her responsibility was to make the final call and determine our fate. She knew when to ask for help and when to order tactical responses. We collected casualties, set up 360-degree security, and called up a very long 9-line CASEVAC request. After completing all this, we awaited our extract. Erin did everything required during this intense exercise. I was encouraged by her ability to remain true to herself without being swayed by what others assumed a female would be able to handle. She and several other females I know in the military shatter gender stereotypes.

Selena, a kickboxer, maintained a perfect balance between training as a fighter and embracing her femininity, even while in military uniform. Throughout her life, she faced challenges that pushed her to fight back, but she somehow also stayed warm. As a musician, she channeled her feelings into songs between rounds on the punching bags. In the Army, she overcame stereotyping that made her feel she couldn't connect with her brothers in arms. In the field, she lived in austerity among her brothers as together we all learned squad-level maneuvering tactics. The military was seeing a lot of firsts for women around this time so many rules were still being developed. Men and women conducting hygiene together in the field can make some people uncomfortable. Not her. Her professionalism and maturity cut through any awkwardness.

She trained to shoot, move, communicate, and kill. Qualifying in rifle marksmanship, ruck marching, and learning to command artillery fire helped her develop warfighting skills most don't have. She joined the military to be an American Soldier. She wanted to serve out of a sense of patriotic duty because the United States had played a powerful role in saving her family from an evil dictatorship. Her grandfather and father inspired her to wear the uniform and represent freedom to the world. She didn't wish to be an outcast or placed into an outgroup because of her gender. Professionally speaking, she believed women should not ever have to be influenced by gender differences. She genuinely connected with others in uniform and didn't let anyone push her to the sidelines.

Negative stereotypes are daunting. Women face many. My Army sisters were often expected to quit during times of physical duress. But they didn't. Incorrectly, they were assumed to have difficulty in the field when it came to hygiene or managing menstrual cycles. Some were told to stay quiet during mission briefs. Men, some would say, do not wish to receive tactical advice from females. None of this stopped them from putting on the uniform and stepping up to the leadership responsibilities before them. They refused to be outsiders. I wonder what women who fly multimillion-dollar aircraft say to critical comments about female drivers.

Positive stereotypes can also play a role in creating misconceptions about service members. Buying the hype of self-serving stereotypes can over-inflate the ego. A common misconception about elite military service members is that they carry themselves with an elitist viewpoint, causing them to look down upon others. Despite what pop culture portrays; this is not necessarily the case. While maintaining a sense of professional pride serves to motivate group cohesion, this doesn't necessarily mean it can't be toggled off. The competitive nature between military peers induces posturing, but ideally only within reason. Competitive jabs are more a modality of psychological play than an attempt to be disparaging.

I bought into plenty of inaccurate stereotypes about military service members before joining. My own assumptions about fighter pilots were obliterated once I got to know one.

SECTION 2: A GOOD MILITARY LEADER

Todd was the first USMC fighter pilot I ever met, and all I knew about him at first was that he was a guitarist in a band. He could also drum and sing and was generally great at anything related to music, except hip-hop dancing. His high and tight haircut made it clear he was a Marine, but if there was anything he wanted to be known for in the world, it was music. He dressed sharp, his green eyes had a piercing intensity, and he was deeply analytical. When I eventually discovered he was a fighter pilot, all these pieces fell into place. One thing that threw me, though, was that he drove an older SUV rather than some roadster. Don't fighter pilots always like to go fast? I asked him why, as a speed demon, he didn't feel the need to blaze around town in a race car. He responded, "I fly one for work."

Intelligent and modest, Todd carried himself with a great deal of confidence, but not to the point that it was overbearing. Being a musician nurtured his artistic streak and softened his intensity. He was one of my first examples of an artist-warrior maintaining a passion for both the craft of warfare and creative expression. Joining the military does not mean one must drop the things that bring joy to life. Individual pursuits of hobbies and creative outlets are encouraged to stay balanced. Staying true to oneself makes for a more robust military because it enriches the culture and prevents repression.

Todd's approachability was a highlight of his personality as he opened his heart and home to others. He welcomed strangers introduced by friends. He is a good man with a generous spirit. His fostering community is especially great for newly arriving military members with no preexisting support group in our city. Service members from various branches recently stationed in San Diego were able to network and connect with others thanks to such hospitality. During holidays it was great making new military friends who would have spent the day alone. Knowing there are people like Todd provides a sense of belonging and connection that otherwise would take tremendous effort to develop.

One time during the local air show he was standing around in his olive drab aviator onesie. I was able to check out his jet while meeting the rest of his squadron. Badass pilots. I asked them what it was like being up in the clouds pulling G's. I was expecting a high-adrenaline description straight out of the movies. Instead, they shared specific techniques for engaging muscle tension in anticipation of each turn. Contracting muscles in their core and legs keeps them from blacking out due to the loss of blood flow that would pool in their appendages. Before each turn, they clenched as they pulled the stick, then released and exhaled. It all sounded so routine. Basic fundamentals. This definitely wasn't what I expected to hear. They spoke about their job as if it was normal. Their humility didn't fit the stereotype.

Once again, my assumptions about the military were readjusted through genuine friendship. My disillusioned thoughts about military pilots were slowly being calibrated to fit reality. It wasn't all action. They put so much work into training, studying, and managing affairs outside of flight time that can go unappreciated. Todd helped me learn about the humbler parts of life in the military that people don’t see from the outside. It was a mature approach to assessing life in uniform. While these were indeed elite fighter pilots, they didn't buy into the hype everyone else believed. They remained grounded even when their heads were literally up in the clouds. Todd modestly told me that fighter pilots like himself are fancy button pushers. I still have trouble seeing it this way, knowing how they tear through the skies in a roar.

Todd continued to break stereotypes I held as truth. He further deepened my appreciation for the common shared humanity of service members by describing his personal growth through pain. He had some tough life experiences outside his career that increased his self-awareness and maturity. He openly shared about being divorced at a young age. Heartbreak cut through any facade or suit of armor he may have had. This shocked me as I never expected to witness vulnerability in a fighter pilot or meet one so disarmingly honest.

His ex-wife realized she hadn't done enough in life to discover herself and decided to do so by partying nightly at clubs and bars with newfound friends. She became caught up in the desire to have a social life that involved drinking until the early morning hours. This didn’t fit well with a pilot who needed plenty of rest before returning to the skies daily. Eventually, their relationship lost its foundation. He realized there was no way to control someone else’s heart. No rank or accolades can mandate someone’s wholehearted, loving commitment.

Even elite professional careers are not able to prevent human frailties. I thought long about my assumptions. With the dissolution of his marriage, Todd refocused on advancing his career as a pilot and pursued genuine relationships with friends of substance. Music also played a large part in his healing process. Sharing that gift with others enriched his life and circle of community. Eventually, he remarried after meeting a grounded woman with a beautiful and humble soul. They played hip-hop at the wedding, and we all tried to dance.

SECTION 3: PSYCHOLOGICAL APPLICATION

Professionals in the military face many stereotypes oversimplifying their identities. Unfortunately, many existing stereotypes discourage recruits who notice they don't align with expectations regarding personality traits or temperament (Peters et al., 2014). Oftentimes this includes assumptions made about expressed masculinity. Tough guy acts are constructed to camouflage vulnerability and are annoyingly fabricated. Stereotyping can also harm physical health in the military as service members feel they must portray strength by refusing medical care, thereby straining their bodies over time (Greene-Shotridge et al., 2007). Professionals in high-risk careers ought to avoid masking legitimate needs just so they can satisfy the expectations of others. Long-term negative impact results in loss of motivation, diminished growth, and even suicide. Stigmas against mental health disorders caused by stereotypes create a sense of isolation that leads to an increase in suicidality (Carpiniello & Pinaa, 2017).

Overcoming stereotypes is healthy for the mind, but it requires a strong sense of self-awareness and the ability to challenge biases. Stripping away the title, rank, and uniform allows for focusing on deeper identity traits. Naked truth. Self-serving biases over-inflate our own strengths because we buy into our own image of success and avoid honestly addressing shortcomings (Karpen, 2018). Stereotypes that invoke a sense of strength are a psychological means of protecting against vulnerability. Social pressure plays a role. Perspective is lost when influenced by peer groups so it's key to recalibrate one's personal viewpoint thoughtfully. Usually, this means being selective about who to receive feedback from. It's also important to reflect on the personal values that matter most. Mental health benefits from "insight, reflection, rumination and mindfulness" (Sutton, 2016).

Self-awareness is a concept in psychology describing how well we know ourselves. It's measured by how capable we are of understanding and predicting our moods and behaviors. It's key in countering stereotypes. Individuals with high levels of self-awareness can focus on pursuing meaningful goals. They are not concerned with being what someone else thinks they should be. "Accurate overall self-awareness benefits the development and well-being of an individual" (Li et al., 2021). Health increases from self-awareness because we know our own needs, limits, and interests. We know how to take care of ourselves.

Self-awareness also helps us face challenges without being afraid of failure or shortcomings. Shock absorption. We become stronger because we confidently believe that our strengths and weaknesses balance out. There is no need to shrink away from tough challenges to cover up weaknesses. Lean into it. Accepting positive and negative personal characteristics increases self-esteem and authenticity (Showers et al., 2016). No need to hide. Fear of admitting shortcomings makes people fragile and imbalanced. Avoiding failure and fearing negative feedback is more likely when someone has fragile self-esteem based on low self-awareness. Having a robust identity helps handle stress, face negative events, self-regulate emotions, maintain optimism, and avoid self-stereotyping (Rivera & Paredez, 2014).

We even form stereotypes about ourselves. Self-stereotyping occurs when someone accepts limitations others project onto them based on a variety of potential stigmas. This deeply affects our health. A variety of stereotypes and outcomes exist. One specific example involves body weight. In the previously mentioned study, obesity increases in individuals who believe stereotypes about themselves at the expense of their self-esteem. Self-sabotage. Their behaviors begin to match what others think about them as they lack the motivation to eat healthy foods and lose weight. Ethnic-racial individuals who internalize negative racial stereotypes about themselves are more likely to be obese because they believe unhealthy behaviors are congruent with their identities (Rivera & Pardez, 2014). Break the cycle! Anyone focusing on positive attributes can overcome stereotyping and maintain healthy lifestyles in line with their personal values.

Self-awareness is complex and involves both conscious and unconscious thoughts about who we are in light of what other people think (Carden et al., 2021). While it's generally healthy to be self-aware, it's especially critical for those in positions of authority.

Objective leaders enhance their decision-making ability. They impact the organization by creating a culture in which reality takes precedence over any other agenda. This invokes a sense of humility which minimizes ego inflation, superiority, and arrogance. Leading from humility is a powerful way to nurture high morale in an organization (Owens et al., 2019).

Stereotypes can have another detrimental effect when it comes to overlooking the universal struggles all humans share. In Todd's case, it led to my assumption that elite service members are impervious to failure or emotional pain. Untrue. Being in the military revealed to me the vast amounts of wounds and struggles that exist. Often, the adversities Soldiers overcome early in life make them incredibly powerful individuals. Seeing them as people, not just uniforms with rank, helped me appreciate the depth and substance they each contributed. Many journeyed into the military from painfully broken lives, violent upbringings, and heartache. They are inspired to stand up for others.

Seeing firsthand how a fighter pilot was burdened with managing a tough career and a difficult relationship at home opened my eyes to a common military struggle. If an average civilian fights with their spouse, they aren't necessarily carrying angst or distraction into a life-and-death situation at work. If a military member is distracted by emotional distress, this can certainly jeopardize lives depending on the job. Being in the cockpit while under a mental fog of anger and frustration could quickly lead to a high-speed, deadly error. Healthy social support is necessary to help service members maintain a clear focus on the job.

Genuine connection outweighs image. Todd

demonstrated how receiving the spotlight for one's career is not necessarily correct, gratifying, or rewarding. Stereotypes are burdensome because they project so many assumptions. They also overlook personal identity. A sense of emptiness exists when all someone is seen for is their professional standing. It begs the question of where their value would lie if the job disappeared. Rather than oversimplifying someone else's identity according to stereotypes, I want to see past the hype. Who are they without titles? Doing so will allow me to understand how personal struggles and adversities contributed to their success. No military career or medal can fully encompass the identity or struggle of a service member, which is why Todd told me the following:

SECTION 4: LEADERSHIP ADVICE

> *"We have cool jobs and some exciting training exercises, but regardless of the hype, we are regular people like anyone else. That's where our value comes from, not from our job."*

Certain military careers may be considered superior when it comes to the firepower, technology, training, and selection process involved. They carry a brand. Exclusivity drives up brand value due to the concept of scarcity or rarity. Not everyone can get in. Also, having associated support roles further implies an elite status. It takes a team working in the background to keep certain jobs going. Rockstars need stagehands.

Millions of dollars may go into training, as well. Placing a dollar amount on resources pertaining to particular jobs does understandably create a value hierarchy. However, there's an issue when the price tag of job training begins to dictate assumed value about the individual service member. It's a disservice to others. Shallow. Combat experience can also add weight to someone's relevance in the military and comes with a slew of misconstrued assumptions about the service member.

Considering how many media headlines or blockbuster movies spotlight elite military careers adds to the weight they carry in the eyes of society. This doesn't just occur on the civilian side looking in. Internally, to the military, the concept of comparing patches, ribbons, and medals feeds into the hype. Competitive tendencies between colleagues cause service members to measure themselves against each other. Taking pride in one's job is an integral part of being a service member, but this can become overblown without balance. Things can go very wrong when a person's entire value is tied to their career or awards. It can be devastating when they feel that ties are severed (by injury, separation, termination, retirement). What about others who opted out of accepting awards or choose not to wear the patches they earned? Several Soldiers I met refused to put on the patches they successfully obtained by graduating from tough military schools. They knew they made it and that's all that mattered. For whatever reason, they felt compelled to hide it.

I also met many Soldiers in the Army who went on multiple combat deployments and earned various awards, medals, and other recognition for saving lives. I've seen them stereotyped as badasses, killers, and heroes, all of which they brush off. They're quiet. Hyping up the idea of American forces in battle is simple to do. Romanticized. Fetishized even. Reality is more complex than that. War was not one-dimensionally glorious to them. The good parts of combat are based on their relationships and love for one another.

Paperwork wasn't a priority. The priority was making sure brothers and sisters came back from their patrols. That's what many miss, the genuine love for each other. Pulling the trigger was their duty to protect a shared military family. Many lost multiple friends and carry silent emotional scars. Several have physical scars from direct-action firefights and IEDs. Asking about their experiences shouldn't be taken lightly because it's heavy for them to relive and discuss. I have seen the expression change on their face when brought back to those hellish moments. The hangover from memory recall can last days.

What puts them back at ease and makes them light up is bringing them back into the present by talking about their families, children, and personal interests. It reminds them of what their sacrifices paid for. Heaven and hell for them are separated by a thin line. They hate when that's overlooked by others, but they may lack words to paint such a picture. Many avoid civilians because it feels impossible to be understood. Silence is simpler.

On the other hand, war is not something they wish to constantly relive either. I noticed that while Soldiers with combat experience indeed have rich wisdom to share about the military, they enjoy being seen for more. There's an interesting balance between talking about military hardship and flipping back to routine life before things get too heavy. Dark humor helps. Military life is both all-consuming and salvific. War to them is just part of the job for which they signed up and being totally numb at funerals for their brothers tends to go unnoticed, perhaps for a lifetime.

One mentor of mine who helped train me during my first few months as a platoon leader was an NCO with extensive combat experience who I call Army dad. War was initially exciting. Deployed to Iraq during the invasion as a young Army Engineer he worked with varieties of explosives he never knew existed before. He supported special operations units from several branches and conducted countless demolitions. (Ask me in person about pistols, boardshorts, and tank tops in Iraq). Insurgents were everywhere. On some occasions, he worked construction projects requiring entire nights of darting between concrete barriers to avoid incoming sniper fire. Every movement was calculated. His adrenaline stayed high for weeks on end in combat. Even decades later, his brain still "relaxes" at a high state of activation.

As a specialist, he had been through bloody situations in war and witnessed the devastating loss of life. On one occasion, he was denied the ability to help rescue friendly forces pinned down by fire because of conflicting mission sets. Men were dying. His plan was to use his vehicle as a shield to guide them out. Various command elements were involved in figuring out the response. He listened on the radio as voices called for help while taking enemy rounds. These same men were a couple of blocks away, bleeding out within his sight as they took fire from an enemy out of visibility. All he could do was watch as they screamed. His unit was ordered to pick up and move out of the engagement area. Not knowing their fate still haunts him to this day.

On another occasion, he recalls washing blood out of Humvees and seeing the pieces of his fellow men. Good men died. Heavy losses occurred in battles he was a part of. The stench of death, gunpowder, and diesel were seared into his mind. Many times, after combat he considered ending his life, feeling unworthy. Survivor's guilt. It takes a lot out of him to bring this up. Asking him to recall war brings him to a dark place where he still hears the cries over the radio. An animalistic rage to tear his enemies into pieces to protect his brothers still burns inside. No medal will ease the pain he feels. No professional acknowledgment helps bring life back into their bodies.

This man is more than just a Soldier with combat experience, he's a living testament to the men he served with. Their sacrifice kept him alive. He learned to stop looking back and asking what else he could have done. Fate decided. He taught me to appreciate the raw humanity of service members underlying their uniforms. He told me about the complexity of wartime decisions and how some people break while others rise. He emphasized the importance of never judging a man based on what he says. Instead, watch how he leads. He focuses on the heart of a leader and couldn't care less about awards, tabs, or aggrandizement. He certainly doesn't give a damn about anyone who arrogantly demands attention for having deployed.

The hype of combat, as witnessed in war documentaries or films, can sometimes make war look too simplistic. The heaviness he feels in his chest when recalling the past isn't captured in those frames. While there is excitement and a sense of adventure in battling alongside brothers, there is also a tremendous weight locked in those memories. To see service members only as symbols of tactical power can mask the raw reality of the insanity they witnessed. Disturbing stories he's shared are hard to repeat. His heart bleeds daily for these brothers as flashbacks race in his mind every night he puts his head down on the pillow to sleep.

For others like him, thoughts before bed fire off like .50 cal rounds: "Why am I still here? Why did I deserve to live? Why didn't those men? Who will avenge them? Why didn't I do more? Was it my fault? What's the point of going on like this?" Decisions made by leaders during battle echo in their minds. This is the human experience of war that no hype of military symbolism can readily encompass. No job title reveals the weight they bear.

Because of my Army dad, I try to remind myself to consider the depth of experience that uniforms don't capture. Of course, I'm human and I get caught up in admiring iconic patches, but leadership potential can't always be graded by resume highlights. When examining someone's military career, it's important to separate the service member from the job description or listed accomplishments. Their identity is not what they do for a living or what someone else measures. Their level of training or years of experience may say a lot about who they are as a person, but it's not a complete picture. This all ties into the stereotyping discussed at the beginning of this chapter.

fStereotypes exist because they simplify the process of defining someone we don't yet know.

Insiders and outsiders to an organization are both guilty of it. While it's understandable that civilians view the military in light of media portrayals, this quickly loses relevance when talking to the heroes themselves. They perform job tasks that most fail to understand, and they train hard to keep up with demands. At the same time, they carry the emotional weight of losses few can imagine. All this is done without visibly breaking. To evaluate them only by their titles and written accomplishments is to only consider small snippets and highlights while ignoring the full burden they carry on their shoulders. It blows my mind that I've been given permission to say all this.

These brothers in arms who helped me navigate the military deeply inspire me because of their refusal to accept even positive stereotypes. Many could easily feed off attention and inflate their egos, but they would rather stay true to themselves. Honor goes to the fallen. Rejecting hype is a great example of professional competency and healthy self-perception. The value of each service member rests not on a job title. Rather, it is tied to the primal human spirit of those still alive today, and those who gave all.

Thanks, Todd (Army dad, too).

On a somber note, I checked in with my Army dad a dozen or more times while writing this book to ensure he was truly okay with me sharing a sliver of his story. There's so much more to his experiences than words on a page can capture. I'm floored by the intensity of what he witnessed in war. We teared up at some stories he shared and wanted to punch a wall at others. Solid leadership during combat is especially vital. Things get nightmarish without it. I'm grateful and humbled he allowed me to hear and share his story. I don't want to fumble this. I'll do my best to honor what you went through in that hellish time.

References:

Carden, J., Jones, R.J., Passmore, J. (2021). Defining Self-Awareness in the Context of Adult Development: A Systematic Literature Review. *Sage journals*, https://journals.sagepub.com/doi/full/10.1177/1052562921990065

Carpiniello, B., & Pinna, F. (2017). The Reciprocal Relationship between Suicidality and Stigma. *Frontiers in psychiatry, 8*, 35. https://doi.org/10.3389/fpsyt.2017.00035

Greene-Shortridge, T. M., Britt, T. W., & Castro, C. A. (2007). The stigma of mental health problems in the military. *Military medicine, 172*(2), 157–161. https://doi.org/10.7205/milmed.172.2.157

Karpen S. C. (2018). The Social Psychology of Biased Self-Assessment. *American J Journal of pharmaceutical education, 82*(5), 6299. https://doi.org/10.5688/ajpe6299

Li, J., Ma, W., Zhang, M., Wang, P., Liu, Y., & Ma, S. (2021). Know Yourself: Physical and Psychological Self-Awareness With Lifelog. *Frontiers in digital health, 3*,676824. https://doi.org/10.3389/fdgth.2021.676824

Owens, B. P., Yam, K. C., Bednar, J. S., Mao, J., & Hart, D. W. (2019). The impact of leader moral humility on follower moral self-efficacy and behavior. *The Journal of applied psychology, 104*(1), 146–163. https://doi.org/10.1037/apl0000353

Peters, K., Ryan, M. K., & Haslam, S. A. (2015). Marines, medics, and machismo: lack of fit with masculine occupational stereotypes discourages men's participation. *British journal of psychology (London, England : 1953), 106*(4), 635–655. https://doi.org/10.1111/bjop.12106

Rivera, L. M., & Paredez, S. M. (2014). Stereotypes Can "Get Under the Skin": Testing a Self-Stereotyping and Psychological Resource Model of Overweight and Obesity. *The Journal of social issues, 70*(2), 226–240. https://doi.org/10.1111/josi.12057

Showers, C. J., Ditzfeld, C. P., & Zeigler-Hill, V. (2015). Self-Concept Structure and the Quality of Self-Knowledge. *Journal of personality, 83*(5), 535–551. https://doi.org/10.1111/jopy.12130

Sutton A. (2016). Measuring the Effects of Self-Awareness: Construction of the Self-Awareness Outcomes Questionnaire. *Europe's journal of psychology, 12*(4), 645–658. https://doi.org/10.5964/ejop.v12i4.1178

4 - COMMAND CLIMATE IS MAKE OR BREAK

"I'm gonna ruck run 12 miles today before a sunset surf sesh, wanna join?"

- ***WILL*** *[USMC MARSOC Officer]*

moral authority: credibility gained by being known as a respectable person

positional authority: deferring to rank when wielding power

observational learning: watching people to note and pick up best practices

SECTION 1: INTRODUCTION TO THE TOPIC

"Look around. Management only cares about their next promotion. Nobody cares about us, it's all about stock options," Sam vented.

Trisha nodded in agreement. I took a deep breath and paused as my colleagues discussed their burdens. I felt similarly and desperately wanted to help, but I didn't know how. Sam is someone I look up to for direction. He is a highly decorated Ph.D. scientist with experience in biotech research, business management, and most importantly, he is thoughtful and kind.

Trisha, an executive-level human resources professional, chimes in to warn us she is leaving the company. "I've never seen this before. HR has been sharing confidential information about anonymous complaints directly to management. Huge privacy violation. This new management is bitter, and angry, and will burn you out. There's nothing you can do to change this place. You need to leave," she tells me firmly. Hearing this weighed heavy on me.

This corporate job started great. What had happened here? The previous manager was amazing. We were encouraged to speak up and improve day-to-day tasks. Management valued our personal experience and perspectives, and we were inspired to be a part of an exciting mission. Life was good. How can one person come into an organization and ruin everything? An entire department instantly demoralized as a healthy company was poisoned by a toxic leader.

We were silenced. Bullied. The new manager intimidated anyone they perceived as maintaining objectivity and confidence, claiming it was defiant insubordination. Anytime an anonymous survey was conducted about the workplace they demanded we reveal who reported any issues. When nobody spoke, the manager said, "Good, so you're admitting no mistakes were made. My next review better be perfect since you're all in agreement." Arrogance and conceit were palpable when this person walked into the office.

Social status and power were conveyed through

overembellished expensive designer clothes and copious amounts of gold jewelry. Constant put-downs and subtle nonverbal cues during meetings furthered the message. Most employees feared losing their jobs and rolled over to keep from being targeted. Sycophants. Anyone who didn't kiss the ring was a threat. At one point the manager confronted Jim, an influential employee who chose to work hard without engaging in office politics. He was immediately isolated from his peers. Behind closed doors, the manager promised to fabricate a report of workplace harassment to Human Resources if Jim continued to demonstrate indifference.

Speaking calmly and with a fake smile, the manager assured him, "There is no such thing as truth here, only perception. I alone have the power to create any perception about you. I can CC and BCC anyone in this company in an email right now to tell them whatever I want. I can even tell executives and HR that you harass people in this department. However, I won't do this if you come to my desk every morning to inform me when you arrive, and every evening to ask permission to leave. Say good morning to me loud enough for everyone to hear each time you arrive. I want the team to hear it."

The manager wasn't smiling anymore but now had a cold, stern gaze. Claiming that multiple coworkers could be persuaded to help support the lies, this leader was making an astounding gamble. Desperate for control. However, Jim remained steadfast and silent, knowing the truth. He was never unprofessional at work. The report was ultimately never made and instead, Jim was terminated for a routine clerical error.

During his exit interview he was handed a check and asked to sign a non-disclosure agreement. Without looking at the check he instantly refused to accept it and politely said all he wanted was to be done with the company. He had no intention of receiving money, only peace of mind. He had packed up his desk several weeks before being fired because he knew he'd never win the games there. Just as he was about to step out of the building an employee from HR chased after him to ask if there was anything he could tell her about what really happened. She seemed kind, but Jim had learned to never trust management. He shook his head and blinked a warm tear. Turning to the door, he stepped outside into the sunshine and breathed in the fresh air. A cool breeze dried his eyes. New start.

Days later, citing wrongful termination, multiple coworkers in the department reached out to their former peer, encouraging a lawsuit against the company. Jim refused and was simply glad to be gone from that organization. Over the next several months, damage to morale became more evident. Eventually, that toxic leader was removed, but not by termination. Instead, the leader was promoted to head a new department in the same company, but with no subordinates to manage. Almost immediately, morale increased.

The lesson: command climate, otherwise known as workplace culture, is directly anchored to the temperament of the leader in charge.

Unhealthy leaders are uninterested in hearing about pain points from subordinates. This includes the refusal to address impractical deadlines, inefficiencies, ineffective policies, and illogical workflow. They focus on enhancing their professional image. People under such leaders are tools to be used. Human limitations are an inconvenience. Leadership like this feels like an ice-cold rain soaking through clothes, boots, and socks. It obscures visibility and sends a deep chill that slows down progress. Healthy leadership elevates the mood and energy level in a department, and individuals in the organization are valued and treated with dignity and respect. Constructive feedback is welcomed to maintain an open dialogue on ways to improve the workplace. These leaders are a warm glowing sunrise drying wet clothes while revealing safe paths through rough terrain.

What type of leader am I going to be? I wondered.

SECTION 2: A GOOD MILITARY LEADER

Will is an attack helicopter pilot turned MARSOC operator and is one of the most laid-back Marines I know. He regularly has friends over for movies or dinner, and I met him at one of those gatherings. He has a lean runner's build, blond hair, boyish looks, and comes off more like a SoCal surfer than a killing machine. His multifaceted tactical training makes him one of the most lethal humans alive. He can bring destruction from the air as a pilot and from the ground as an operator.

On a casual day in Oceanside, CA, he likes to ruck various high-mileage routes through uneven terrain, making sure to throw in rounds of surfing, mountain biking, rock climbing, and anything else that gets the blood pumping. He always pushes himself to get better. On our mountain biking trips, I circumvented the drops and hills he blazed through because I couldn't handle the difficulty. Never once did he mention my lack of skill. He was just pumped to have a friend alongside him. This was one of my first examples of getting to know what a "team guy" is like. He made me feel welcome regardless of my lackluster athletic performance abilities. He could have laughed at me but didn't. He encouraged me. In his mind, there was no point in putting someone down to get an ego boost.

Will's welcoming spirit is one of the profound characteristics that struck me when we first met. I experienced his kindness when he let me crash over and couch surf anytime I needed a place to stay. Like myself, countless others came to his home simply to be encouraged and get the recharge they needed. He even hosted skateboarding events for younger teenagers from the neighborhood to have a safe place with good influences. There was always something fun happening at the "RadPad."

Where did all this love come from? It's sourced in a deep place. Will can afford to be genuinely warm and hospitable because of his confidence. He's not threatened or intimidated by the world. He's not afraid of the dark struggles others carry. He wants to help. His home is open to anyone in need and if they need the shirt off his back, it's theirs without question. He places his love for community above all else and is driven by it. He welcomes the uninvited and makes a space for those who have nowhere to go. He's genuinely an awesome person and a rare friend. At one of his backyard firepit get-togethers some other military officers came over and the contrast between his leadership style and theirs was clear.

Will, a marine officer and my friend, has a

unique style. He was relaxed and totally unconcerned with impressing anyone. His face wore a sincere smile, and his embraces were warm. Across the firepit, the other officers seemed mechanical by contrast. Stern. Authoritarian. They seemed rigid and on edge, burdened by having something to prove or being unable to exit work mode. They were uncomfortable when conversing. They spoke tersely and offered little eye contact, keeping mainly to themselves. However, they did make some condescending remarks about others at the party.

Will didn't need showmanship. So, what does temperament say about a leader when it comes to organizational psychology?

SECTION 3: PSYCHOLOGICAL APPLICATION

Leaders must be aware that their attitudes and demeanor shape the work environment. We can make both good and bad decisions that impact the lives of those around us. The words we say create a template for others to follow. More than this, nonverbal communication is thought to contain the majority of our social impact. We can’t hide the truth, not for long. Our body language portrays the level of tension we carry. Eye contact demonstrates connection or disconnect depending on duration and intensity. Vocal tone, volume, and word choice convey the stress we carry.

The point isn’t to be perfect. Rather, be self-aware. Leaders are human like everyone else. We all struggle with ongoing stress and tension in life. What we do with our stress is the question. Do we manage it? Or do we drop the weight of it onto the backs of others? How many subordinates are forced to manage their leader's emotional issues? Is that really what they are getting paid for? Instead, choosing to shield subordinates from the brunt impact of negativity is powerful. Whether we need to protect them from leaders above us or even from our own emotional distress, it's important to be thoughtful in how we treat those we lead. Unaware leaders are exhausting. Leaders who attack subordinates are the worst.

Fear is the main source of toxic leadership. When threatened, humans posture to make themselves seem big and strong, like wolves with their hair standing up on end. Weaker competitors strive to over-assert themselves when compared to winners, who are more relaxed in temperament (Buades-Rotger et al., 2021). Weak people unnecessarily act aggressively to convey strength. This finding contradicts many expectations that dominant individuals inherently act tougher and are more aggressive. Instead, confidence helps induce a sense of calm. This is because there's no need to exert aggression when no threat is detected. Confident people can relax and smile at the success of others because it fuels them to keep growing. It's built into our biology. Dynamics throttling calm and aggression are neurologically wired into our brains.

Aggression is not an inherently bad characteristic in leaders. When used correctly, it serves the pro-social purpose of fueling change. Motivation. Leaders wanting such positive qualities must understand how aggression relates to brain activity and how it impacts stress levels in coworkers. Testosterone-fueled aggression managed with a calm brain (activated prefrontal cortex) yields socially supportive behavior meant to build others up (Choy et al., 2018; Cooper et al., 2010; Somerville et al., 2010). Energy goes towards driving prosocial progress meant to encourage others through difficult challenges. However, the opposite occurs when self-control is lacking. Destructive aggressive behaviors increase when testosterone impairs prefrontal cortex activation, lowering impulse control (Mehta & Beer, 2010).

A similarly powerful emotion is anger. Anger is neurologically promoted by fear and sadness to motivate action when provoked (Zhan et al., 2018). This misunderstood feeling serves the purpose of creating healthy boundaries. When uncontrolled, anger can be harmfully used as a defense mechanism to keep from feeling deeper, unwanted emotions. It's common for people to cover up their fear with anger. When someone fears vulnerability, they will lash out to protect themselves. Their protective actions may be either defensive or offensive depending on the context and what specific fears they carry.

Leaders who bring unresolved emotions to the workplace force everyone around them to experience their dysregulated mood states. Leaders like this use anger and aggression as a means of control. What they don't understand is they are displacing their feelings onto the wrong targets. Fear clouds their judgment and invokes unnecessary aggression. Leaders who have nothing to fear won't use aggression for self-preservation. They regulate their mood states and react appropriately to others. Anger and aggression are modulated to fit the situation.

Calm, confident leaders who regulate their emotions possess higher executive functioning in their brains. They don't allow primal urges to impact their judgment. Before acting, especially when stress is high, they weigh their reasoning. Complex intellectual thought occurs in the front lobe of the brain just behind the forehead. It's housed within the prefrontal cortex and helps control emotions. Inhibitory responses (the braking mechanism of the prefrontal cortex) allow the mind to slow down and read the situation before reacting. Higher-order thought allows the brain to assess perceived threats accurately. Strong, healthy leaders calmly throttle their aggression this way. This is important to keep from draining the energy out of subordinates.

Tense situations are exhausting. Emotional, mental, and physical energy is consumed during heightened nervous system activation. Anger and aggression affect us this way because they induce the fight-or-flight response, meaning that we spend a lot of our energy on high alert. Biologically speaking, these feeling states necessitate heightened levels of muscle activation to fight off threats in the environment. Mentally speaking, hypervigilance induces constant situational awareness. Our brains scan our surroundings for danger, much like a radar system. Such mental states become exhausting over prolonged periods of even a few minutes. Increased activation states are helpful when short-lived. Extended durations of these feeling states wear on the body and our relationships.

Leaders who create work cultures based on aggressive emotional states inherently exhaust the energy levels of their staff. Everyone must keep an eye out for incoming attacks. Chances are these leaders are projecting their own unresolved emotional issues onto other people. Understanding the existential threat they fear will help them calm their fear response. If no environmental threat actually exists, it may be a response to subconscious memory or internal beliefs. Something inside of them is causing them to fear vulnerability. Again, if a leader feels weak, they will overcompensate with strength. Subordinates will feel the tension as soon as they walk into the room.

Leading from a sense of inadequacy severely impacts the work culture because it conveys the message that no one else in the department is ever good enough. Performance must continually accelerate to compensate for what's lacking. These work environments force subordinates to bear the strain of competing for relevance. Expectations are never satisfied. Such leaders commonly steal credit for success. Again, this goes back to their desperate need to build an image. Insecure leaders wish to compensate for their own inadequacy and vulnerability. They use anger to stimulate work performance and mask whatever weakness they perceive in themselves. No one has time to rest. Weakness in others is inexcusable and will be attacked. Instead, everyone must feign strength to help create a false image. Nobody wants an aggressive leader calling them out on failures. Confusingly, subordinates also must never be too strong, or that will threaten the boss. Such a high-pressure dynamic piles on the stress.

Confident leaders never do this. Even when they have the biological recipe needed for physical dominance, their self-control mitigates any need to be overbearing. They are level-headed, even while handling high-intensity situations. There is no desire to step on others to assert control. Any organization will benefit from such leadership, not just the military. In the corporate world, some business leaders over-exaggerate their power and behave in aggressive manners meant to dominate others. For example, when it comes to sales departments that fuel competition between peers there may be those who thrive on speaking down about others to highlight their own successes. Contrary to the belief this behavior exudes success, it reeks of insecurity and fear.

Elite military members are especially good at balancing healthy assertion and aggression. Since I've known him, Will has never flexed to prove his strength. He faces rivalry with a sense of calm, friendly confidence. I wanted this for myself. Contrasting with my own insecure need for posturing, his demeanor revealed how much I struggled to manage fear. He inspired me to change. I wanted to grow out of my need to prove my worth to others. I grew tired of compensating for what I lacked. It was exhausting. I wanted to learn how to switch this off. Joining the military once again made sense because there was a solid example of a service member who lived out the qualities I wanted in myself.

Will had real-world survival and tactical skills, yet he would have no problem being the quiet guy in the room. There was no overwhelming need to show off. Focusing on the fine details gave him a tremendous advantage in goal setting. He excelled in finances, friendships, education, and physique. Humility keeps him from bragging about any of this. His life displays the results. Through a healthy diet and impeccable fitness, he built discipline worth emulating. He would always strive to beat the standard. I envied how shredded he could get. Even today at 35, this motivates me to keep pushing myself to get better.

Based on his work ethic alone, he is an example of an officer I would do well to follow. Most importantly, however, is the emphasis he places on creating a healthy work environment. Mistakes happen. He learns from them and accepts feedback from teammates. He reminds himself to humble his pride. Leaders always have a choice in how they decide to lead. While we listen to others or ignore critical feedback? Striving to keep morale high, he always wants to shield subordinates from as much stress as possible when it trickles down from higher levels. I admired his approach because he trusted his team to get the mission done. Anything else was just an unnecessary distraction in the workplace.

Will's leadership advice rings true through every job I've had, civilian or military:

SECTION 4: LEADERSHIP ADVICE

> *"Command climate dictates how good or bad your job will be, period, full stop. Good leadership will increase morale, and the job will be fun. Bad leadership does the opposite, and unfortunately, there isn't much you can do to change it other than stay motivated and wait it out."*

He was so right it hurt. I was amazed whenever I saw the vast extent to which an individual leader in the military could control the lives of everyone around. Work culture (command climate) stems directly from the personality and temperament of those in positional authority. Rank determines who sets the tone for the group. Little can be done to change the environment short of replacing the leader, which in extreme situations can be healthier for the organization. Barring any such immediate change, the workplace will reflect whatever mood the leader puts out.

Not knowing what kind of leader one will get makes joining the military a bold move. Once the contract is signed, freedom goes out the window because the government considers our physical bodies pieces of equipment. To detail this concept further, intentionally getting an injury such as a bad sunburn to avoid work is a crime. My body is no longer my own. I belong to a chain of command having a greater purpose than my personal agenda. The healthier the chain of command is, the better life will be. A unit's leader is entrusted with utmost control and legal authority. Hopefully, they've earned this through proven trustworthiness.

Baron von Steuben, a founder of the American Army, is known for having directed military officers to show compassion and consideration for the subordinates they lead. The best command climate exists when leaders accept risk to ensure subordinates have freedom. In the Army, we call this having "wide left and right limits." Autonomy is encouraged, and people are treated with dignity and respect. Failure is accepted without ridiculing those who are driven to take risks, and freedom is provided to subordinates, if only in the smallest ways. People are spoken to like adults capable of making reasonable decisions suitable for the organization's goals.

Good leaders take holistic approaches to keep workers healthy and avoid burnout. Such leaders are awesome to work for because they demonstrate how much they care. They provide time to rest, mitigate redundant tasks, and streamline the workflow. Service members are encouraged to take time off to decompress and return to work recharged. Work is purposeful with clear direction provided. Every order they give is filtered to ensure unnecessary burdens are removed. Thought is put into how subordinates are impacted by new demands. This type of leadership benefits the organization especially by inspiring career longevity.

Bad leaders are unaware of the impact their directives have on others. Focus is placed on getting the results they desire regardless of morale. The worst possible situation is when zero autonomy is given to others. No one else can voice their insights or make adjustments. Anyone who attempts to speak up is shut down. This type of leadership attempts to control others through fear and intimidation with threats of punishment. Subordinates are siloed from each other, and relationships are fractured to ensure no parties below the leader are capable of consolidating power. Using tactics involving shame, insecure leaders thrive off belittling and weakening others. Peers fear that resources are limited so they attack one another. Sibling rivalry is a similar psychological phenomenon in which children compete for scarce parental affection. This is a horrible work situation and is excruciatingly exhausting to endure.

Signing a military contract means accepting risks, to the point of death. This covers being placed in a high-stress work environment. Throw in an unhealthy leader and the situation spirals downward. Negative work environments are pervasive and create overwhelming tension that bleeds into personal life. Leadership, especially in the military, maintains control around the clock because we are always on call. Tensions at work come home with us. It may seem impossible to change the situation, but there is always hope. Mitigating such negative effects, even in small ways, is important. Detox. When things are hard, having career and personal goals will bolster motivation to thrive.

Things that helped me:

- Journaling
- Writing letters to mentors
- Online college classes (especially on leadership)
- Goal setting with daily countdowns
- Meditating/breath control
- Salt baths by candlelight & mental visualization
- Budget planning
- Streaming motivational videos
- Working out to audiobooks
- Studying human psychology
- Learning a new language
- Optimizing diet with new recipes
- Fitness (stretching, mobility work, active recovery)
- Jiu-Jitsu (especially for aggression management)
- Playing guitar, writing music
- Reading books
- Regularly scheduled calls to friends and family

Leaders need to prioritize rest and recovery. Stress never stops. Healthy outlets manage anxiety levels and protect subordinates from becoming unfair targets. Metabolize aggression. There's always the potential to remain positive amidst trying times, which I found through personal experience. Practice is required. Whether the job or leadership is stressful, nothing can control one's attitude. Avoiding stress is unrealistic, so proactively channeling angst into something productive is the way to go. Hitting a hard workout or long run puts the energy to good use. Using frustration to seek out advice on leadership development brings actionable, strategic solutions to employ. I learned to accept anger toward particular situations and allow that to fuel my healthy habits. If I felt stuck in a bad situation, I remembered to think about all the little ways I could improve my life.

Learning the difference between managing a stressful work environment and demanding change takes wisdom. Of course, in the event of unethical or inappropriate behavior in the workplace, there are systems for reporting to help ensure a safe work environment. I encourage anyone to speak up when they see abuse of authority, especially while serving in a leadership position. Confronting unhealthy behavior is the only way to help strengthen the organization and minimize damage to morale. More on this later in the book.

Positive work environments encourage dignity and respect. Workers are given a voice and can express themselves freely. They find purpose in their daily tasks. They can bring forward ideas and contribute to change. Motivation increases whenever workers feel engaged like this in the workplace. Leaders humbly ask where improvements can be made. Subordinates speak up and give meaningful feedback. Focus is placed on removing friction points in the workflow based on logic, not politics. Growth in the organization occurs because resources and training are provided. Leaders enable self-development in subordinates, whether through training, education, or certification programs.

I have been a part of healthy departments in both the military and the private sector. In such an environment, my supervisors took notice of my skill sets and allowed me to work autonomously towards goals that fit my strengths. This made me feel motivated to push harder. My coworkers experienced the same, and we all felt good about our jobs. Because of the appreciation we were shown, emotions were calm and stress was minimal. Challenging situations at work were met with collaborative teamwork. Because workers felt positive about the work environment, loyalty to management increased. Our gratitude for good treatment invoked a stronger dedication to the organization. We liked our leaders, so we worked harder for them. Transparency and openness created room to breathe and relax, in turn making it easier to be more productive.

Military jobs are uniquely geared for high levels of stress on the mind and body because war involves taking life. Unlike corporate work environments, being nice in the military isn't a requirement. Customer service is not a focal point of the training pipeline although it's been addressed in recent years. When bullets fly and explosives detonate, there's a time for violence of action, raised voices, and urgency. This doesn't mean we don't feel emotions; we compartmentalize them temporarily. Mental skills and tools are necessary to enable this. Emotional well-being plays a big part in sustaining readiness in the troops. When leaders overlook the long-term effects of high-stress urgency, they risk creating an unsustainable work culture. Eventually, because of this ignorance, ongoing work stress wears down unit cohesion. It can result in mental health issues, depression, and suicidality.

Working with combat veterans taught me a lot about the significance of mentally healthy leaders. Some Soldiers hardened by war may remain mission-focused and have little patience for human error. Emphasis on procedure is important because they know that mistakes lead to miscalculations in war, ultimately costing human life. Perhaps a Soldier has witnessed friends die in battle and now has little patience for mistakes. With a punitive tone in their voice, they demand subordinates fear, angering them, continually pushing while scrutinizing details. They demand attention to detail and hard work. While this is meant to save lives in war, there's a propensity for burnout under their command. Overemphasis on procedures can ignore the personal touch needed to inspire subordinates.

Balancing people and policy is an art. Self-aware leaders manage the ratio of tasks to relationship building. I was surprised by some leaders who lost friends in battle and yet patiently led with compassion. Focusing on people rather than procedures, they made work sustainable over long periods. They maintained a calm work environment while remaining focused on achieving goals. Discipline was rewarded with trust when standards were exceeded. If goals are missed, then swift punitive action takes place. But it wasn't personal. This leadership style is most suitable for self-driven, mature individuals.

In the military, I learned the difference between leading and managing. Leaders inspire hard work. Managers monitor tasks. There's no perfect formula because every personality is unique, but morale is certainly measurable. Until someone takes command there's no way to predict how they'll lead. Personality and emotional intelligence dictate success because those traits determine which soft skills they possess. Soft skills are personality characteristics that influence how one person relates to others. Emotional intelligence is one soft skill all leaders need. This soft skill allows leaders to read the mood in the room and adjust accordingly. They know when to push and when to back off.

Other soft skills include empathy, clear communication, flexibility, and many more. In the military, kindness goes a long way. It positively impacts morale which is important when assessing leadership efficacy. High morale translates to increased commitment to the organization. However, not every leader sees it this way. Some have no concern for personability and instead sternly enforce standards. They're no fun to be around. When a leader does care to be nice, it's a welcomed breath of fresh air.

As a leader, I always had a choice in how I treated others. When unable to remove job stress, I could at least not compound it further. One of the biggest things Soldiers appreciate is autonomy. They love it when a leader trusts them enough to give them the freedom to maneuver. It made sense to me. Who doesn't appreciate being treated like an adult? Plus, it gives Soldiers a real chance to develop their own leadership skills. Will's advice inspired me in this area. I strove to enable squad and team leaders to function autonomously and build leadership potential. Enabling them to lead meant that I provided ongoing guidance while allowing them to adjust the workflow. If they met the commander's intent, I could avoid micromanaging them.

I'm human and struggle with stress like anyone else. As a military leader, I needed to ensure I never used my position as a way of enabling unhealthy behavior. No matter how angry or aggressive I felt, it was important I never used rank as a means of winning an argument or getting my way. I never wanted to lose control of my feelings, raise my voice, or curse. Doing so would make those things an acceptable part of our work culture. Instead, I knew to step away from stressors to regain my thought and control my breath.

Energy remains trapped in the body until we either snap at someone or burn it up as fuel. I always aimed for the latter by putting energy towards physical exercise. Sweating it out during a workout kept me from acting out in anger toward others. Leaders who act out frustration at work tend to become bullies. Being at the top of a food chain has obvious perks, but abusing such authority is never acceptable. I respected friends like Will and wanted to lead in a way that made them proud.

The command climate I created was only as good as my continued self-awareness. Shortcomings and character flaws on my part impacted the Soldiers even if I wasn't aware of it. They could see I was under pressure if I closed myself off. Learning to compartmentalize sources of stress was critical to maintaining effective leadership. I found it was important for me to shield them from the negativity pressed upon me. Way easier said than done. I eventually learned to filter out the before speaking to those I led. Being cautious of my words and attitude, I attempted to never aim frustration at them but rather attack problem sets. This strategy helped me maintain objectivity and create a work environment that valued innovative solutions. As a leader, being calm is more beneficial than aggression in the long run.

I modeled my leadership style after friends who inspired me to join the military. Will led in a manner that enabled subordinates to excel as subject matter experts. Trust and humility were foundational to making this happen. He was not concerned with using others to build his image. Instead, he worked as hard as possible to ensure he shared the burden. He enabled his teammates to do their job. His personal values were reflected in his work as he genuinely treated others well. While some leaders strive to look better than the competition, leaders like Will simply have fun being authentic. We can feel the difference between confidence and arrogance in a leader.

As a military officer, I wanted to live with intensity but remain a calm leader. This was never an easy balance to maintain, especially when stress, exhaustion, and frustration were part of the mix. Soldiers I led suffered through physically demanding work and on top of that had to manage their roles as parents and spouses at home. As a leader, I needed to help minimize the stress they carried. Feeling out their mood allowed me to know when to push and when to back off.

Mindfulness practices helped me process intense emotional states as appropriately as possible. For example, out in the field during training exercises when things went sideways, I took regular tactical pauses. During long convoy movements or high-tempo mission sets, stress built. When nearing a boiling point, I dropped to the ground and cranked out push-ups. Other times I lifted heavy things or reorganized cargo. Before I opened my mouth, I needed to get energy out of my body. The job was exhausting enough. I didn't want to make it more stressful for those I led.

Consistent physical outlets help digest stress and aggression before it negatively affects others. Will taught me to crush myself in workouts which helped me remain friendly toward others. Thanks also to what I learned on the mats in Jiu-Jitsu, I took deep breaths to maintain control of my fight-flight response. My mentors choked me out frequently to check my ego. Wisdom gained on the mats carried into the military. I refused to feed chaos. Countless times I was able to keep my mouth closed while letting someone else vent. Tension inevitably subsided once someone felt they got everything off their chest. It was all water under the bridge within a few minutes, and we could focus on attacking a new problem set. Military training never runs out of problem sets.

Aggression is welcomed in the military and is best channeled into practical efforts pertaining to fitness. Being fit as a leader inspires others who can visibly assess and appreciate the work ethic. Dependability in combat rests upon one's ability to meet high physical demands. Many different body types exist, so there isn't one set formula to follow. When progress translates to functionality in the job, it encourages others to do the same. Basics include running, pushups, sit-ups, pullups, rucking, and swimming. There's an endless discussion to be had here, but suffice it to say, fit leaders motivate others.

Joining the military was a deep dive into developing my ability to manage difficult situations up and down the chain of command. Sometimes I had leaders who frustrated me; other times, Soldiers I led did. There was no shortage of opportunities to test my self-control, so whenever I emotionally reacted, I learned and moved on. With friends like Will in my life, I wanted to be a leader who rose above hotheadedness and used it as positive fuel. When people look at a leader like Will, they know he's no joke because he beats discipline into himself. Subordinates know he can turn up the heat if needed because he has no issue whipping himself into shape. He has nothing to prove, so he can invest mental and emotional resources into pulling everyone else up.

In conclusion, command climate makes or breaks everything. Military environments are rough, and it's easy to make a knee-jerk decision without realizing how it will affect others. Leaders make mistakes, but each one can be used as a learning opportunity. Ego can be your greatest opponent. Removing emotions from decisions helps, but it does not guarantee you will not fail. There will be times when you screw up and need to fix the damage. Sometimes you will get things right. Sometimes you won't. Learn with an open mind. Believe things will get better with time.

Despite mistakes or shortcomings, stay focused on the type of energy you put into the workplace. If others notice your frustration, let them know you are working to address a challenge. Build a work culture centered on problem solving. Remind yourself to communicate clearly and respectfully. Doing so helps uncover solutions as tensions run high.

According to Will, and he stands correct, my path in the military was uncertain because leadership constantly changes. What he wanted me to know was that the leader who wielded power above me would create the conditions in which I had to work and live. What could be predicted was the certainty of change. Command climate in the military is sourced from a subset of leaders that change every couple of years. This creates a revolving door of leadership that could completely change styles over the course of one's contract. The brilliance of such design is that no single leader remains in position for the entirety of one's contract (usually).

Pandemics causing freezes in movement can impact this too, which I experienced during my contract. Normally, leadership is staggered so multiple positions change out at different times. During the COVID-19 pandemic, this halted. Instead of one leader changing out every few months, several new leaders showed up or left simultaneously. This is great when leadership is awesome, and taxing when it is not. Thankfully, pandemics like COVID-19 are infrequent events.

Leadership is a complicated responsibility with rough patches I still don't fully understand. But it took such challenging situations to help me grow. Military work environments are potent tests of the human spirit, resolve, and endurance. Leadership can influence this for better or worse. I know how awesome it feels to be around good leaders, so I took notes and did my best to emulate the characteristics they employed. I'm still working towards that goal and plan to continue for the rest of my life.

Thank you, Will.

References:

Buades-Rotger, M., Göttlich, M., Weiblen, R., Petereit, P., Scheidt, T., Keevil, B. G., & Krämer, U. M. (2021). Low competitive status elicits aggression in healthy young men: behavioral and neural evidence. *Social cognitive and affective neuroscience*, 16(11), 1123–1137. https://doi.org/10.1093/scan/nsab061

Choy, O., Raine, A., & Hamilton, R. H. (2018). Stimulation of the Prefrontal Cortex Reduces Intentions to Commit Aggression: A Randomized, Double-Blind, Placebo-Controlled, Stratified, Parallel-Group Trial. *The Journal of neuroscience : the official journal of the Society for Neuroscience*, 38(29), 6505–6512. https://doi.org/10.1523/JNEUROSCI.3317-17.2018

Cooper, J. C., Kreps, T. A., Wiebe, T., Pirkl, T., & Knutson, B. (2010). When giving is good: ventromedial prefrontal cortex activation for others' intentions. *Neuron*, 67(3), 511–521. https://doi.org/10.1016/j.neuron.2010.06.030

Kirland, FR. (1990). The Gap Between Leadership Policy and Practice: A Historical Perspective. *Defense Technical Information Center*, https://apps.dtic.mil/sti/pdfs/ADA515376.pdf

Mehta, P. H., & Beer, J. (2010). Neural mechanisms of the testosterone-aggression relation: the role of orbitofrontal cortex. *Journal of cognitive neuroscience*, 22(10), 2357–2368. https://doi.org/10.1162/jocn.2009.21389

Somerville, L. H., Kelley, W. M., & Heatherton, T. F. (2010). Self-esteem modulates medial prefrontal cortical responses to evaluative social feedback. *Cerebral cortex* (New York, N.Y. : 1991), 20(12), 3005–3013. https://doi.org/10.1093/cercor/bhq049

5 - TRUE IDENTITY

"Lay on the bottom of the pool pretending you're a sea creature. That helps me stay calm while people waste energy panicking."
- ***MIKE** [Navy Rescue Swimmer]*

Exposure therapy: resolving fears by engaging directly with them

Interoception: awareness of feelings inside our bodies

Self-Concept: who we believe we are based on unique traits and characteristics

Social Identity: who we perceive ourselves to be in relation to our peer group

SECTION 1: INTRODUCTION TO THE TOPIC

Cadre wanted to evaluate our aptitude for leadership during our time in the schoolhouse. I was tasked with running a live fire range for our BOLC class. This was my first time doing it. Without any guidance or framework, I had to figure it out from scratch. I was a brand-new officer and I didn't know anything yet, but I knew who did! My first decision was to identify any Lieutenants with enlisted experience in the military. Of those I identified, I asked who had run a range before. Within minutes I found a subset of men and women with whom I formulated a plan and moved forward to execute. Because of their support, it was a success.

During the execution of the range, one cadre member decided to test me. We were waiting on ammunition to be delivered, so I gave everyone a break to eat chow. He came up to me while I was briefing our entire class. After I finished speaking, he started screaming in my face accusing me of not correctly running the range because everyone was sitting down and wasting time. I stood there confused and waited for him to finish. Once he did, I wiped the spit off my face. I calmly told him ammunition delivery was enroute. In the meantime, we were taking a quick pause to coordinate our next movement and have breakfast. Some classmates volunteered to go wait for ammunition while others went to set up targets and establish firing lanes. I wasn't sure where the error was, so I simply maintained eye contact awaiting more info. Instead, he abruptly stormed off.

Was I a terrible leader already? My mind raced through the operation plans. We were on track. Transportation times were all covered, and everybody was on time this morning. The packing list indicated all necessary items were present, including uniforms, gloves, ballistic eye protection, ear plugs, helmets, body armor, canteens, and camelbacks for our water sources. We had designated who the lane safeties were and who would be helping run the range with me. Food for the whole day was packed in our assault packs (backpacks). We had even covered all the potential risks, from getting frostbite when handling metal objects in the cold to dehydration. I know we covered basic safety procedures like ensuring we never flag another person with the barrel of a weapon and never touch a rifle when someone is down range adjusting targets. Where'd I drop the ball exactly?

Realistically, I don't think there was a right or wrong answer. He was going to yell at me regardless. Still, I felt like I screwed up somehow, and in front of all my peers, no less. But because of my peers, I was confident in my ability to run a range. Collaborating with my classmates, we proceeded with a thoughtful, complete plan. I listened to the guidance offered by anyone who was prior enlisted. Applying attention to detail, I was sure to establish concrete timelines down to the minute.

This instructor effectively made me question my intelligence, work ethic, and communication ability. My confidence wavered as I questioned if I really had an objective outlook. Was I lying to myself? What was I missing here? I felt deflated and utterly blind to my ignorance; until Austin approached me.

As a combat veteran and former enlisted marine, Austin is one of my favorite people in the military. He always encouraged me whenever I felt like I didn't fit in because of my age or inexperience in leadership. He knows what he wants to see in a leader and makes it very clear. I leaned on him constantly to coach me through stressful events. Out of 60 students in this 19-week course, he was at the top of the list of people I trusted to give heartfelt guidance.

"Hey brother," he calmly spoke in his rich Southern accent. "Did you see how uncomfortable you made that guy?" Still confused and embarrassed, I asked him to clarify. "While you stood there and stared directly at him, he kept yelling louder and louder to make sure he got the entire class's attention. When you didn't budge or blink, he flinched. He walked away so awkwardly. That was awesome. Don't think twice about what he said. I know what he was trying to do. Brother, you're doin' a great job."

Austin has been to combat zones multiple times and doesn't suffer fools. He continually reaffirmed my belief in myself and does so even today. His words help me remember who I am outside the military training environment. To this day, this is one of my most powerful memories in the Army.

SECTION 2: A GOOD MILITARY LEADER

Another great friend I was inspired by before joining the military is Mike. With Irish heritage shining as bright as his red hair, green eyes, and freckled white skin, Mike is a motocross adrenaline junky who sails boats, rebuilds engines, and travels the world to have outdoor adventures of any kind. Always serious about his fitness and diet, he walks around with abs and usually a bag of granola with oats. We first met at a loud beach bar in San Diego through a mutual friend as we conversed by shouting over the cover band. He was one of the first Navy friends I made, and I knew right away he was a great guy. He invited me to go dirt bike riding the next day, and I agreed. Since I had just obtained a motorcycle license, I thought it would translate to dirt biking. That was incorrect, so I mostly just stood around and watched.

Having a strong self-identity, he joined the military around 18 and left home. Oceans awaited. He tested his swimming abilities in a rigorous training pipeline and passed, becoming a rescue swimmer. Amidst all the unknowns ahead of him, he held true to his goals. His mindset kept him grounded. We talked about military life and how much it grew him as a person. He quickly learned to be comfortable exploring new places around the world with his Navy crew every time the vessel docked for "liberty," which is basically their monthly time-off. They grew close on deployments. His friends were all awesome, which added to my desire to join. We went hiking, boating, and swimming, and all the while, I admired how everyone felt like family. They did everything together.

Anytime they went out, whether to explore nature or hit the town to go bar hopping, they kept tabs on each other. Training bonded them. They took their careers seriously. Knowing who had 24-hour duty coming up next helped determine who would be the designated driver. I could see how important it was for them to support each other because at work they dealt with life-and-death situations. Attention to detail was vital. Mike was always dependable, and anyone who worked alongside him knew his work ethic was solid.

Mike is a teammate that anyone would want. I dug his mature insight. Whenever I asked him for stories about leadership in the military, he always had great examples of what to do and what not to do. He was thoughtful and very matter of fact. On the job, he learned to read situations quickly and accurately to avoid clouded judgment from adrenaline build-up.

His focus stayed steady. He kept track of both the technological equipment he used and the temperament of those in the aircraft with him. His training taught him to stay aware of his environment. The way he depicted things so clearly allowed me to deepen my understanding of what it means to serve in the military. On the one hand, it means becoming part of something much bigger than oneself, and it comes with a surrender of control. On the other hand, it also means having a voice and exercising the responsibility of speaking up when things aren't right.

Mike's most desirable feature by far is his calm temperament which is what fuels his sense of control. He's unshakable. I am convinced that if the world was ending and everything was going horribly wrong, he would be in complete serenity with a tactical plan. As a Navy SAR (Search and Rescue) swimmer, he knows how to handle the most powerful natural element on the planet, the ocean. He tests his mettle by surfing ever-increasing waves (10+ feet), and the more he gets crushed, the more his appetite grows. There are days he still goes out when he knows conditions are too much for most surfers to handle. He brushes it off, saying he was sketched out but still had fun, even if he almost died. When Mike chuckles and says, it was a rough day to swim past the breakers; I know this means I would drown within seconds.

Threats of death just don't seem to register in his brain, and I love him for that. Being around him gets me out of my head. His sense of calm helps calm me down. He's present and knows how to stay grounded even when there's no more ground around. He will find the sketchiest cliff, jump over the sign that says don't pass this sign, and take photos of his feet dangling over the drop-off. Again, that is Mike doing what he does. I'm grateful he's still alive.

When I asked him to teach me to overcome my anxiety in the water, he never hesitated to provide guidance. After all, he is trained to save people from dying in raging seas. He even got me to jump off the bluffs at Sunset Cliffs into the ocean 20 feet below. Without judgment, he helped me understand how important it is to breathe slowly and steady my heart rate. One time he coached me on getting comfortable in the water by exhaling myself down to the bottom of the pool where I could hang out chest flat on the bottom. He wanted me to build a relationship with water that was restful. He pointed out how much energy I wasted fighting against a force I could never control. Again, his mind was always calm, and I strove to find that path alone. Hanging out with him helped me reflect on where I could improve my understanding. I wanted to be like Mike.

While strapped to the back of the aircraft, he flew over the ocean in some gnarly situations. A few times, this included surprise storms, at night, in complete darkness, on aircraft carriers. Service members can die in such situations. There were moments he swore could be his last as helicopter pilots had to land their aircraft on a ship swaying in cold, black swells. Having almost a decade of military experience, Mike spoke up when he needed to educate a new pilot on risk-taking and when it was too dangerous. Even though he was enlisted and the pilots were officers, he didn't see rank as a reason to avoid professional criticism. If Mike says a situation is dangerous, then there's no way anyone could disagree, or at least they shouldn't if they were sane. He's the last person to be afraid of an adrenaline response, so I'll take his word over anyone's. Mike knows how to ride the razor's edge in life as well as back off at the exact right time.

One time, while flying in stormy night conditions, he was overridden by some pilots who he said were being too risky. The weather worsened, and when the flight eventually ended, everyone knew he was right. They almost lost control of a situation their experience level could not handle. He jumped out of the aircraft, fuming that his experience was ignored because of rank. For Mike, saying "I told you so" would not ease his anger because lives could have been lost. I took this to heart when I became an Army officer. My respect for him as a dear friend translated to fierce protection of the Soldiers I was leading. I never once pulled rank during my time in the Army. Instead, I trusted insight from subordinates with more military experience. This helped me navigate many dangerous situations.

SECTION 3: PSYCHOLOGICAL APPLICATION

Mike wanted me to remember that my life experiences before I joined the military deeply enriched my mindset. He encouraged me to reach out anytime I felt stuck or isolated during my journey. He knew from personal experience that being away from friends and family would cause me to forget key aspects of my identity. Military training pipelines are unique environments in which members are pulled from external social influences and secluded as a unit. Psychologically, this promotes cohesion between service members. Individuals begin to find commonalities with each other, and the desire to strengthen similarities increases. The transformation from civilian to Soldier begins this way. These training environments help build a military identity as we alter our self-concept according to our new social group (Alcover et al., 2020). We are never the same again.

Individual identity changes in social groups. In the military, seclusion from others in society develops a territorial mindset in which civilians are categorized as outsiders (Vincens et al., 2020). This is known as building an "us versus them" mindset. We are instructed to run internal evaluations to flag any unwanted behaviors. Peer reviews are a part of military training programs in which students anonymously report positive and negative behaviors in one another. Students are then ranked, top to bottom, based on these scores. Several peer reviews occur before graduation. Nerve-racking! Anyone routinely ranking at the bottom of the class runs the risk of being dismissed. In the military, being part of an outgroup is detrimental to successful graduation should peers agree to vote someone out of their ranks.

It's normal for people to want to be a part of a group, and the military uses this to help strengthen bonds. Desire to belong within a social group is based on the protective need for acceptance and can be measured by perceived cohesion among individuals (Meuret et al., 2016). Cohesion can be measured by how well peers get along or understand one another. Exclusion from the group can cause social anxiety resulting from stigma about those who don't fit in.

Social networks are known to provide protective factors that increase the social support of those perceived favorably (Stevens et al., 2017). Tribalism began this way. Anyone deemed unacceptable risks losing shared resources. They become outcasts. Existential crisis. Our brains seek to avoid such threats. Fear of rejection motivates conforming behavior to help minimize perceived differences. Standing out in isolation from the pack makes for a more obvious target.

Fitting in with peers is only one aspect of uncertainty and discomfort related to military training. Not knowing what challenges and stressors exist on the road ahead also induces anxiety. All these variables combined help ensure that trainees are tested for the ability to manage chaos in combat. The mind is constantly trained to be aware of threats while managing behavior to abide by military standards. It's important that service members maintain control of themselves while collaborating with others, no matter how intense a situation becomes. Social pressure can be positive or negative depending on how one gets along with peers. Finding social support within training pipelines helps increase courage when facing difficult situations. We are tested to face situations we fear to build our identity as military leaders. It's a group effort.

Believing we can overcome hardship alongside others makes us successful leaders. It's important to make courage a part of our identity despite our brain's desire to seek comfort (Norton & Weiss, 2009). This is done by viewing fears as challenges or "reappraising anxiety as excitement" (Brooks, 2014). Mike is a living example of these powerful mental tools. I study him like a social experiment whenever we hang out. My brain will interpret things like ocean waves as scary while he sees them as fun and exciting. I know he naturally has this inclination, but I wondered how much he grew from his time in the Navy. He inspired me to join the military as a way of conditioning my brain to be a little more like his.

Leaders use slow breathing to control their emotions. Calm helps them maintain focus. Deep breathing is a known psychological tool to reduce anxiety during stressful events (Ma et al., 2017). Some people like Mike do this innately. Swimming early in life certainly paved the way. I, however, must actively remember how to breathe. The more intense a situation becomes, the more I lose control of my breath. Sometimes I unknowingly hold my breath. *Deep inhale...and...suddenly...I...forget...to...BREATHE! Ahhhhhhhhh.* I can very intentionally reset myself with practice by actively reflecting on all the advice and coaching I have received. It's not natural for me, but it's getting better. Anytime I'm in the water getting overwhelmed by the ocean, I hear Mike in my mind telling me to relax and become a sea creature.

Mindfulness is especially key to remaining calm and in control of our emotional states. One Harvard University study on meditation used MRI brain imaging to convey the importance of mindfulness (Desboreds et al., 2012). Images visually confirm the helpful benefit of learning how to reflect and meditate because this downregulates areas of the brain associated with anxiety. Even better, these practices carry over into everyday life and continue to enhance our ability to face adversity.

Before I shipped out for BCT, Mike gave me a great piece

of advice related to this that increased in value as I progressed throughout my journey in the military:

SECTION 4: LEADERSHIP ADVICE

> *"You're going to get stressed and forget who you are during military training pipelines. It's totally normal. Remind yourself who you are, because nobody can take those qualities away."*

It amazes me how often I find my way back to this advice. It guides me through many overwhelmingly stressful situations in which I've found myself lost and confused. Why did certain people not like me? Why was I not fitting in with certain leaders or peers? Do I have what it takes to make it through? Should I give up and quit? Doubt after doubt slammed my brain like out-of-control ocean waves. Breathe, slow down, and control what I can.

After a year in the military training pipeline, I noticed I was losing confidence. The endless noise of people throwing around opinions and complaints began to drown out my inner dialogue. Fears that other people had were slowly seeping into my brain. People are naturally afraid of falling behind. There's no shortage of competition in which peers seek to surpass each other and stand out as number one. This is a fundamental truth of the human social dynamic. These aren't necessarily bad or corrupt people; they just have a desire to be ahead of others. My innate response is to find the road less traveled and enjoy the peace there. I prefer to avoid crowds. When training in a busy, high-traffic military program, the cacophony can be mind-numbing. I often had to call a trusted friend or relative to help remind me who I was amidst the noise.

One specific example of losing sight of myself happened in OCS. It's one of those situations in which opinions around me clouded my self-awareness. A peer in my class kept boldly professing his desire to kill in war. He wouldn't shut up about it. His blood lust was intense, and over months, his aggression kept building. I assumed the distance from his wife and kids was getting to him but there were many other classmates enduring the same distance with much less anger. After another one of his rants, I felt compelled to discuss the weight of killing in combat based on what others have told me. Yes, many have killed with ease and accuracy, but they also understand it to require sound judgment. It was more than scratching an itch to take life. While it's certainly muscle memory to pull the trigger, and it's compelling to protect others, the long-term effects of killing another person are profound. I felt it was appropriate to honor the weight of the decision made to take someone's life because the men I know who killed their enemies still think about it today.

When I brought this up, he immediately erupted into anger and accused me of being a soft, emotional wimp. I can't disagree with him about being sensitive, but I wasn't saying that it's wrong to kill people in combat even though that is how he interpreted what I said. He then began telling our peers I was weak, anti-war, and against killing terrorists. I started doubting my own argument. This was the situation Mike had warned about; that training pipelines can make us forget who we are.

Am I against killing enemies in war? No. Do I

believe my friends who killed enemies in combat are bad people? No. What about the fighters who mentor me on the mats, are they wrong for enjoying hand-to-hand violence? Not at all. They are teaching me to appreciate discipline in using and controlling violence. I thought about how much I love Jiu-Jitsu and mixed martial arts because they enable me to protect others if necessary. To a lethal extent, I imagine how appropriate it would feel to fire my weapon to stop someone with the intent of killing Americans or allies.

I was up for discussing all this, but my colleague wasn't. He was visibly upset and ranting loudly. By this point, I realized he could no longer conduct a meaningful conversation because he was emotional. Peers started looking over, wondering what was going on. He started shouting about me being a coward. Thinking he might be right, I felt like a freak in my uniform. Maybe I had made the wrong move by joining the military. I don't have intense blood lust making me thirst for shooting someone in the face. I do enjoy getting destroyed on the mats, but that's different. No one dies at the gym. I joined the Army to find brotherhood. Killing would only be a potential means of protecting my military family, not a predominant goal. I started to doubt myself in big ways until I thought about my true identity.

I experienced abuse as a child. I can say I wouldn't hesitate to put down an enemy that victimizes innocent people, yet my actions would not be thoughtless and inconsequential. Even while killing enemies in war is the right thing to do, later, after the battle, I would contemplate the situation and reflect on it in the quiet of my mind. I know my friends do. How could I not revisit my decision to take a life when veterans tell me they still do? It impacted them. They spoke about how they fell back on training and executed their kills perfectly. They also told me that after the missions, they thought about who it was they just took out of this world and what impact that had. These are warriors, not wimps; I wondered what he'd say to their faces. Again, none of this registered to the man I was attempting to dialogue with, so I shut up.

Mike's advice came in clutch during this situation. Here I was in a military training pipeline that isolated me from friends and family. I was inaccurately accused of having certain beliefs. My peers were told I wasn't dependable in war. My antagonist wanted a reaction. Emotionality. I kept my mouth closed and reflected on who I was before I joined the military, not wanting to pour gas on the fire. Remembering my values and beliefs helped me resist confusion by the misjudgments of others. Finding peace within myself, I chose to stay true to the self-understanding gained by talking to others who knew me.

Distancing myself from unnecessary tension paid off. I regained my confidence. At a healthy distance, I saw this man burn bridges by antagonizing others and gossiping. He became even more confrontational and talked down with indignation, especially toward the end of our time in training. He pushed his peers around and it was becoming more obvious. As graduation approached, frustrations were high for everyone because we all wanted our freedom. Once grades were finalized and we received our orders, there was less incentive to play nice with peers other than the fact that it's good to maintain professionalism at all times. Some people lost their sight. This was one man who let anger drive him toward damaging relationships.

Finally, justice. He ran into someone just like him. Collision. An obnoxious screaming match ensued and a near physical altercation clearly demonstrated the hot-headedness of both men. Classmates watched and rolled their eyes. Everything made sense now. Observing all this drama unfold helped me remember and appreciate my authentic identity as a sensitive person who doesn't look for fights. I'm totally okay looking weak to anyone who thinks emotional reactivity shows strength.

I'm not saying there's never a time and place to boldly demonstrate power, but the context will determine good judgment. Sometimes being explosive and loud is necessary to convey dominance. War is a perfect example. Violence can be essential to enforce protection. However, this doesn't mean the assertion can't be quiet. Not all battles that comprise a war are conducted the same. Some are covert while others are explosively visible. In whatever scenario enemies are killed in war, there must be a thoughtful approach to prevent collateral damage. We train with weapons to consider who or what stands behind our targets to ensure we don't indiscriminately kill. Rules of engagement.

Emotional regulation and self-control keep Soldiers accurately focused on their lethality. Ensuring each service member is emotionally healthy strengthens their capacity to engage targets appropriately. Good judgment is key. I personally know what it's like to struggle with self-control. My emotions used to run my life, and after countless embarrassing situations, I hated my own behavior. Because I was afraid of looking weak, my mouth ran without considering the consequences. Words alone never prove true strength. I especially took notice of the quiet demeanor of blackbelt-level fighters sparring at the gym. They let their skills speak while calmly crushing opponents. With that realization, I desired to slow and control my responses. They were happy to oblige.

> *Fist bump. Choke. Tap. Again.*
> *Fist bump. Choke. Tap. Again. "$&%#!"*
> *Fist bump. Wrist grab. Throwdown. Choke. Tap. AGAIN.*
> *(Hesitant)Fist bump. Slam. Diaphragm crush.*
> *Tap! Tap! Tap!...pause...breathe...$@^#&*$#!!*

My ego died a slow death. Getting wrecked on the mats instilled a sense of stillness that slowly humbled my aggression. Every submission helped. My pace in grappling slowed down and I learned to relax while being attacked. My focus was on my breath and trusting subtle techniques to regain control of the situation.

In the Army I looked hesitant to engage in any conflict, but I guess I really am. I train on the mats to learn what to do if a threat presents itself while also learning how to control my own aggression. Because I was physically attacked as a young child, I have a deep disdain for physical violence. Expressing aggression is somewhat uncomfortable for me because I know what it's like to be unfairly hurt by it. In developmental psychology class, we learned that abuse in childhood off lines the motor responses meant to fight against a violent threat. This is what happened to me. I never learned to defend myself when I was younger. In adulthood, Jiu-Jitsu plays a vital part in awakening my motor neurons through quite unpleasant flashbacks during my sparring sessions. My coach even commented on my obvious freeze response which helped me finally open my eyes to it. The journey has been hellish, but healing. I'm still growing through my past and am grateful for the leaders showing me the way. I'm not ashamed of my avoidance now that I understand how to manage it. Ultimately, I can't change who I am, and I certainly can't let others try to change me. Instead, I embraced what I brought to the military and looked forward to healthier peer interactions in the future.

Later during my time as a leader in the Army, Soldiers I led commented on my steady silence during times of emotional chaos. They expected me to erupt, but I gave no response. Why was I calm? It's because I was thinking. Whenever they commended my calm demeanor, it surprised me. For in my head, I was crazily running through various thoughts about the situation. It certainly didn't feel peaceful to me. Externally I remained stoic because I just didn't see how any reaction could help. In those cases, I'd stay quiet and note what needed to be handled to solve the problem. My frustrations could be minimized that way. For instance, when last-minute changes to our missions threw off all the prior planning we had invested our time in, I simply nodded, knowing that many more changes would inevitably follow. Getting upset every time this occurred would be a tremendous waste of energy. Soldiers noticed this and told me this kept them from wanting to punch the walls. We just rolled with whatever came. Of course, I had my moments of venting, but I mostly kept from leading with emotionality.

Not everyone in the military liked this. In training, my instructor docked me points during my turn as a class leader because he said I failed to show anger and yell when people screwed up. He said he had no idea what I was doing with all my anger. I took this as a compliment, but never told him that. Mostly I tried to not take things personally. Even when Soldiers screwed up, I tended to believe that the best approach was to address the consequences with a conversational tone. Shouting would raise their defenses even higher. I know it does for me. Whenever situations or people did irk me to the point I felt anger rising, my frustrations were transferred into my workouts. After calming my physiological response, I directly addressed the issue or people involved. But not until my heart rate was back to rest. In emergent situations I tried to keep yelling to a minimum, but adrenaline gets high in the field. So in those moments, I really got to test my discipline and seek out ways to experiment on my threat response.

My secret weapon was Jiu-Jitsu whenever it was available to me. In EBOLC, nobody in my class knew I was part of an underground fight club. Every lunch break I escaped to go get beat up by a group of salty, seasoned, combat veterans. Tough love. They taught me to control my breath, my anger, and my emotions. Eventually, after seeing how I was getting overwhelmed by all the angles of attack, they had me spar with my eyes closed. I thought my coach was joking. He insisted. Being blind on the mats forced me to stay calm and learn to feel my opponent. Amazing growth on those mats. I'd come back to class with a red face and drenched in sweat after every lunch break. Classmates stared at me in confusion and asked if I had been working out. Yep. My face beamed with a telling smile.

Mike always told me how potent my ability to read my own emotional state and that of other people would be in the military. I felt it was a burden. He told me to never forget that I possess a skill in understanding human psychology that most others are missing out on. He said it would pay off. Leaders with high self-awareness pick up on underlying social dynamics in a room. Subtle queues are noticed. Egos can then be navigated to bring solutions and overcome barriers.

I really did have to credit hardships in childhood for this ability. Reading people's emotional states can be a side effect of unsteady childhood situations that demand heightened attention to help guard against emotionally unpredictable adults. It can be a superpower. However, if not managed well, it's easy to become preoccupied with negative emotions. Training the mind to organize all this data takes time. Quieting the radar (ie. downregulating situational awareness) is necessary to rest the body. Sometimes the best way to do this is by exerting pent up energy through sport or exercise. If it wasn't for my Jiu-Jitsu coaches, I would never have made it this far, and psychological growth accrues every single time I roll.

Because of my own struggle with anxiety, I studied psychologically extensively. When it comes to understanding body language, books by former CIA and FBI interrogators or hostage negotiators are especially helpful. They give advice on profiling peoples' behaviors based on various physiological cues. Mike loved that

I knew all this. He said I would analyze people in the military and find ways to help reduce stress. I'd be able to avoid falling into it because I would know when someone was trying to get a reaction out of me. Books are great, but grappling reinforces my awareness of physiological stress. On the mats or in life, when someone is trying to intimidate or pressure me into losing focus, I need only remember that no one can take away what I know. With calm breath, I read the situation, contextualize the threat, and conduct myself accordingly. Technique trumps strength (...usually).

Embracing my quirks while in the military, I reminded myself to trust my gut in tense situations. Quietly reading people allows them to reveal who they are. It's easy to spot emotionally reactive people and various control tactics they use. Sound logic doesn't require violent enforcement or overexertion when working with a group of intelligent adults. Anyone who is defensive is trying to manage fear. Bullies, for instance, fear losing control and being hurt.

Our brain has helpful neurobiological features built in. For instance, the prefrontal cortex manages logic and complex thoughts. The amygdala, hippocampus, and a series of other structures manage primal urges. Balancing these brain features takes work, but knowing all this helps us understand how to stay in control of emotions. Easier said than done.

Throughout my time in the military, I had to remind myself that no one has the authority to tell me who I am or control my attitude. They can influence my environment, but never my mind. Mike wanted me to remember that anytime the situation around me was chaotic or painful, this didn't need to shift my internal thought process. Reflecting on my true identity and unique characteristics allows me to ground myself amidst uncertainty. I found peace in that truth then, and I still do now.

As much as I know myself, I still need to lean on trusted friends for reminders. Life isn't meant to be lived alone, and social support helps provide powerful motivation to overcome challenges. This is frequently why people first join the military. As a community, we can push one another past our perceived limits. Doubt and self-limiting beliefs vanish when we see others marching alongside us. Conversely, in isolation, we can lose sight of the ability to overcome difficulties. Suicide rates are currently increasing among both veterans leaving the military and active-duty personnel. Isolation and disconnection from the community are variables being further investigated. Again, losing sight of intrinsic value and capabilities can lead to despair and diminished hope. To illustrate my point, Researcher Danielle DeSimone published these findings on Wednesday, September 1, 2021:

"Suicide rates among active-duty military members are currently at an all-time high since record-keeping began after 9/11, and have been increasing over the past five years at an alarmingly steady pace. In 2021, research found that 30,177 active duty personnel and veterans who served in the military after 9/11 have died by suicide - compared to the 7,057 service members killed in combat in those same 20 years."

Being a part of a peer environment doesn't ensure social support and meaningful connection. It's still possible to be alone in a crowd. Keeping the company of a few trusted friends is important to fostering healthy support. Even in the absence of this intimate circle, there can be reminders and advice to reflect on. Hence, the reason I am writing. This book is a collection of thoughts I constantly mulled over whenever I felt alone or disconnected. Sometimes I felt like I didn't fit in with groups of people around me. At that moment, I thought about all the service members who inspired me to join. Others like them exist somewhere in the military, and it's only a matter of time before I'd find them. I kept hope and focused on making it through whatever challenge I was currently facing. Sure enough, I eventually made lifelong friends.

While in the military, there is always an avalanche of opinions and critiques. This can become overwhelming, so it's important to recalibrate perspective in light of true identity and inherent strengths. Nobody knows the struggles, adversities, and difficulties another person has faced before joining the military. Those tough times shape the character we bring to our units. Reflecting on past accomplishments and experiences is key to reminding ourselves we can make it through what's ahead. Calm the incoming anxiety even as waves incessantly pound down. When getting pulled under the surface, remember to own that domain. Don't waste energy fighting a wave that will never stop. Stay present in the discomfort of it all. Mindfulness eases the speeding thoughts and helps us focus on what brings peace.

Thanks, Mike.

References:

Alcover, C. M., Rodríguez, F., Pastor, Y., Thomas, H., Rey, M., & Del Barrio, J. L. (2020).

Group Membership and Social and Personal Identities as Psychosocial Coping Resources to Psychological Consequences of the COVID-19 Confinement. *International journal of environmental research and public health, 17*(20), 7413. https://doi.org/10.3390/ijerph17207413

Brooks A. W. (2014). Get excited: reappraising pre-performance anxiety as excitement. *Journal of experimental psychology. General, 143*(3), 1144–1158. https://doi.org/10.1037/a0035325

Desbordes, G., Negi, L. T., Pace, T. W., Wallace, B. A., Raison, C. L., & Schwartz, E. L. (2012). Effects of mindful-attention and compassion meditation training on amygdala response to emotional stimuli in an ordinary, non-meditative state. *Frontiers in human neuroscience, 6*, 292. https://doi.org/10.3389/fnhum.2012.00292

DeSeimone, D. (2021, September 1). Military Suicide Rates Are at an All-Time High. *USO.* https://www.uso.org/stories/2664-military-suicide-rates-are-at-an-all-time-high-heres-how-were-trying-to-help

Ma, X., Yue, Z. Q., Gong, Z. Q., Zhang, H., Duan, N. Y., Shi, Y. T., Wei, G. X., & Li, Y. F. (2017). The Effect of Diaphragmatic Breathing on Attention, Negative Affect and Stress in Healthy Adults. *Frontiers in psychology, 8*, 874. https://doi.org/10.3389/fpsyg.2017.00874

Meuret, A. E., Chmielewski, M., Steele, A. M., Rosenfield, D., Petersen, S., Smits, J. A., Simon, N. M., Otto, M. W., Marques, L., Pollack, M. H., & Hofmann, S. G. (2016). The desire to belong: Social identification as a predictor of treatment outcome in social anxiety disorder. *Behaviour research and therapy, 81*, 21–34. https://doi.org/10.1016/j.brat.2016.03.008

Norton, P. J., & Weiss, B. J. (2009). The role of courage on behavioral approach in a fear-eliciting situation: a proof-of-concept pilot study. *Journal of anxiety disorders, 23*(2), 212–217. https://doi.org/10.1016/j.janxdis.2008.07.002

Stevens, M., Rees, T., Coffee, P., Steffens, N. K., Haslam, S. A., & Polman, R. (2017). A Social Identity Approach to Understanding and Promoting Physical Activity. *Sports medicine (Auckland, N.Z.), 47*(10), 1911–1918. https://doi.org/10.1007/s40279-017-0720-4

Vincens, N., Stafström, M., Ferreira, E., & Emmelin, M. (2020). Constructing social identity through multiple "us and them": a grounded theory study of how contextual factors are manifested in the lives of residents of a vulnerable district in Brazil. *International journal for equity in health, 19*(1), 83. https://doi.org/10.1186/s12939-020-01196-2

6- COURAGE TO STAY AUTHENTIC

"Next time you're told that front-line leaders can't make tactical decisions on the ground, respectfully ask, 'Sir, if you say we're to always defer to you before we make decisions, what happens in war if you get shot in the face?'"

*-**BRAD** [Navy EOD Commander]*

transactional leadership: rely on a rigid structure that uses rewards and punishment to keep followers moving toward a desired goal

transformational leadership: inspiring followers to pursue goals beyond job requirements or expectations through genuine, heartfelt conviction

SECTION 1: INTRODUCTION TO THE TOPIC

"How can I help?" I asked a group of Soldiers during a discussion on mental health and resilience. They shrugged. Silence. No one had experienced this before. Lockdowns across the globe were limiting humanity's ability to stay connected due to the pandemic. Remote bases like ours struggled even more. All we had was ourselves. If we stayed locked up alone in our rooms when not at work, how could we decompress? Social isolation correlates with depression. Some Soldiers believed there was no hope for improvement until the lockdowns were lifted. I was undeterred. It was my job as a leader to find out where morale could improve. One way was to listen to the most vulnerable population, the junior enlisted Soldiers.

Eventually, they spoke. One Soldier said he believed his low rank made him unimportant to the organization. Others agreed. I noticed it was a common response from anyone in the E-1 to E-4 rank. Another said she felt too exhausted to speak out because of a tense marriage dynamic at home. Again, some nodded. Other frustrations were shared. It was messy, but progress always is. I let them know they were important, no matter the rank. Squad leaders and team leaders echoed this. NCOs spoke up, offering sincere support. Pulling from past combat deployments, they shared the mindset advice that pulled them through dark times. Nothing bad lasts forever.

I sprinkled in some psychology related to how brain signals change during depressive states and why it's important to understand the mechanics involved. Know your opponent. Understanding the wiring of our brains makes it possible to come up with real tools and strategies to combat difficult emotions. We can share these tools. I encouraged those struggling to view themselves as examples to others who feel lost and alone in life. They could spark inspiration by deciding to rise and overcome. Speaking up takes courage.

Initially, there was some resistance to seeking

help, but with peer support, hesitation eventually melted away. Social connection was key. Reaching out to a trusted friend during times of solitude can be vital. If more help is needed, the military has additional mental health solutions and services solutions available. Questions about Behavioral Health Services came up. Soldiers desiring further professional counseling began scheduling appointments. Stigma was important to address and there is a lot more work to be done here, both within and outside the military.

Contrary to common assumptions among Soldiers, receiving psychological help in the military would not negatively impact their careers. Privacy is protected. Soldiers don't have to share what they are going through with their chain of command. During the pandemic, we found a large influx of appointments were in the queue. Counselors were usually booked out for at least several days. If the wait was several weeks long for an appointment, we continually checked in with those who struggled alone, and if things worsened, we'd make moves to get them immediate care. For anyone, regardless of whether they were seeking help or not, we urged social connection.

As a leader, I stayed honest about my own struggles with being demoralized by the isolation. I missed Jiu-Jitsu, my fight house, and my coaches. Being in the Army and stationed on a remote base out in the middle of a desert had removed me from the best medicine I had to strengthen my mental health. Even without the lockdowns, our schedule gave me little time to travel out and see them. Despite not being able to grapple daily, any genuine social connection, especially at the gyms on base, helped me stay balanced.

I told the Soldiers to step up and build a social support network together, especially around fitness. Even without pandemics and lockdowns, this is vital to mental health. The lockdowns simply emphasized preexisting mental health struggles all humans quietly wrestle with when isolated. Eventually, travel restrictions would lift, but we all still needed lifelong solutions.

I'm proud of the Soldiers who were so open about what they needed. Honesty is inspiring. Though young, many intimately knew deep suffering. Hearing them speak about the adversities they overcame before joining the military was gut-wrenching. Knowing what it means to wake up every day in pain gave them insight into helping others. They also knew it was necessary to speak up now and ask for help because in the military you aren't meant to suffer alone. We share the burden. Lockdowns necessitated commitment to help each other. Stories from these Soldiers can save lives if they choose to share them.

Military training inherently uses shared suffering to build powerful relationships. Being close to the troops day and night provided insight into their personal lives. We become familiar with quirks, personalities, and preferences. Being aware of sudden changes in temperament is important. Just as we check the gauges and fluids of our vehicles before using them, leaders also gauge morale. Leaders must constantly be mindful of variables impacting morale and seek to address those issues. One way of doing this is by allowing Soldiers to speak freely.

When orders are given, it's critical to allow for dialogue or questions from subordinates. Openness ensures Soldiers on the ground can voice concerns. They're the ones doing the work. Allowing them to question the tasks they are handed is a sign of respect for their hard work. Give them the why. Sometimes misunderstandings lead to frustration. At other times, small details having a great impact are overlooked during planning. Without pausing to examine such areas, stress builds up. Yes, orders are made to be followed. However, Soldiers are authorized to bring up issues pertaining to their safety, even in combat. If no safe alternative is available, then the order stands. But until then, there is potential to optimize planning. Open dialogue with experienced Soldiers builds strategic solutions while ensuring the commander's intent is met. Giving Soldiers a voice earns leaders trust and credibility.

SECTION 2: A GOOD MILITARY LEADER

Brad was a stout Southern boy with a big heart who thrived in the pursuit of adventures that quite literally spanned the globe. I met him a few weeks after my nasty 30 mph bike crash. The crash culminated in my helmet cracking against a guard rail which stopped me from toppling over a steep mountainside. For three days after the crash, my equilibrium was gone. I drunkenly stumbled around in a fuzzy haze. Standing up resulted in the necessity of having to grab walls to keep from falling. Free tequila. Mid-sentence, I would forget what I was saying or who I was talking to. My brain felt foggy. The sound was muffled in my ears. Within a few days, I felt normal again. That's when I went to the cafe next door for a drink.

Brad sauntered in with cleats clicking against the

concrete floor. He was wearing tactical digicam cycling attire and had the steady swagger of a fighter emerging victorious from battle. *Who is this dude? Bet he rides a sick bike.* We briefly made eye contact. He beamed a smile; I sheepishly looked away. I was still physically recovering from my injuries and felt nauseating fear whenever I thought about cycling. I desperately wanted to revisit my crash site and reflect on what happened, but I was terrified. I looked at Brad again and believed he could help me face my fear.

Within minutes of dialoguing, I knew he was solid. His direct eye contact conveyed his intensity for life. His smile demonstrated confident openness. This man knew who he was, which was great for me. I needed a sure guide to help me down uncertain paths. As soon as I told him about my accident and the resulting anxiety, he jumped at the opportunity to ride along with me back to the crash site. “Sometime in the next few weeks?” I asked. “Today,” he responded emphatically.

My heart sank because I didn't feel ready. Just that morning, I had attempted to ride a single block in my neighborhood. My legs wobbled when I tried to mount my bike. The whoosh of cars driving by sounded like deadly missiles to my hypervigilant brain. Immediately, I got off my bike and walked into my apartment, defeated. This sad attempt was just a few hours before I met Brad. Now he wanted me to do it all again this afternoon, and even more. I tried to reason with him, but he wouldn’t take no for an answer. He sunk his teeth into the opportunity to help me.

Reluctantly I agreed but asked him to ride ahead of me so I wouldn’t slow him down too much when we approached the crash site. I let him know I was nervous and didn't want to annoy him if I needed to slow my pace down to a crawl. His response was powerful. He calmly and solemnly told me he'd stay right behind me to keep his eyes on me the whole way. He didn't care how slow I needed to go. His main goal was to protect me and ensure my success in destroying fear. The humility and strength of his response warmed my heart and fired me up to face the challenge. I knew I was safe with him, and there was no way I would back down now.

Hours flew by. Sure enough, as promised, he was at my apartment later that day, biking up my driveway. He arrived smiling with fierce joy and all the confidence in the world. I needed to see that because my heart was pounding out of my chest. He knew I trusted him to help me crush my fear. We mounted up and rode out. My anxiety skyrocketed as cars drove by, but I slowed my breath, at least, whenever I remembered to focus on it. Thoughts in my head mocked me for being so afraid in front of a military warrior, but I reflected on the patience Brad had. I believed that just over my shoulder was not a critic, but a friend. Though I barely knew him, he fully deserved my trust. I leaned on him for confidence, and luckily, he had plenty to spare.

We climbed the hill and curved around the bend. The surface of the road was still covered in the fine sand grains upon which my tires had skidded when I lost control that fateful day. *Panic*! I started to feel like my tires were as thin as razor blades. Then, looking down at my wheels, I remember how my brakes locked up. *Flashback*! I visualized how the pavement burned through both tires until air at 120 PSI burst out in high-pitched hisses accompanied by puffs of what looked like steam. Metal rims grinding against the asphalt and unable to steer, I had somehow managed to stay upright for several seconds before crashing.

Then I saw the spot! My eyes widened as I looked at the exact yellow reflector on the guard post that bashed my skull. The craziest thing was how calm I felt before the crash and the clear focus of it all. Acceptance. Time had slowed down in that instant. I was at peace with the upcoming impact. I wasn't afraid. I was simply ready to accept the inevitable, hospital or funeral. I told myself to get ready and do my best to keep my body from toppling over the edge, which I knew was at least a 10-foot drop. I remember thinking it would be easier to get an ambulance on the road than a helicopter to drop a litter and carry me out.

I vividly remember the gleam of the yellow plastic reflector on the grainy wood. It slowly got bigger and bigger as I toppled into it. Before I struck the barrier, I told myself to turn my head away and downward so the damage wouldn't be as bad. I was hoping for an open-casket wake. My right temple smashed against the inside of my helmet. My body folded in twists. I blinked, and chaos became stillness. I felt nothing. My ears were ringing and my body was numb. Holes burned through my cycling outfit. Blood slowly began to pool inside the pink patches etched into my skin. No pain registered, and I wondered which bones were broken. The entire right side of my face tingled like it was ice cold. Raising my hand up to feel it I hesitated. Not yet. I was too afraid to touch it and assess the damage. If my brains were hanging out, I didn't want to know. Within seconds I saw white stars twinkling everywhere as fog came rolling in. Then my breath sounded muffled in my ears like I was sitting outside of my body. *Woah, is this it, I thought.* Whiteout. Laying on my back staring at the clouds in a dream-like state, I waited to wake up from existence.

"Jesus, mate!" a voice said. "Are you &%*ing okay?!! %$&# me!! I watched the whole $#&@ing thing happen! Had you gone over the edge you'd be dead on the cliffside for sure!" I squinted and slowly tried to look up. "$@%#'n hell! Don't move, I'll be back with my truck to get you!"

The Aussie who witnessed the crash was a shouting, cussing angel. I stared in a blank daze and slowly blinked, thanking God for letting physics, centrifugal force, and gravity keep my body on the safe side of the guardrail. That was a lot of math and providence all at once.

I inhaled deeply as my mind returned to the present, squeezing the handlebars to keep perfect pressure on my brakes, 20 percent on the front and 80 percent on the rear. My heart thudded in my chest and my brain scanned for threats. True to his word, Brad never left my side. He stayed right behind my shoulder to cover my back from any cars or cyclists coming down. I slowed, still staring at the reflector, as the blue ocean shimmered brightly a few meters away. What a beautiful place to have almost died. This must be what heaven looks like. I exhaled fully, only slightly releasing the brakes.

We did it. We passed the crash site. Riding down a few hundred feet to the tide pools at the bottom of the hill, Brad and I stopped to talk. He checked in with me to ask how I was doing. I was beaming with relief that we had made it through. He said we needed to ride back and do it again a few more times. I trusted him and agreed. He kept behind me and covered me the whole way through. A few weeks later we were going on 60-mile rides together up the coast.

After that day, Brad and I became fast friends. He's been to war and knows what's truly important. When I joined the military, he was a constant sounding board, especially because of the combat experience he'd had. Any advice he gave me was seasoned with the awareness that troops on the ground matter most. No brief or map touches on the importance of understanding the reality on the ground. Brad saw death and saved lives. He knew what it meant to care about the troops. He also saw what could happen if leaders lost their cool and failed to make good decisions. Rank does not enable someone to prevent death. Calm, clear concentration is what it takes to read a situation in real-time and disarm the threat. Brad has this ability inside and outside the military.

As a Navy EOD (Explosive Ordnance Disposal) technician, Brad was trained to diffuse explosives through high-intensity situations. This job involves a potentially deadly unknown object at his hands and the potential of nearby enemies. As an Army Combat Engineer, I learned that obstacle emplacement, including razor wire (aka concertina wire) and minefields, requires observational positions to await the enemy. To accomplish their mission, observers coordinate direct fire weapon systems upon enemy arrival.

This same concept involves the IEDs (Improvised Explosive Devices) used by enemy forces to kill

Americans overseas. Whenever an IED was discovered, it was obvious the enemy was nearby and ready to kill using guns, rockets, and a remote detonator. EOD technicians must be able to approach explosives with a clear, cognitive focus amidst enemy threats. While they assess and diffuse the explosive, they are prepared to respond to direct fire from short-range targets or long-range snipers. Even still, they must take care to avoid lethal mistakes and disarm the threat.

A leader like Brad exercises thoughtful insight when risking his life and the lives of those around him on every mission he leads. If he cuts the wrong wire or fails to recognize a daisy chain of explosives, his mistake could take not only his life, but also the lives of men dozens or hundreds of yards away. He requires autonomous thought and executive decision-making power to keep everyone safe. His authority as the subject matter expert supersedes anyone else involved who doesn't have the expertise to neutralize the threat. Any hesitation or oversight on Brad's end can have a deadly fallout that impacts many more people than expected. Service members like Brad must have the freedom to think quickly on their feet; they train to remain calm and in control.

This level of training and combat experience makes Brad a powerful teammate and capable leader who personally understands the value of autonomy. This kept him alive in war and provided him with the capability of saving the lives of others. Leading from this knowledge, he strives to motivate others to think for themselves while staying calm in the chaos.

SECTION 3: PSYCHOLOGICAL APPLICATION

Brad helped me develop courage. As I faced fear, he inspired positivity while driving me toward accomplishing a goal. He knew how to reduce the noise in my brain just enough to get me going. I borrowed from his calmness, which gave me an anchoring point, psychologically speaking. He keeps himself steady and compartmentalizes stress to remain mission oriented. Such a demeanor is palpable and benefits those who observe it. One study states that the psychological strategies of "EOD Operators were comparable to those of Olympic athletes" and "frequently used strategies during training and military operations were goal setting and emotional control" (Taylor et al., 2019). Relying on his leadership helped me stay resilient and courageously overcome my fear far beyond my expectations.

Transformational leaders inspire followers to pursue visions of success beyond what's normally possible. They authentically care. Work tasks aren't all that matters to them. Transformational leadership at work increases job satisfaction by helping others overcome personal challenges (Choi et al., 2016). They make far-reaching goals seem doable. Organizations thrive with these types of leaders because everyone gets on board with shared goals. Subordinates evaluate organizational goals as important and perceive them as attainable (Steinmann et al., 2018). Rational and kind, transformational leaders earn high levels of trust. Buy-in for their ideas increases. When a subordinate's personal goals are achieved, the leader's goals are supported. Workers become proactive and seek to attain goals that benefit the entire team. As a result of heightened levels of job satisfaction, commitment to the organization increases. This is great for everyone.

The military needs transformational leaders. We all want authentic bosses who inspire us especially when our safety is on the line. Genuine concern makes us more resilient. People want to stay with an organization that motivates them and keeps them strong. Researchers highlight the value of transformational leaders as they are known to "lower stress and burnout" (Sangal et al., 2021). Maintaining highly motivated, healthy teams is the goal. Such leaders want subordinates to envision the best versions of themselves and push to become exactly that.

Subordinates under strong leaders are explicitly taught how to remain assertive and courageous, just as Brad had shown me. Strength at the lowest levels helps build a strong organization. Difficult goals are achieved through self-efficacy and by knowing how to cope with stress (Bergman et al., 2021). Tenacious goal setting follows. When the focus is placed on promoting a work culture with a growth mindset the entire team grows stronger. Military leaders with this capacity empower fighting forces and promote readiness. Even at the risk of facing injury or death, resilience induces courage.

Stress can be helpful in attaining goals if managed well. Leaders make all the difference. Helping subordinates manage stressful challenges enhances their accomplishments. They know when to endure stress and for how long before it becomes counterproductive. Acute stress can impair the ability to learn and remember new information (Vogel & Shwabe, 2016). While invoking stress can be a tool to test knowledge retention, it's important to understand when this is overdone. A calm state of mind helps promote learning because the brain has quieted down any distractions allowing for optimal focus (Sun et al., 2015). Calm leaders like Brad are great in high-stress environments.

Here are two powerful pieces of leadership advice I received from Brad:

SECTION 4: LEADERSHIP ADVICE

> *"Relay the reality on the ground. If a leader tells you they'll dictate exactly how to win a battle during training, ask them what happens when they get removed from the real fight." (Speak Up)*

Brad taught me the importance of being an officer who is quick to stand up and call out a bad decision whenever it will negatively impact those in the fight. Battle, in and of itself, has obvious lethal threats, but this is compounded by psychological confusion and emotional distress. Training military leaders to think on their own is critical to ensure survival when chaos ensues and communication is disabled. If a leader is taught only to survive because of explicit direction, they'll fail as soon as they lose their comms.

Contingency plans for communication issues are well-known in the military and ensure we stay as connected as possible with our units. We call this a PACE plan for **P**rimary, **A**lternate, **C**ontingency, and **E**mergency. For example:

(P)rimary: Radio – mounted inside the vehicle
(A)lternate: Radio – manpack carried by a Soldier
(C)ontingency: Runner

(E)mergency: Flare (white star cluster)

This plan ensures tactical coordination in malfunctioning equipment, electronic warfare (signal jamming), or loss of friendly forces. Leaders are kept in the loop to coordinate support elements. However, none of this matters if restrictions are placed on making critical adjustments in the heat of a fight. Imagine straining to manage communication channels in a deadly firefight when you've been told to sit and await guidance. No way. Such a leadership dynamic exposes friendly forces to further losses.

As a junior officer, I once heard a leader dictate that during training exercises he must approve and authorize all actions during our combined arms missions. Combined arms tactics involve a multifaceted approach to warfare involving various military tactics and units. Lots of moving parts. Nobody rebutted. I looked around the room at all the experienced Soldiers around me and was shocked at the silence, including by service members with actual combat experience.

Later that day I phoned Brad, who has fought in war and been in situations where he needed to check high-ranking leaders to prevent casualties during explosive situations. He picked up and I told him I was frustrated about a leadership situation. I asked him if I was crazy for getting so emotional about this brief. "No way, you guys definitely should've said something." He told me I was justified in my reasoning and responsible for speaking up. He continued, "Good leaders don't make themselves irreplaceable. They enable subordinates to win the fight in their absence and are never to be a linchpin in success." His words calmed me down.

During the brief I wanted to speak up, but I was afraid. I believed I didn't have the experience or rank to say anything. Brad educated me on why my lack of combat experience didn't matter. He told me that in battle, it's necessary to prioritize those on the ground who are first in line to get shot or blown up. This begins in training, right where I was. The military is a people business that must protect the lives of those most likely to lay theirs down. These individuals, regardless of rank, must have the autonomy to make decisions that will keep them alive in an ever-shifting theater of chaos and battle scenarios. If a leader makes themselves the choke point for decision-making, severe consequences follow.

Brad encouraged me to respectfully speak up and let the leader briefing us know we are dangerously limited by his protocol. If we are discouraged from thinking autonomously, then whenever this leader is ever taken out of the fight, our platoon, squad, and team elements will quickly fall apart. Decision-making criteria cannot be isolated to one person lest the rest of the organization suffocate when they are not directed to breathe. I felt relieved that Brad had such a common-sense answer. I resolved to speak up. If I'm ever told I can't think for myself because my superior has done all the thinking for me, I'll know what to say.

Brad knew I was unsure how to speak up genuinely in the military because I had observed others intimidated by rank and titles. The same fear occurs in private corporations as managers or executives go unchallenged when friction points occur. He taught me that constantly filtering oneself is unbearably stifling. His unapologetic advice was:

> *"Be yourself and let your personality burn bright because that's what the military needs most. Don't let people force you to conform your mindset and attitude to theirs." (Authenticity)*

Brad directed me never to stop being who I authentically was to fit in with someone's expectations. I didn't have to kill my personality out of fear; it made me stand out from the crowd. Hiding my intuitive response from leaders would degrade my ability to lead. There's a time and place to fall in line with others. However, one doesn't have to trade their autonomy for acceptance. A good leader will always listen to insight if it's founded on logic. Even if this means they must let go of control and hand it to others.

Authentic leaders can be transformational. When they inspire meaningful change because they care about the well-being of those they lead, reciprocity results. Subordinates who are grateful to be motivated truly invest in making the team successful. Even when nobody's watching. Inauthenticity is exhaustingly repressive and leads to depression (Mun & Kim, 2021). Masking feelings to try and make a leader happy is never right. It temporarily delays friction while draining mental resources. Research shows that "authentic workers show more positive signs of well-being (i.e., work engagement and job satisfaction), low-authenticity workers show adverse relations with well-being (i.e., burnout and boredom)" (van den Bosch, 2018). The military needs authentic people who are true to themselves and genuinely connect to others.

I noticed whenever my morale sank during my time in the military; it was tied to my inability to express my emotions. Having to bury a feeling state only causes it to explode in intensity. This requires increased effort to maintain the status quo. It's vital to emote feelings in an intelligent way to mitigate rigidity or avoidance. Having a voice in the workplace is important. Eventually, I learned to speak up about errors in logic while providing thoughtful solutions. Once I began to honestly express the reality of what was happening, I provided a helpful voice of reason to my commanders and the Soldiers I led.

When something didn't make sense, I could let my leadership know so we could work on a compromise to accomplish the mission while minimizing wasted effort. An inch goes a mile. Creative solutions were possible whenever I led with authenticity. My personality came out in my work, and my energy level increased. This is something I wanted to give to others. Whenever Soldiers in the platoon spoke up about existing issues, I encouraged them to devise solutions and own them. This way, they felt autonomous, further driving their motivation. They were free to ask me for necessary resources, and I would put in the requests to get them covered. My biggest goal was to be an enabler and stay out of their way.

Life in the military taught me the importance of speaking up authentically. Fear is stifling and leads to artificial compliance. Leaders must be willing to risk professional standing when voicing reason. Job experience should not be a limiting factor in having the right to speak up so long as the dialogue is well thought out and respectful. Once I learned my personality could be expressed through both good and bad situations, my fear decreased. In time I was able to make small, meaningful changes in the workplace based on logical observations, and most importantly, I motivated others to do the same.

Being a leader who encourages others to express themselves through contributions in the workplace is rewarding and exciting. Transformational leadership makes the organization come to life. The military needs people who can think innovatively and help improve the experiences of everyone around them. Freedom of thought and personal authenticity enhances survivability in combat. My friend has lived this throughout combat deployments and inspired me to follow in his footsteps.

Thanks, Brad.

References:

Bergman, D., Gustafsson-Sendén, M., & Berntson, E. (2021). From Believing to Doing: The Association Between Leadership Self-Efficacy and the Developmental Leadership Model. Frontiers in psychology, 12, 669905. https://doi.org/10.3389/fpsyg.2021.669905

Choi, S. L., Goh, C. F., Adam, M. B., & Tan, O. K. (2016). Transformational leadership, empowerment, and job satisfaction: the mediating role of employee empowerment. Human resources for health, 14(1), 73. https://doi.org/10.1186/s12960-016-0171-2

Mun, I. B., & Kim, H. (2021). Influence of False Self-Presentation on Mental Health and Deleting Behavior on Instagram: The Mediating Role of Perceived Popularity. *Frontiers in psychology*, *12*, 660484. https://doi.org/10.3389/fpsyg.2021.660484

Sangal, R. B., Bray, A., Reid, E., Ulrich, A., Liebhardt, B., Venkatesh, A. K., & King, M. (2021). Leadership communication, stress, and burnout among frontline emergency department staff amid the COVID-19 pandemic: A mixed methods approach. Healthcare (Amsterdam, Netherlands), 9(4), 100577. https://doi.org/10.1016/j.hjdsi.2021.100577

Steinmann, B., Klug, H., & Maier, G. W. (2018). The Path Is the Goal: How Transformational Leaders Enhance Followers' Job Attitudes and Proactive Behavior. Frontiers in psychology, 9, 2338.https://doi.org/10.3389/fpsyg.2018.02338

Sun, S., Yao, Z., Wei, J., & Yu, R. (2015). Calm and smart? A selective review of meditation effects on decision making. Frontiers in psychology, 6, 1059. https://doi.org/10.3389/fpsyg.2015.01059

Taylor, M. K., Rolo, C., Stump, J., Mayo, J., Hernandez, L. M., & Gould, D. R. (2019). Psychological Strategies During Military Training Are Linked to Resilience in US Navy Explosive Ordnance Disposal Operators. Journal of special operations medicine : a peer reviewed journal for SOF medical professionals, 19(1), 61–65. https://doi.org/10.55460/JAEQ-3MJZ

van den Bosch, R., Taris, T. W., Schaufeli, W. B., Peeters, M., & Reijseger, G. (2019). Authenticity at Work: A Matter of Fit?. The Journal of psychology, 153(2), 247–266. https://doi.org/10.1080/00223980.2018.1516185

Vogel, S., & Schwabe, L. (2016). Learning and memory under stress: implications for the classroom. *NPJ science of learning, 1,* 16011. https://doi.org/10.1038/npjscilearn.2016.11

7- SOMEONE BIGGER, BETTER, & STRONGER

"You're probably fine, pull your shorts down. I'll take a look at it."
- ***RYAN** [Navy Flight Surgeon]*

Envy: resentful jealousy about good things another person possesses

Collaboration: working together as a means of achieving shared goals

Intrinsic Motivation: being inspired by internal, personal beliefs

Peer Counseling: when equal members of a social group help each other

SECTION 1: INTRODUCTION TO THE TOPIC

In company formation, we stood around with our gear waiting inside a large metal warehouse to secure weapons, night optics, and supplies for our field exercise. It was 0500, and the cadre silently stood by, observing as we led ourselves. The armorer opened his window, and we lined up in alphabetical order to grab what we needed. This required careful documentation of all serial numbers on sensitive equipment, including radios, GPS trackers, weapons, optics systems, and more. Not to mention we needed to maintain accountability for all ammunition, food, water, and other expendable items we would be using throughout our week in the field. We all trusted one man in our formation to lead this effort, John, our one and only Ph.D.

John joined the military with the title of doctor but didn't disclose this at first. Never one to brag, he simply fell into formation like any other Soldier. Eventually, we found out about his credentials. I pride myself on being a studious bookworm, but he just blew me away. Not only is he the most educated person in our program, but also on our entire base. Every cadre member gives him respect for joining the military after already achieving such an accomplishment. On top of his academic credentials, he's also extremely fit and leads in physical ability.

His knowledge about information management and analysis came in super handy. On the civilian side, he streamlines tedious procedures to get quick and accurate results. In the Army, he kept us organized. When stressful field training exercises left us exhausted, hungry, and cold, having to ensure proper accountability for hundreds of pieces of equipment becomes that much more challenging. If a single item was missing, none of us would be allowed to go home to shower or eat. We would need to remain in the field and search the forests for whatever item was lost. Depending on the piece of equipment, this could even lock down the entire base, including all civilian workers. Relying on John to help get us home with minimal personal time lost was great for our morale. It also helped us look good to cadres, who would go easier on us as a result.

In a competitive training environment, it's tough to line up against a Soldier everyone deems the best man for the job. Whether they dominate tactically, physically, or academically, it's best to give them credit and carry on. Anyone who is not the best and then takes it personally will suffer a great deal. Technically, we were all competing for points on the OML (Order of Merit List). When cadres highlight the accomplishments of a specific student it says something to everyone standing around. We learned to respect such students because they earned it. The same was true in this case with John. In turn, he used his credentials to get our tracking systems organized and develop logic workflows to expedite our mission planning. He was a powerful resource and ally to lean on.

He also taught me the importance of acknowledging that any Soldier standing next to me could be far more brilliant than I realized. Two key reasons this is awesome: One, I can learn from them. Two, I can be a part of their team and contribute with whatever skills I possess. When someone better shows up in life, I don't have to be intimidated, isolated, or antagonistic. Ego is minimized. Working together alongside the strongest individuals in an organization helps create a collective force that enhances overall potential. We augment one another's abilities. No one person carries the team. If they do, that certainly won't be sustainable over an extended period.

Military units require cohesion to achieve shared goals. Every individual has something to contribute and deficits to address. Where one person may be lacking, another excels. Putting aside pride and selfishness ensures we allow the group to function cohesively.

SECTION 2: A GOOD MILITARY LEADER

With the broad build of a rugby player, Ryan's as sturdy as a Douglas-fir, which makes sense because he's from Washington. But don't be fooled by his gentle smile, friendly laugh, and blue eyes, because when he's in competition mode, he's a downright killer. For instance, when it comes to ice hockey, he may forget all about the Hippocratic oath. I met him just after deciding to sober up from the post-college party scene. This was one of my first friendships that didn't involve binge drinking on a party bus or blacking out at some downtown nightclub.

Upon our first conversation, I learned he was a flight surgeon in the Navy and was new to San Diego. Work had been so busy he didn't have time to make many friends outside of the military. Following my gut, I shook hands with him, looked him square in the eyes, and said, "We're gonna be friends." To this day, that was one of my best judgment calls. Free medical advice is only one of the many perks of being friends with Ryan. Another is being able to constantly throw around, "Well, my friend who's a doctor says," with which I have unashamedly bludgeoned people.

Ryan is a symbol of success in pretty much everything I failed at in life. First, he has quads the size of my torso and is a giant man bred from some heritage of Viking ancestry, making him *BIGGER*. Second, he's great at every athletic thing he tries, from surfing to soccer, whereas I didn't learn to train my body until I was 25, making him *BETTER*. Third, he's an educated doctor, whereas I was a pre-med student who failed to launch because, in college, I chose alcohol and debauchery instead of studying, making him *SMARTER*.

Rather than envy him for absolutely crushing life, I wanted to learn from him and emulate his achievement wherever I could. Personal growth enticed me, so I envisioned a path forward. He inspired me to play sports, surf, and read books. He almost encouraged me to eat an apple a day. Ultimately, joining the military was an eventual manifestation of my desire to share in his experience of wearing a uniform. Whether on team green or blue (Navy or Army), it's still one family. I was inspired to serve in some capacity just to know we were brothers in arms. As a medical officer, he was always down-to-earth and fun to be around, which made our friendship awesome.

When he PCS'd (Permanent Change of Station, i.e., moved) to Camp Lejeune in North Carolina to work with the Marines, I visited him a couple of times because he's one of the best friends I have ever had. He introduced me to kiteboarding, one of the coolest sports in the world. Being harnessed to a giant kite is the closest feeling to having a pet dragon. You lean back with your entire body weight under a giant curved wing as it casts a large swooping shadow alongside you. When the wind gusts through it lifts you up straight into the air.

Depending on the gusts and size of the kite, it's possible to be lifted tens or hundreds of feet up.

Kitemares can happen when control is lost and the wind carries a kiteboarder out into deadly situations. When I was learning on his rig, Ryan was sure to hold me by a strap to ensure I didn't get dragged off into the ocean. Once, he found himself riding ocean waves over several large sharks. Luckily the wind didn't putter out, or he would have been swimming with them.

He also introduced me to flight in a private aircraft because he's a pilot and can do that sort of thing. This was fitting because on that trip we visited the Wright Brothers National Memorial at Kitty Hawk where the first manned flight occurred. Renting a two-seater aircraft, he flew me back to the international airport in Raleigh. Random fun fact: fuel used in small planes is light blue in color. This flight turned into a neat adventure when, after flight checks and take-off, we began buzzing around the clouds like a mosquito as the wind rocked us back and forth.

My anxiety immediately shot up. Lacking complete control is terrifying, especially when you are thousands of feet above the ground. Ryan stayed solid. Whenever I felt sketched out by the situation, I looked over to read his facial expression for reassurance. This didn't help because when he's thinking he keeps a deeply furrowed brow. Every time I looked at him he was monitoring wind conditions and flight gauges with a focused look that kept me guessing. Eventually, I stopped worrying and trusted him to get me there safely. We landed smoothly right at the gate of my next flight. VIP parking. Raddest friend ever.

Pilot, doctor, and kiteboarder; Ryan represented to me what a military-trained professional could become. He was super adventurous and stayed disciplined on the job. Serving in the military enabled him to become a doctor without the financial burden, a certified pilot with hundreds of hours of training, and a tactically proficient leader. This image is a recruiter's dream come true. What I learned most from him is that there's always someone better who has enviable accomplishments under their belt.

In the military, there were tons of people who could outperform me, whether physically, mentally, or tactically. Rather than be stuck in competition mode determined to win at one-upmanship, it's better to humbly learn from them. Stay inspired. I learned to use the greatness of others as fuel. Ryan taught me to keep an open mind and remain coachable because he was willing to show me the ropes. Early in life I often acted like a know-it-all because I desired relevance, but that was hindering my growth. My pride kept me uncoachable. I needed to stop trying to act smart and put in the work to grow smart as a critical thinker. I needed to find people to lead me toward becoming the version of myself I desired to be. However, no matter what degree or achievement I obtain in life, there will always be a Ryan out there who dominates across the board. People like this are powerful sources of inspiration. Keep progressing!

SECTION 3: PSYCHOLOGICAL APPLICATION

Healthy leaders inspire growth. They see deficits in skill in terms of potential for further development. Everyone is given room to improve. Subordinates are encouraged to share responsibilities and help team members attain goals. It takes a village. Such leaders strengthen organizations by addressing weaknesses with patience. They are accessible. They don't allow rank to make themselves unapproachable. Everyone in their unit is encouraged to contribute without belittling others. Research studies find that teams and organizations operate optimally when everyone involved synergistically combines efforts regardless of hierarchical status (Shuffler et al., 2018). Each member has unique skill sets that other individuals may not have but are able to develop, if motivated (Ng, 2018).

Even in competitive professional work environments, good leaders manage subordinates with mentorship in mind. This gets tricky. Some team members may want to force their way to the top by excelling at the expense of others. Emphasizing collaboration is key. Professional synergy involves creating clear roles while allowing overlap to ensure healthy team relationships with mutual support (Nancarrow et al., 2013). Everyone has a hand in helping the organization succeed. Success is shared. Team cohesion increases when leaders disperse roles and responsibilities among individual members to ensure "leadership is not solely located in a single individual" (Klasmeier & Rowold, 2021). Forcefully attempting to outperform others in an organization can undermine concerted efforts and detract from the shared mission. No one person will be the best at everything. Rather than outperforming others, seeking to improve and develop teammates should be promoted by leaders.

Shared goals trump individual goals. Being in the military means serving a greater purpose than one's personal goals. Supporting peers in their advancements is a powerful way to do this. It makes the organization stronger. To do so requires surrendering the desire to win at everything. A healthy mindset is vital. Studies show that "individuals with high self-esteem" are prone to helping others, thereby enriching the environment they work in (Li & Liao, 2017). Selfishness is a characteristic of those who feel threatened by a potential loss in relevance and therefore seek to secure their status by hindering others.

Humility demonstrated by solid leaders may be emulated by subordinates. Several humble behaviors desirable in leadership are "self-awareness, appreciation of others, low self-focus, teachability, and self-transcendent pursuits" (Maldonado et al., 2021). I see all these in Ryan. Realistic and self-aware, he knows he's not the best at everything. He acknowledges limitations. This also means he is keenly aware of just how much potential he possesses within his strengths. He enjoys challenges that give him the chance to test his mettle, physically and mentally. While he does seek out difficult paths in life as a means of personal growth, he enjoys helping others along the way. Investing in others is rewarding.

Being confident in who he is means he doesn't walk around with a need to dominate or belittle others. Wins or losses don't ultimately define him. He sees everyone's growth potential just as he harnesses his own. While he will compete like a champ to win at everything he tries, that rests more upon his self-discipline than insecurity. He can readily help others and cheer them on towards their goals because he knows this doesn't detract from his greatness. Confidence removes any need to feel threatened. I feed off his positivity and enthusiasm for life because he shares it with me. He helped me see my own potential as I joined the military and pursued my graduate degree.

The imposter phenomenon convinces people they are incapable of succeeding in their work, so why even bother putting in the effort Zanchetta et al., 2020)? Instead of taking risks, they clam up. Fear of being exposed as incompetent heightens ego defenses, such as arrogance, in those with fragile self-esteem (Cowan et al., 2021). Leaders with this insecurity drive down their own potential and limit others around them. Selfishly, I have tried many times earlier in my life to over-inflate myself at the expense of others. I was afraid of the strength others had. I also learned to fear my own strength. Much of my life at a young age involved being bullied and physically abused. Growing older in adulthood didn't remove the fear associated with these events. I needed Jiu-Jitsu and counseling for that. Once I received information about the scarcity mindset and how that ruins the world, my perspective slowly began to shift.

Scarcity-minded individuals choose to focus on the fear-based interpretation of reduced survival opportunity because they believe vital resources dwindle via competition and consumption. Stated another way, more people accessing a given resource means less for me. This can even apply to love. An abundance mindset is an optimistic rebuttal to this, invoking innovative thought as a means of creating solutions to address needs. This involves viewing increased consumption of a product as enabling a growing market with the potential for a variety of similar products. For instance, the more people who consume freshwater on our planet creates more demand and potential for technology to produce fresh water from oceans. Abundance thinking chooses industriousness over having to fight. (On an aside, war can be seen as bringing forth an abundance of innovative technology, but that's a complicated topic I'd need to research more.)

As an aspiring leader, I wanted to orient my thoughts towards gaining knowledge from others and being coachable rather than fearing loss of relevance. Competition intrigued me. I saw how private corporations address competition both internally within a sales department to increase productivity, and externally to drive hard against adversaries. Now I wanted to see how a warfighting organization uses competitive drive between individuals to build a singular vision of victory against the enemy. How does a group of alphas unite?

I wanted to let go of fear, insecurity, and having to feel superior individualistically. Joining the military was one of many steps I took as I attempted to rectify my behavioral patterns. Being in the military helped me relearn how to become part of a team and family. When I asked Ryan to meet me later for coffee on the day we first met, I shared with him my disappointment in how I lost discipline in college. My potential suffered. I told him that because of my immaturity, I forfeited both the opportunity to go to medical school and to join the military. I lost faith in myself and desperately wanted it back. Ferociously, he inspired me to shift my perspective and keep an open heart:

SECTION 4: LEADERSHIP ADVICE

> *"It's never too late to pursue goals and dreams, so don't get discouraged by comparing yourself to others. You'll be able to do anything you set your mind to. Go for it!"*

Hearing this encouragement from someone I looked up to, meant a lot. I figured he'd say I'm too late and that I should've joined the military earlier in life. He'd already gone to medical school and accomplished so much in life. I was nowhere near approaching my own goals. None of this mattered because he didn't believe in comparing oneself to others. Rather, he helped me appreciate the value of the unique roads we each have in life. Forget expectations. This negates prescribed timelines for how life is supposed to look. I wasn't meant to be in the military at a young age because that version of myself would've made a horrible leader. Joining at 32 was the right time for me.

I met countless people in the military with unique stories and timelines for their lives. We all had our own journey. There are no uniform criteria dictating who joins when. While many enter the military at 18 years old, some sign contracts in their 40's. While some Soldiers have multiple graduate degrees or doctorates, others never pursue education past high school. So what? In any case, they successfully work their jobs in the military. They're growing towards their future goals.

Measuring paths with others is like comparing apples to oranges. Variables pertaining to each person are different, so the equations can't be matched up. This happens in the civilian sector as well. How does a doctorate from an obscure university compare to an undergraduate degree from a top school? What about a brand-new M.D. compared to an experienced D.O. having deployed in the military? An entrepreneur at 20 years old selling a multimillion-dollar idea is a totally different leader than a 50-year-old executive still building a retirement plan.

While in the military, I compared myself to my peers with various accomplishments, including those who graduated from enviable courses like Airborne, Air Assault, Ranger, and Sapper Leader Course. Other awesome professional accolades are being in Special Forces, being a diver, or being a pilot. Not having proven myself in these ways decreases my value to the organization, doesn't it? I haven't been invested into it to the same extent. Can I blame the pandemic? Lockdowns abruptly shut down schooling opportunities when I graduated from Engineer BOLC in 2020, but it's still just an excuse isn't it? As a leader, how else can I measure myself besides my resume? What's the best way to quantify my value to the military?

I wanted to get to the bottom of all this, so as a platoon leader, I went straight to the source. I asked the Soldiers I led how bummed they were to have a 'slick sleeve' leader, meaning I had no tabs or schools under my belt. Believe me when I tell you they are straight shooters. When something needed to be said, they'd say it plainly. Bracing myself for their response, I didn't hear what I expected.

They told me they didn't care about the schools I had gone to or the tactical training I brought to the table. No award or accolade would determine what they thought about me. *What?* I was shocked. There was, however, one key thing they cared about above anything else. Did I care about them? That was it. I couldn't believe how simple their response was. I asked them the question again, to clarify, because there must be some confusion. "Don't you want a leader who has all the tabs and made it through all the tactical schools?" Again they said it didn't matter at all. They cared about one thing when it came to having a leader: knowing someone cared about who they were as human beings.

Damn. Hearing this one hot summer day as we sat by our parked vehicle convoy in the desert waiting for the mission to start is still one of the clearest, most profound memories I have. It makes me quite emotional to remember the sincerity in their sweaty, dust-covered faces. One Soldier who was awarded The Purple Heart for wounds sustained in combat spoke up and everyone quieted down.

"Sir, Soldiers care about one thing in a leader. Are you good to us? Sometimes leaders with all the tabs bring egos that make the job suck for us. Yeah, you might stress over stuff, but you don't take that out on us. It doesn't matter what patches you don't have. At least we know you care about the Joes."

Woah. Thank God I didn't join the military as the tool bag I used to be in life. I'd be a mess of a leader if it wasn't for good friends and examples like Ryan who guided me.

I was floored. This Soldier is a humble warrior who possesses a rich perspective of the military, and he took notice of my affinity for connection. Here I was comparing myself to peers based on missing training experience, feeling like I didn't measure up. All the while, the people who matter most didn't see it that way. I asked how he knew I cared. He said whenever I ask the Soldiers questions about their lives outside of work, I was letting them know I cared. I asked about their families, hobbies, morale, mental health, educational goals, etc. These questions were important to me because it broke the monotony around us. Our unit frequented the field, and it was more tolerable if we all spoke as friends while passing the time together. It was easy for me to talk to Soldiers, but I was oblivious to what it meant. That's my leadership style, and despite lacking military credentials, it made all the difference.

Feedback from the Soldiers helped alleviate any sense of inadequacy I felt by comparing myself with others. Whenever I felt the compulsion to put myself down in the light of others' successes, I remembered that the Soldiers never judged me on that at all. I'm grateful they were open enough to share that with me. Otherwise, there would have been no way for me to measure myself except by my resume or military OER (Officer Evaluation Reports). These are helpful when contrasting experience levels between military officers, but may not capture who they are as leaders.

Earlier in my military journey I planned on attending some schools to beef up my OER, but the pandemic delayed even my peers with hard slots. A hard slot just means that somebody has a confirmed seat in a class as compared to being put on a waitlist. Everything shut down. Morale suffered as a result because Soldiers hate nothing more than to be told they have to sit down and do nothing. That's the equivalent of being back in BCT on timeout. With all the travel restrictions, there was quite a bit of red tape to wade through before anyone could start heading to schoolhouses for more training.

After over a year of this, my focus shifted entirely to maintaining mental health while getting through the lockdowns. Military life became all about staying healthy and keeping others around me healthy. This inspired me to keep tabs on how everyone was doing outside work where I knew they could be isolated in despair. Suicides were increasing around the planet because of the pandemic. Many people in society were losing hope and lapsing into alcohol or drug abuse. Depression soared. As a leader, I wanted to avoid that for myself and the Soldiers I led. During lockdowns, I decided to not drink alcohol and instead chose to work out three times a day while pursuing a graduate degree in psychology.

Investing in my goals outside military training put me at a tactical disadvantage. When it comes to comparing OERs, many people in the military far exceeded me because they pushed hard to get themselves into schools when lockdowns were lifted. I was on a different path. To compare myself would be an endless practice in feeling incompetent, especially because most of my military contract involved being under global lockdowns. If I sat there wishing COVID never came about I would burn with frustration at lost opportunities. Did I really want to go down that path? What about my regrets before joining the military when I was busy being directionless and making poor decisions?

Swearing in at 32 and in 2019 means I missed most of all the wars. It also meant I was vastly displaced from my age group. When I was an O-1, most everyone my age in the military was an O-4 or O-5. There was no way I could catch up and it was all my own fault. Not knowing myself in high school meant I wasted college years partying vapidly to find my identity. Looking at the young faces around me, I admired men and women who courageously joined at 18. It took me three decades of life to build just barely enough courage to join.

This is where Ryan's advice hits home. Stop comparing. It's never too late to achieve great goals in life. Age waivers help bypass military cutoffs, and even if rejected, there are always other opportunities to serve in life. It really is never too late to begin an exciting journey or challenge. No two people walk identical paths in life, so measuring oneself against another is useless. The specific path doesn't matter as long as we are moving toward a purpose. Learning to appreciate greatness in others instead of being bitter or envious inspires the pursuit of similar wins in life.

Joining the military in my 30s was a great place to jumpstart a change I wanted in my life. It forced me to grow. Leadership experience was incredibly dynamic and beyond anything I expected. Many of my friends exemplified the growth I wanted. The military helped Ryan pursue medical education while receiving valuable job experience. His example encouraged me to further my own education while serving. It opened my eyes to a variety of professional and educational options that are available. I pushed Soldiers to take advantage of any program they found interesting. I didn't want them to waste time like I had.

With so many opportunities afforded by the military, I recommend it to anyone needing a professional rest or launch point. Many amazing people of various ages serve across all branches. They have plenty of wisdom to share. Many have done things few will ever do, and they are available as mentors. I learned there is always someone bigger, better, and smarter than me, and they inspires me to likewise pursue excellence. I also learned to understand that metrics on resumes don't show the whole picture. Soft skills and other subtle nuances impact success in leadership. Heart matters most. No quality overshadows the universal ability to lead with a genuine love for others.

Thanks, Ryan.

Quick aside on the intro quote to this chapter. When I was visiting Ryan on a trip to the Outer Banks of North Carolina, we went on a run on the boardwalk. Actually, I think this was somewhere in Virginia Beach before we drove through OBX (the Outer Banks of North Carolina). Well, about a mile into the run, I realized that my board shorts were rubbing on my privates. It was specifically a part of the shorts with reinforced stitching, so think sandpaper rubbing. After a few miles we ended the run and I noticed a pink spot outside my shorts.

The skin on a very delicate part of my anatomy was rubbed down to the blood vessels. Because of the delicate neurological tissue involved in said structure, I felt peculiar feelings of pain, stinging, and a nauseating tingle. I was horrified and told Ryan I had just uniquely injured myself. He paused, waiting for clarification. I sighed slowly as my eyes dropped downwards. His eyes then dropped downwards in recognition. Without any expression, he matter-of-factly offered to take a look at it.

Time stopped. I wrestled with the awkwardness of whether I should show my friend my penis, especially this friend, Ryan, who I know is always bigger, better, and smarter than me at everything.

References:

Cowan, N., Adams, E. J., Bhangal, S., Corcoran, M., Decker, R., Dockter, C. E., Eubank, A. T., Gann, C. L., Greene, N. R., Helle, A. C., Lee, N., Nguyen, A. T., Ripley, K. R., Scofield, J. E., Tapia, M. A., Threlkeld, K. L., & Watts, A. L. (2019). Foundations of Arrogance: A Broad Survey and Framework for Research. *Review of general psychology : journal of Division 1, of the American Psychological Association, 23*(4), 425–443. https://doi.org/10.1177/1089268019877138

Klasmeier, K.N. and Rowold, J. (2022), A diary study on shared leadership, team work engagement, and goal attainment. J Occup Organ Psychol, 95: 36-59. https://doi.org/10.1111/joop.12371

Li, S., & Liao, S. (2017). Help Others and Yourself Eventually: Exploring the Relationship between Help-Giving and Employee Creativity under the Model of Perspective Taking. Frontiers in psychology, 8, 1030. https://doi.org/10.3389/fpsyg.2017.01030

Maldonado, T., Vera, D., Spanger, W. D. (2022) Unpacking humility: Leader humility, leader personality, and why they matter. Business Horizons, Volume 65, Issue 2, March-April 2022, Pages 125-137. https://doi.org/10.1016/j.bushor.2021.02.032

Nancarrow, S. A., Booth, A., Ariss, S., Smith, T., Enderby, P., & Roots, A. (2013). Ten principles of good interdisciplinary team work. Human resources for health, 11, 19. https://doi.org/10.1186/1478-4491-11-19

Ng B. (2018). The Neuroscience of Growth Mindset and Intrinsic Motivation. Brain sciences, 8(2), 20. https://doi.org/10.3390/brainsci8020020

Shuffler, M. L., Diazgranados, D., Maynard, M. T., & Salas, E. (2018). Developing, Sustaining, and Maximizing Team Effectiveness: An Integrative, Dynamic Perspective of Team Development Interventions. The Academy of Management annals, 12(2), 688–724. https://doi.org/10.5465/annals.2016.0045

8 - KINDNESS IS STRENGTH

"Bro, don't feel stupid. The scene when his partner got killed made me cry too."

- ***TREVOR*** *[Navy Rescue Swimmer]*

Ego Defense: behaviors meant to mask weakness or vulnerability

Empathy: ability to feel the emotions another person is experiencing

Prosocial Behavior: positive actions that strengthen relationships

SECTION 1: INTRODUCTION TO THE TOPIC

"You like being an individual, don't you? Always doing your own thing when everyone else falls in line." Dozens of classmates stood around and listened as two of the most dominant students in our group shouted accusations and insults at me. They hated me and made it known. These two friends had joined forces during their time in the Army schoolhouse to stand above everyone else. I was one of several targets. They condescended to almost everyone else as well. I thought about getting the chance to fight them both.

Training in Jiu-Jitsu and kickboxing makes it easy to tell when people aren't fighters. These guys are too square with their hips, making their base (center of gravity) unstable. A trained fighter will turn their hips at an angle in preparation to throw a strike or kick while being able to absorb impact. No way they'd ever throw a real punch. Suddenly, I felt guilty about these fantasies of violence. My coaches, whom I respected, would scold me forever for striking someone first out of aggression. After scolding me, they'd properly choke me out to ensure I respected the gym hierarchy. We don't train martial arts to start fights. We train to finish the fight a bully starts.

Taking a deep breath while the accusations flew, I remembered to keep my mouth shut, and then I carried on with my workout. Anger burned inside me, but I didn't want to carry around resentment. This would only detract from my focus during military training. I had joined the military to learn how to lead through uncomfortable situations while keeping a cool head and it was time I started speaking up more. *These guys may have more military experience than me,* I thought. *But that doesn't mean I don't have a voice here. I've been a doormat my whole life and it's time I speak up for myself.*

After our group PT session I approached Phil, the bully who was the biggest physically. Two thoughts preempted my action plan: One, I needed to wait for an opportunity when they weren't both present because they always fed into each other's angst. Two, engaging the larger of the two opponents reminded me I wasn't intimidated while conveying the same message to him.

We were all walking to our cars when I called his name. "Hey, Phil", I sternly said. Shooting a glare at me, he stopped and waited for me to walk up. He's over a foot taller than me, which never feels awesome in an altercation. Without breaking eye contact (never break eye contact first), I told him we needed to have a private talk. I calmly stated I joined the Army to learn how to lead and was open to advice. I told him I respected his experience in the military and didn't mean to give off whatever impression he found so upsetting. This took him by surprise. He said he appreciated my saying so. All the tension left his face, and he never attacked me again.

We all were growing through our time there in training, and many opportunities arose for either conflict or cohesion. Observing varying degrees of leadership aptitude among so many officers, it became clear to me who was strong and who was weak. The strong leaders were those exhibiting patience, self-control, and kindness in high-stress situations because no one else threatened them. I wanted to work towards becoming more like them.

SECTION 2: A GOOD MILITARY LEADER

Trevor was an anatomical dichotomy. He had the burly size and build of a running back and the disarming face of a blue-eyed toddler which earned him the nickname "Babyface." He's one of the kindest human beings I have met, which initially took me by surprise. I met him at the gym when I asked for a quick spot. Because of his girthy stature, I assumed he was a meathead. Well, he sort of is, but not in a knuckle-dragger way. He's a gentle giant more likely to give a hug than throw a punch. Maybe everybody from the Pacific Northwest is raised to be kind, but I chalk it up to his strength and presence. He can afford to be a total softy because his physique does all the tough talk.

I interrupted his workout and asked him to put a 45 lb. plate on my back so I could do some weighted pushups. Once he did, I thanked him so he could return to his workout. I proceeded with my reps. After completing my set, I laid flat to slide the weight off my back. To my surprise, I felt someone pulling the plate off for me. It was Trevor standing there next to me with a big dumb smile on his face. He didn't go back to continue his workout.

I took my headphones out and apologetically told him I didn't mean for him to stop his exercise for me. I only intended for him to put the plate on my back and walk away. He said he wanted to stand by to make sure I handled the weight safely and could get it off my back. Now, I know I'm smaller than him, but come on! This was Trev being his protective, considerate self. Anyone who is this patient during rush hour at the gym is a quality guy. Right then and there, I knew he had a big heart. We became fast friends and eventual roommates.

Trevor and I began working out together. He took me to the gym pool for some of my first swim lessons since childhood. Watching him slice through the water with his huge frame was a trip. He taught me the combat side stroke while patiently guiding me through details related to breathing practices, form, and pace. Stuff like, keep my core tight, make my body as straight as possible and use big scissor kicks with small flutters. It felt awesome having an expert Navy swimmer giving me private lessons. I remember looking around the pool at other swimmers around us and realizing that my friend was the most powerful one in the water. That built up my confidence to keep attacking my fear of the water.

A human heart is the size of a single fist, and Trev has big fists, so he's got a huge heart. This makes him one of my all-time favorite people. We watched two movies together and these are still two of my favorite memories of hanging with him. One was *End of Watch*, and the other was *Lone Survivor*. Both movies were emotionally raw experiences because I badly wanted to have brothers in arms. Also, the friend I had with me was a military hero in my eyes, making some of that content hit close to home. Especially heavy was the nonfictional, devastating loss that occurred in Operation Red Wings (June 28, 2005). Those riveting images cut deep as that historic event echoes loudly even today.

I teared up sitting next to Trev. Ok, fine. I sort of, maybe, just cried a little bit during parts of both movies and tried hard not to turn and see Trev's expression of shock. It would be humiliating to get laughed at by a military friend who I assumed had killed off his ability to feel as a part of training. Totally not the case. He was also struck deeply by the loss of brothers in those films, both symbolically portrayed and the actual loss. He told me he teared up too so I shouldn't feel stupid. This is one of those rare and much-needed experiences of human vulnerability that I wish could be shared more between guys. He felt like a sibling more than a friend. I still draw strength from that memory. I joined the military to build more friendships like this. My belief is that the reason men are more prone than women to substance abuse and suicide is that they lack genuine connections.

Trevor taught me a lot about what it means to wear the uniform, metaphorically and literally. Service members are still human, and our heartfelt feelings are a source of strength, not weakness. He was comfortable being real, and he knew exactly when to be tough and when to be kind. By no means is this guy a pushover. On several occasions, he had to confront guys he worked with for running their mouths and putting others down. He drew a line and told them never to cross it. He warned them that if they did, all the desks would be moved to the corners of the room, and the door would be shut so he could smash them. I guess on a few occasions when they didn't believe him, he made believers out of them.

One big thing I learned from him is to never wash out of Special Forces selection and then go around telling coworkers how bad the job sucks or say that because of some random fluke, selection just didn't work out. Fast way to get pummeled, but it's common. Bitter people put others down as a means of venting toxic fumes. It blatantly belittles and disrespects professionals who are proud of their jobs. If someone belongs on the teams, they won't wash out of selection. When things don't work out, stay positive and work hard at whatever job comes. Returning to selection in the future is possible. Otherwise, carry on with a new life. It's a bad idea for anyone to tell others they are better than them and deserve an elite position, especially if Trev's around.

The more we hung out together, the more I was aware of just how civilians differ from those in the military. There's a strange nuance that's hard to describe but easy to distinguish. Primal connection. It involves accountability to teammates and looking out for one another as family. Comradery is programmed into military training pipelines, and it comes out in daily life outside of work. For instance, one time when we were working out together, Trevor told me he was going to the drinking fountain to get some water and would be right back. He wanted to be sure I knew where he was. Civilians don't do stuff like that, I thought. We would just walk off and get water. He did this every time he went to get a drink so I'd know where he was. The way he always checked in said something about his loyalty.

I loved that about him, and it contrasted with my own self-centeredness. At first, his genuine softness made me uncomfortable because I feared vulnerability. Acting tough was my way of pretending I couldn't be hurt. Demonstrating concern for others is what takes strength. I wanted to have the same selfless connection with others that Trevor had. How could I learn to become like that? How could I learn the value of being a dependable battle buddy? Knowing he signed a military contract pumped me up to do the same. More signs added up that I needed to ship out for a stint in the armed services. I wanted to be more like these friends of mine.

SECTION 3: PSYCHOLOGICAL APPLICATION

For much of my life, I didn't know what strength meant. I assumed bigger people had more strength, a direct proportionality. Being smaller in stature for most of my life fed into this thought process. Such oversimplification is understandable. Physical strength might be visually expressed in the form of physique and musculature, but that depends on body type. Some people put on muscle mass a lot faster than others, but they may not necessarily have the stamina or strength a smaller person has. Also, strength may not translate to athletic ability or coordination. Strength can be assessed and quantified in numerous ways, but that still only covers the physical aspects.

Trevor taught me to see strength differently by treading lightly. Strength means more than flexing power; it means offering a helping hand while standing up for what one believes is right. It's shown by refusing to back down from a challenge that brings growth. It means having self-control. Strong people control their emotions and refrain from letting aggression get the best of them. They use their mind to guide their actions carefully. When physical aggression does need to come out, it's intentionally focused.

Strength is also demonstrated within the mind. Mental strength is a powerful concept that can even beat out physical strength. When the body begins to experience pain and wants to quit, our thoughts carry us through. We overcome our fears this way. This is why so many times in tough military training pipelines it's not always the biggest and strongest people who make it through, sometimes the smallest person has the most grit. Even with tremendous physical strength, it's important to develop strength of mind.

Mental toughness is a manifestation of strength transcending physicality. It's built from a combination of both performance ability and personality traits such as positive metacognition (reflecting on how one thinks about oneself) (Bruns et al., 2016). Simply put, being aware of our capabilities helps us determine the level of challenges we believe we can overcome. Unrealistic self-appraisal results in failure due to a lack of preparation. Alternatively, it can lead to fearful avoidance of engaging in challenges because we believe we are too weak to win the fight. It's best to know the upper and lower limits of our abilities so we pursue meaningful challenges with optimal difficulty.

Mental strength can be built by testing one's abilities while gaining new skills and experiences (Budin, 2017). Challenge perceived limits. It's best to have guides or teammates present to help avoid becoming overwhelmed by challenges. The military addresses this through mentorship and peer relationships, especially between new officers and experienced enlisted service members. Challenges alongside battle buddies are key to building strength with just the right amount of resistance. Competitive athletes strive for mental toughness to enable their persistence, creativity, and emotional stability (Stamatis, 2020). From workouts to competition, great teammates remember to look out for their peers and keep a positive atmosphere even while pushing hard to obtain tough goals.

Leaders demonstrate tremendous strength to subordinates through self-discipline and self-control. They create a healthy work culture that defines strength in terms of remaining calm and considerate towards others. It takes practice. In one psychology study, "Practicing small acts of self-control for two weeks led to a significant improvement on a laboratory measure of self-control" (Muraven, 2010). This style of leadership contrasts directly against uncontrolled or reactive aggression, which may be thought of as mental weakness involving impulsive and uncontrolled outbursts of anger as a reaction to a threat (Kip et al., 2021). A bully, for instance, operates from a state of fear to create a facade of strength. However, contrary to their goals, the façade is a bright beacon that reveals weakness. On the other hand, openness and kindness are powerful indicators of strength because they allow vulnerability without fear of reprisal or harm (Schretlen, 2010).

When I asked Trevor how toughness is portrayed within the military, he helped me understand the balance involved. Strong people have enough self-confidence to offer kindness towards others, but they know when to enforce boundaries. He taught me the importance of using strength honorably, to defend against harmful behaviors and maintain a code of conduct meant to protect others. Bullies toe the line until someone stands up to them.

SECTION 4: LEADERSHIP ADVICE:

"Some people pretend to be tough by putting others down because they feel like they're superior. That pisses me off. I've had to beat guys up for doing that when they refused to stop after I warned them. It takes a lot to make me angry because I've got a long fuse, but when that fuse burns down, it's a big explosion."

Earlier in this chapter, when I confronted Phil with a soft request to work together instead of remaining combative, that was an idea Trevor helped spark. Earlier in life, my normal reaction to someone being condescending is to shut down or ignore them. If that didn't work, I made some feeble attempt to say something back or retaliate. Feigning strength involved being petty and obnoxious. However, at this stage in life, I wanted to emulate healthy friends who exuded genuine confidence. I thought about Trevor, how he first used calm words to create peace before ever looking to get into a fight. Kindness isn't weakness, it portrays strength. This changed everything. After speaking to my classmate, we went from tense enemies to allies. That same guy became the strongest asset on my team when it was my turn to lead a platoon training exercise in the field.

During one mission set involving an ambush with simulated explosives, Phil made a selfless decision to support me when he could've stayed quiet and watched me fail. By reciprocating kindness, he went out of his way to provide tactical guidance before I almost detonated a (simulated) charge that I incorrectly placed due to my own miscalculation. I was about to clack off an explosive charge with a devastating backblast and (simulated) fatal casualties. "Simulated" means that during the exercises instructors made verbal calls to remove Soldiers from a training exercise when they deemed them casualties according to what would happen if the explosion had occurred in a real-world scenario. It's always critical to know the parameters related to blast radius, lethal range, kill zone, fragmentation, etc.

For instance, M18A1 claymores explode with almost a thousand steel balls cutting through vehicles, structures, bodies, and trees for 100 meters. They also inflict damage on whatever is immediately behind them upon explosion. This is where I was about to screw up as a leader. With my hand on the detonator, Phil stopped me from killing off my entire platoon. Had I pushed the detonator, this high-visibility failure could have potentially jeopardized my upcoming graduation even though it occurred during a training exercise.

Every EBOLC (Engineer Basic Officer Leadership Course) student must lead an offensive attack mission while being graded on leadership ability and tactical execution. That day it was my turn to lead. It was around 35 degrees and the freezing rain was drenching us. We'd been in the woods for several days, wet and cold.. Today we staged an ambush and needed to place explosives throughout concealment in the wood line. This involved low crawling with our weapons toward the road intersection where we believed the convoy would move through. Luckily, the brown fall leaves were wet and soft, dampening any sounds we made. As the OIC (Officer in Charge), all mistakes made by the platoon are my fault. I scoured the tree line for the best spots to place each Soldier as I coordinate the EA (engagement area). Tree trunks must be wide enough to provide cover from enemy return fire and the surrounding foliage provides concealment to keep them hidden. Cover stops bullets, concealment does not.

All this planning must be done carefully and quietly to avoid exposure because cadres are anticipating our attack. At one point, getting distracted by all the distance measurements involved, I found myself about 20 meters from the road and almost made contact with the enemy. Cadres were standing around with their weapons in hand scanning the tree line. I froze. Quietly aiming my rifle at the center of the mass, I slowly and quietly backed up into the woods. Had I fired off one of my blanks, it would have ruined everything and led to mission failure. Eventually, I concealed myself again and was able to identify better positions to place our personnel.

My classmates helped me prepare all night for the day's mission. Now, I was specifically in charge of establishing attack positions and coordinating support by fire elements while ensuring no fratricide occurred. This means at no point during the attack do any weapons risk injuring a friendly force. This is a detailed, dynamic process as attack elements will be bounding forward toward the enemy through existing lines of fire. Support by fire elements must sequentially keep shifting their sectors of fire to sweep ahead of the attack force. Always ahead of friendlies and always before friendlies walk into that window where our bullets are flying. TRPs (Target Reference Points) are set up ahead of time to ensure Soldiers shift their rifle sights at exactly the appropriate location and time. In this case, I picked three distinct trees about 20 meters apart and in a whisper asked each Soldier if they acknowledged those were the TRPs. Once they each confirmed, I moved on to the next task.

My RTO (radio telephone operator), who I relied on to keep everyone informed was having communication issues with the radio. He was my link to the rest of our friendly elements spread through the woods. Not being able to contact them was complicating the mission execution. Terrain and foliage play a big role in disrupting comms. Without radio connection, having to physically run all my directions to each element in person was exhausting and time-consuming. Even in the cold, I was sweating from running back and forth between squad leaders. I needed to hurry. Cadres had me on the clock, and I was about to miss my window to assault the convoy.

Finally, having worked on my PACE plan and established new communication guidelines, all elements were set and ready to rock. The convoy was enroute, and I needed to set antivehicle charges. I slung my rifle to my side, grabbed the claymore satchel, and then bear-crawled to the detonation site. The wet leaves offered a soft cushion and relief from being on my feet for days carrying weapons and an assault pack. This was no time to rest. I began to prime the claymore and positioned the blast window. Instructors stood by and took note of every step.

Just as I primed the blast charge, I felt an adrenaline rush knowing the battle was about to start. Then Phil, my former antagonist, crawled his way over to me and whispered, "Stop! You're about to kill the entire platoon. This claymore is too close to us." I looked behind me. Over a dozen wide-eyed Soldiers were staring at me through their rifle iron sites mounted in hand atop downed tree trunks. Crap! I totally forgot to factor in the back blast. Shrapnel and ricochets would theoretically hit all 20 or so Soldiers behind me and virtually kill off my entire platoon.

Phil, who utterly despised me a few weeks ago, had just saved me from becoming a headline failure in our program. He went from wanting to see me fail to wanting me to succeed. When I met him, I thought he was a weak bully. Now I think differently. His act of kindness just amplified his strength in my eyes.

"Hurry up, let's move," he said, grabbing some detonation components. I grabbed the rest, and we continued to crawl up together, setting the explosives at the correct range. Cadres in charge of grading me during this exercise looked up at each other and chuckled at what had almost happened. They were ready to fail me right then and there. Once we set the charges, still laying flat on our stomachs with rifles in hand, I looked Phil in the eyes and thanked him for what he just did. He gave a quick nod. "Let's go," he said, "We don't have much time. Start the assault."

We quickly crawled back to our element and awaited the convoy. A few minutes later, a diesel engine rumbled as the vehicle approached from a distance. I scanned my EA. The attack element to my right was set behind cover, ready to bound through the enemy. Support by fire was divided into two flanking locations 30 meters apart, tracking the appropriate TRPs. Everyone lay completely still on the wet leaves as the rain trickled down the canopy onto our backs. All eyes locked on me, awaiting the command. The vehicle pulled up to the preplanned positions, putting it directly in front of the claymore. Clicking the detonator in hand I triggered the claymore. Cadres in charge of grading me unpin and toss out a simulation round to signal the explosion.

BOOM! The enemy, yelling in the distance through the tree line, begins firing their rifles at us. I pull my trigger, fire a three-round burst, and shout as loud as possible while laying down, "Attaaaaaack!" Rifles came to life and M4s, 240 Bravos', and M249s blasted away in the rain as machine guns chewed up belts of ammunition firing hundreds of rounds. Brass flew, and more simulation rounds exploded. We unleashed everything we had in pulsating, back-and-forth sequences making sure our weapons systems "talked" to each other. That meant there was never a moment when shots weren't being fired.

After several minutes of cacophony, the smell of gunpowder filled the cold, moist winter air. Vehicles were disabled and the enemy was killed. The attack element that bounded forward cleared past the enemy shouting back "LOA!" (Limit of Advance). While walking by any downed enemy, they were sure to remove their weapons to prevent getting shot in the back. At this point, they laid down and pulled security with sights aimed down either side of the road. Next, the support by fire element bounded through the enemy to join in on pulling perimeter security. At this point, I received accountability numbers for any friendly casualties, ammunition, and water. Then we checked the enemy for weapons, intelligence materials, and casualty status. After each enemy was checked, we crossed their feet and arms to mark them. "Endex," the cadre shouted as we were given the signal that the exercise was now complete.

Everyone stood up and horseshoed around the instructors. We completed the mission and debriefed right there in the woods. Rain became sleet, and our jaws trembled as we shivered. "Control your shivers. Have some self-discipline," one instructor shouted coarsely. "Who was in charge here?!" they barked. I stepped up knowing what they were about to point out. They yelled out I would have failed the entire mission if my battle buddy hadn't helped me reset the claymore position. I immediately acknowledged that mission success was entirely because of Phil. I had to give credit where it was due. It was a good moment to check my ego and own my failure. I felt stupid, but mistakes are part of leadership training.

Cadres then told us to get ready to head back to base. *Heck yes!* We were done with all our field exercises for this training set, so we headed back to our shelter and barrel fires to prepare for the ride home. Before we knew it, we were boarding buses back to housing for hot showers and hot food. There's a special pleasure about stepping into a furnished room after trudging through the wilderness for days at a time. Recovery is everything. I mastered the art of taking salt baths in candlelight to help my body relax and reduce inflammation. Rolling out sore muscles keeps cramping to a minimum and speeds up healing.

Another awesome part of getting out of the field is clean, dry clothing. Laundry never smells as good as the day field training ends. Electricity is never more appreciated. Simple comforts are luxuries. Heating and air conditioning are the icing on the cake. Winter field training especially fits perfectly with reclining on the couch wearing thick wool socks and sipping hot chocolate while wrapped in a warm blanket and watching snowflakes drift down outside. I put on a movie as the heater kicked on. Snuggling into the cushions, I stuffed my cold nose into a fold of the blanket and breathed in the clean scent. Damn, the littlest things mean so much.

Field training is miserable for a reason, and there's an obvious draw the military has when developing toughness. Discomfort is built into field exercises, including long nights, heavy rucks, and exposure to the elements. Aggressive mission execution is required even when exhausted. Violence of action is a vital aspect of winning wars. Strength is powerfully displayed to deter enemies seeking to destroy friendly forces. They become targets of intense and explosive coordinated attacks. We train to drive through the enemy with fury and unrelenting momentum. Ferocity. In scenes like these, one version of strength is demonstrated through lethality and utter destruction.

Strength and power can also be subtle. Silent. Resolve, grit, and confidence can overpower an enemy force. Stoics preach this. Strength can look more like a slow burn than a kinetic blast. Psychological strength may manifest in a steady, persistent exhibition of tactical strategizing. Unconventional forces in the military exhibit silent strength with surgical precision against powerful enemies while requiring a tiny fraction of the manpower conventional units have. There's more than one way to defeat an enemy. Even kindness, sourced in inner strength, can turn an enemy into an ally. Bit of a stretch, but I need to conclude this chapter somehow by tying this all together.

Understanding various manifestations of strength develops a robust perspective in life. Heart isn't easily measurable because motivation can come from deep personal beliefs beyond any surface characteristic. This is a great reminder to never underestimate an opponent. Fights are multi-dimensional. Properly assessing an opponent's ability is important before engaging in confrontation, physical or mental. Misjudging strength will have dire consequences when the rounds begin to fly. Studying the enemy is one thing, knowing ourselves is another.

Kindness has surprisingly become one of the most powerful indicators of true strength I have come to witness in the military. Dominance is nonverbal. Strong leaders in control of a situation can afford to be gentle in their approach. They don't rush. Using calm to their advantage, they take time to assess critical challenges and threats thoroughly. They communicate clearly. Tactical procedures are described in full detail. Questions are welcomed. They don't exclude anyone from group dialogue. Their kind treatment of subordinates enhances their credibility. Solid guidance. It increases loyalty to both themselves and the organization. Unit morale grows tremendously when a kind leader is in charge. This translates to a powerful unit ready to meet any opposition with optimism and resolve to accomplish the mission.

Trevor demonstrated how to refrain from using strength to be mean. He taught me never to misuse rank or social influence to harm others. He also taught me that there's a limit to the soft approach when someone else is being harmed. When friendly warnings are ignored and violations continue, someone strong must put an end to the inflicted damage. Even still, they remain in control of their aggression and can pull back as necessary, knowing how to respond with appropriate levels of violence. Whenever I meet someone in the military who leads with kindness, I know that I can trust them to lead me in the right direction. I also know to stand clear of the back blast if they ever do need to react with a show of strength.

Thanks, Trev.

References:

Ayer, D. (2012). End of Watch. Open Road Films (II).

Berg, P. (2013). Lone Survivor. Universal Pictures.

Budin W. C. (2017). Building Confidence. *The Journal of Perinatal Education, 26*(3), 107–109. https://doi.org/10.1891/1058-1243.26.3.107

Burns, K. M., Burns, N. R., & Ward, L. (2016). Confidence-More a Personality or Ability Trait? It Depends on How It Is Measured: A Comparison of Young and Older Adults. *Frontiers in psychology, 7*, 518. https://doi.org/10.3389/fpsyg.2016.00518

Hagen, R., Havnen, A., Hjemdal, O., Kennair, L., Ryum, T., & Solem, S. (2020). Protective and Vulnerability Factors in Self-Esteem: The Role of Metacognitions, Brooding, and Resilience. *Frontiers in psychology, 11*, 1447. https://doi.org/10.3389/fpsyg.2020.01447

Kip, H., Da Silva, M. C., Bouman, Y., van Gemert-Pijnen, L., & Kelders, S. M. (2021). A self-control training app to increase self-control and reduce aggression - A full factorial design. *Internet interventions, 25*, 100392. https://doi.org/10.1016/j.invent.2021.100392

Muraven M. (2010). Building Self-Control Strength: Practicing Self-Control Leads to Improved Self-Control Performance. *Journal of experimental social psychology, 46*(2), 465–468. https://doi.org/10.1016/j.jesp.2009.12.011

Schretlen, D. J., van der Hulst, E. J., Pearlson, G. D., & Gordon, B. (2010). A neuropsychological study of personality: trait openness in relation to intelligence, fluency, and executive functioning. *Journal of clinical and experimental neuropsychology, 32*(10), 1068–1073. https://doi.org/10.1080/13803391003689770

Stamatis, A., Grandjean, P., Morgan, G., Padgett, R. N., Cowden, R., & Koutakis, P. (2020). Developing and training mental toughness in sport: a systematic review and meta-analysis of observational studies and pre-test and post-test experiments. *BMJ open sport & exercise medicine, 6*(1), e000747. https://doi.org/10.1136/bmjsem-2020-000747

9 - DO IT OR SHUT UP

"Thanks for being flexible. I had to stay late to make sure all the requests my guys made were approved."

- ***JARED*** *[Navy SEAL Officer]*

Assertiveness: being bold in stating needs or desires

External Locus of Control: outside circumstances determines one's actions

Internal Locus of Control: ability to control actions comes from within

Self-Efficacy: belief in one's own capacity to accomplish specific goals

SECTION 1: INTRODUCTION TO THE TOPIC

"Jump in already!" Mike shouted from the dark blue water below. Sunset Cliffs in Ocean Beach is a beautiful seascape with huge houses resting along the coastline. Tourists are everywhere, some were taking notice of our cliff jumping. The police will fine us if they catch us. Maybe Mike can get us out of it because he's in the Navy. Tiptoeing on the edge of the sandstone bluffs, I keep hesitating.

He knows I'm afraid of water. I'm especially scared when I don't know what animals are lurking under me. Stingrays, jellyfish, sea urchins, lobsters, sea lions, I could go on. All these sea creatures live in this spot. Did I really want to drop in on their home? Besides, how can I be sure I wouldn't break my legs on the rocks below? The tide was going out, leaving less water to break my fall.

"Trust me. You're going to be fine. We all made it." He doesn't understand how hard my chest is pounding. The others yell at me to hurry up and get in with them before the water level drops. I think even more about the rocks hiding in the murky blue. Imagining the feeling of a cold splash followed by shattering bones on slippery jagged rocks has me frozen. I envision oysters and barnacles slicing my flesh as I land on them. Dark blue shadows in the water make it hard to make anything out. I pace back and forth like a scared animal.

Mike has had enough of my fear. He climbs out of the water and jogs back up the cliff. Calmly he looks me in the eyes and points a finger down into the ocean pool below. "Look bro, you're going to be fine. Just land right there in that spot. You'll be safe. Trust me. I checked around to make sure there were no rocks." He always sounds fearless. Danger probably doesn't even register with him. He slaps my arm before running to the edge and leaping in again. I peer down to make sure screams don't follow his splash. He pops up through the surface and shakes the water out of his hair.

"Go!" he roars with a smile.

Ok, here we go. I take a few steps back, then run to the cliff's edge with my chest pounding. *Here! We!... No, don't!* I stop right at the edge, too afraid to do it. I sigh angrily. I'm sure Mike does too. Panning around to ensure no cops are watching, I see more tourists watching my display of cowardice. Everyone in the water is splashing around together. I tell myself I have to go through with it. A young girl walks up to me, says it'll be fine, and jumps in. *Ugh!* Why can't I do this?! I really want to just go for it.

Thinking about tough decisions, I reflect on how it's ok not to feel ready. Jump anyway. Danger is part of the excitement. The anxiety in my stomach won't go away until I crossover into the unknown. The more I hesitate, the more it builds. *Stop letting fear ruin your fun* I tell myself under my breath. I hear Mike's laugh down below and it pierces the fog in my mind. With a fierce rebellion against sanity, I run toward the edge and leap up into the sunlight. Surrounded by blue sky, the wind roars in my ears before I submerge below into the blue-green water. Water breaks around me in a cold rush of bubbles. Then it's just me floating there in the quiet ocean. In that brief still moment, I resolved the tension inside.

I slowly floated back up to the surface, craving more dives.

SECTION 2: A GOOD MILITARY LEADER

"Some of you sitting in this audience right now are at a Kairos moment in your lives," the pastor said. "You know it because you've come to the same crossroads repeatedly. Life is forcing you to keep facing the same problem. Until you take action, your life will not change. Timing is never going perfect. You must have the courage to finally take that leap you have been hesitating over for so long. Your entire life history will change trajectory once you follow through. What difficult decision keeps you circling the same Kairos moment in your life?"

Thud! Jared jabbed my ribs with a hard elbow. I shuddered at the impact. Jared, like Mike, was helping me overcome my fears and take a step into the unknown. Turning my head, I saw him gazing straight forward, smiling. I had talked enough times about joining the military. He wanted me to take action.

Jared is a Navy SEAL officer and a fierce athlete with a passion for leading by example. He also has energy reserves that never run empty. Built broad and lean, he's a competitive Naval Academy swimmer with tan skin and black wavy hair. What I found most profound about him is that his tremendous courage is a blessing he has carried his entire life. His mom said even as a toddler nothing had ever scared him, and no matter what happened in life, he faced it head-on with a big, fearless smile.

He strives for mastery in his endeavors from all things physical, mental, and spiritual. Nothing about him is average except for his seemingly calm demeanor, which is an active attempt not to seem superhuman. I couldn't envision a more driven leader to motivate and inspire elite warriors in battle. Keeping a framed copy of The Constitution of the United States hanging on his wall, he's a patriot who values our nation's founding. He seeks to honor the principles instilled throughout American history. He keeps a wooden paddle on his mantle with the Navy Special Warfare insignia, the

SEAL Trident, and his BUD/S class number.

We met at a seminar on personality testing sponsored by a local church. We learned about our personalities and suitable professions by using a well-known diagnostic test. The exam classified traits based on discrete typologies: being extroverted vs. introverted, etc. Pretty straightforward. Jared was invited to attend by his Naval Academy peers. I'd already met them earlier that year. We all sat together. Because of the tightly cramped seating arrangement, things started awkwardly.

For whatever reason, chairs were so tightly packed together that only one of us could sit up straight lest our shoulders, biceps, and elbows completely smash into each other. Jared and I didn't know each other at this point, and it seemed problematic to fight for space in a turf war. We had absolutely no room between us, but something told me this wasn't the type of guy to challenge. He was clearly in shape and had an edge that was difficult to immediately identify.

So, for hours, without speaking a word to one another, we nonverbally agreed to switch between sitting up straight or leaning forward with elbows on knees just to have some breathing room. Alternating between these positions kept any tension from building as we respected each other's space during those hours. I wanted to be annoyed, but we both chuckled at how ridiculous it was. After a full day of this, we knew we could get along as friends.

One of the most impactful impressions Jared made upon me occurred when we first met for a beer. He and I pushed the time to around 2000 because he wanted to stay behind after work and sign off on all the requests put on his desk. His platoon had requested various approvals (leave, training, etc.), and he was doing all he could to greenlight them. His desire to get his men what they wanted was impactful. It demonstrated his willingness to sacrifice personal time to prioritize everyone else in his unit.

I told him this surprised me because I never expected paperwork to be a part of the job of a Navy SEAL. Knowing only what I saw in movies, my assumption was that his job entailed tactical training day and night. I was ignorant, but luckily, he was patient. He taught me about the responsibilities of all military officers and emphasized that the biggest priority is always the troops. Their needs always come first. Without them, there is no unit to lead.

I learned many valuable lessons from Jared. Whether exemplifying leadership characteristics or explicitly teaching me a skill, I always gained knowledge from him. He's intellectually sharp and provides the why behind anything he stands by. As an analytical person, I found this incredibly satisfying. Whenever he made a point about something, I knew he had done his research, and his judgment was sound. He was adept at skills and concepts from a broad swath of topics about both the military and life in general. I'll share some of the things he taught me:

- Action speaks louder than words; talk less
- Subordinates come first
- Don't ever leave your buddy behind
- Never bully, but don't fear a fight
- Seek wisdom from experienced members of the team
- Don't interview SoF operators about work during time off

- Keep a trauma kit in the car (tourniquets, IV, bandages)
- Lean into the target when shooting at a standing position
- Use proper ammo on steel targets
- Flashbangs are fun
- Don't grunt during workouts
- Know knots
- The incline of a shoe sole dictates its purpose
- When buying a road bike, purchase last year's model
- Never run downhill to look fast; instead run uphill fast
- Never shoulder check a Navy SEAL during a trail run

So yes, more on that last point. During one of our many trail runs together, some obnoxious, shirtless moron came barreling down the hill out of control and made the mistake of bumping Jared. Of course, this same man had just struggled walking up the mountain, but since he had slowly made it to the top, he now wanted to feel fast on the way down. Continuing down the trail, he kept cutting people off and stomping around without concern for hikers who couldn't look up in time to see him coming around corners. Nobody appreciated this. Running down a mountain without concern for others on a busy trail is an ego problem. Navy SEALs are effective at rectifying ego problems.

In mid-sentence, Jared bolted down after this man and after quickly catching up, returned the shoulder check. The runner faceplanted. In a daze of dust he looked up, completely shaken, as Jared chewed him out for putting everyone on the trail at risk. Endangering others is irresponsible and stupid. Many people were relieved to know he put this man in check. Like an instructor, Jared scolded him on trail running etiquette and received a jittery apology. Then, he helped the man stand up, dusted him off, and ran back up the hill to meet me. What a great lesson in assertive leadership.

I could go on and on about what I learned from my friend. If there was any single person at the top of my list who inspired me to join the military, it was him. He helped me recognize my many deficits during a chapter in my life when I was becoming more self-aware. His example showed me how I could develop myself further through service in the military. If I wanted to be an apprentice to like-minded individuals, I would need to sign the contract and go for it. He encouraged me to do so and reminded me I had talked about it enough. It was time to sign the contract or move on.

SECTION 3: PSYCHOLOGICAL APPLICATION

A study on over 100 Navy SEAL candidates sought to explore how they related to high-stress situations. Those who found stress a catalyst for motivation had positive outcomes in training. The authors found that having "stress-is-enhancing mindsets was a predictor of greater persistence through training, faster obstacle course times, and fewer negative evaluations from peers and instructors" (Smith et al., 2019). Another study showed that tension and apprehension are overcome by Special Forces candidates who utilize optimism to overcome overwhelming challenges (Hormeño-Holgado et al., 2019). Getting to witness the potential that a positive mindset has in the lives of elite warriors really impacted my life. It was difficult to excuse my own self-doubt in light of their accomplishments. I wanted to push past my limits.

Special Forces Army personnel, when compared to the general military population: drink less alcohol, smoke less nicotine, eat less fast food, and experience less anxiety (Cooper et al., 2020). They benefit both psychologically and physically from their disciplined lifestyle. Purposeful direction provides them with a framework with which to build optimal habits. They pay careful attention to what they consume mentally and physically. Rather than limit themselves according to normative societal standards, they pursue excellence. Feeling fear like anyone else they choose to dive into pain and uncertainty instead of hesitating. Jared told me to never say "I can't" because it would signal my brain and body to shut down. He was explicit about the words he allowed to be spoken around him.

Jared was very intentional with every action he took in life. His assertion kept him in charge and left little to chance. Assertiveness in leaders increases likeability and influence because it relays a sense of agency (Bongiorno et al., 2014). They can be trusted to achieve results and get the job done. They know how to use aggression for good. Balance must exist with assertiveness and self-efficacy to prevent problematic behaviors of aggression (Khademi Mofrad & Mehrabi, 2015). Experienced leaders who understand this demonstrate authority without intending to use it offensively to control others. They create a positive example for others to follow as they promote the development of confidence in the workplace. Such leaders encourage followers to seek out solutions to problems by believing they possess the ability to bring about change.

By being assertive, Jared took ownership of his

life. He stayed positive through injuries and pitfalls. He never gave up on fighting for what he wanted to accomplish. Despite any challenges facing him, he expected himself to find a way to overcome them. He would never make an excuse for lacking ability or potential because he believed that success was rooted within him. Psychologists call this idea the locus of control. This is one of the most powerful concepts I have researched. Locus can be either internal or external. Locating where we believe the locus lies determines if we can drive our own success, or if outside circumstances dictate our fate.

In the military, it's easy to blame failure on leaders or faulty equipment. Taking ownership despite any complications is a great way to stay in control even in times of chaos. Doing so can even benefit our physical health on top of keeping our minds in a positive place. One study found that "patients with an internal locus of control are less depressed than patients with fatalistic views on their health/pain" (Wong & Antiescu, 2017).

Another stated that the internal locus of control is "a powerful positive resource associated with better health outcomes, especially influential for lower-income individuals" (Music et al., 2020). Overcoming adversity heavily relies on the ability to reach inside ourselves and draw up a plan to rise above our circumstances. An external locus of control heavily influences veterans struggling with PTSD as this increases the level of avoidance and desire to numb themselves from pain (Smith et al., 2018). People who fail to do this can lose hope in things ever getting better. Believing the universe is against our existence is a depressing way to live life.

Personally, I hit a point where I wanted to take full control of my potential even if that meant accepting dangerous risks. For much of my life, I deferred to causes outside of my control to explain my limitations. I cowered. Lack of ownership led to wasted time and opportunities and is a big reason why I hesitated to join the military for so long. Jared accepts no such limitations. He believes the locus of control is internal. Outcomes are directed through one's power of will and discipline. He is a realist who knows life can hit hard; but damn it, get up and hit back. Don't just lay there and let bad things happen.

Jared never makes excuses about things being too hard or painful. He also doesn't allow others to make those excuses in his presence. He knows that is cancer to morale. Frequently I needed to check myself quickly before voicing a complaint around him. When I felt the pain in my legs during a run, I wanted to grunt loudly to get the frustration out. My body was telling me to quit, and I often doubted my ability to keep going. Jared's determination to push through pain made me aware of my self-limiting beliefs. I liked that I was second-guessing my limits now. He inspired me to challenge myself. I felt compelled to push myself well past my breaking points because he didn't believe in them.

Once I joined the military, I constantly reflected on his audacity and courage. It pushed me to never quit or give up. Even now, as I write this book and reflect on my time in the military, I see how I still seek improvement in this area. He gave me a timeless piece of advice that helps now just as much as it did when he first called me out:

SECTION 4: LEADERSHIP ADVICE

> *"If you say you are going to do something, do it. Don't keep talking about it."*

Here is a man who helped elbow me over the line of hesitation to sign my military contract. I joined the military at 32 in big part because of him. He saw my weakness and fear, but unlike most people, he explicitly called me out on it. "Join the military or stop talking about it." I was never again allowed to tell him a plan I had if no action was to follow. This challenge hit me right between the eyes. I needed that and am still grateful to this day that he dropped that ultimatum on me.

Fearing inadequacy kept me in avoidance, hiding from opportunities to prove my abilities. Failure scared me. I made myself small. Avoidance is a painful way to go through life. Challenges remain unresolved. It leaves many unanswered questions on the table. I nearly became someone who would always look back, wondering how life in the military would be. Talking about joining was cathartic, but I soon became content with pretending. Until I met Jared, I never realized how obvious my hesitation was. I learned there's a difference between being thoughtful and being avoidant.

In the military, I noticed Soldiers talking about things that needed to change and then not taking action. Venting is normal in the military culture, but sometimes it makes us feel like we are doing something productive when we are not. This can be detrimental to our progress in the organization. Especially when subordinates refuse to tell leaders about situations requiring improvement. Both enlisted and officer personnel are guilty of this, including me. I would discuss my vision for change without providing results. We all see how things could be better, but we don't want to think about the variables involved. Oversimplifying problems makes it seem like somebody must not be doing their job. In reality, they may be waiting for more information or a perspective we have to offer.

After being in the Army for a few years I began to see myself complaining about situations that could be improved. Feeling overwhelmed by the difficulty in bringing change to the organization I relegated myself to becoming a bystander. But sitting idly by was not why I joined the military. At one point, after observing my ongoing inaction, I decided to speak up. I wanted to personally address the Soldiers' issues with accessing support for college education. I stopped talking about it and began executing a plan of action. Before I knew it, several leaders got behind me to push the initiative forward. Several Soldiers immediately signed up for school, and for months, many more came trickling in.

Many Soldiers felt they shouldn't speak up to ask for resources because the training tempo was so high. They rejected my offer when asked if they wanted to talk to leadership about this. Nobody wanted to take the first step. After hesitating, I eventually took it upon myself to do so. Online college classes helped me tremendously, especially during the global pandemic and shutdowns. I wanted to give that gift to others. I made the discussion happen and coordinated talks with the Army Educational Center on base. The civilians working there were incredibly helpful. They came to our company and gave presentations to the Soldiers about college benefits. Several subsequently enrolled for online degrees. As each Soldier becomes more educated, the Army does as well.

This example is one of my favorite times of taking action as a leader. Many other attempts failed along the way. My ideas regularly got shut down for a variety of reasons. Sometimes resources were scarce. Other times the ideas were not scalable to encompass all Soldiers. Even still, there were golden moments when Soldiers privately thanked me for trying. They saw me actively attempting to secure resources or commitments to aid them. Even though multiple times my requests were discarded, the failure wasn't what caught their intention. Action did.

They were glad I at least tried to get things done. Their encouragement meant a lot because Soldiers see everything, and they notice the finest of details in how one leads or doesn't lead. I made plenty of mistakes along the way. But I am amazed at how colossal errors in my own eyes are not weighty to them at all. Soldiers notice effort, and that's what counts to them. Actions.

Words mean things, as we say in the military, or at least, they are supposed to. Soldiers are not just cogs in a machine without expectations, needs, and goals. They are spouses, siblings, children, parents, and so much more. Leaders shouldn't waste time sharing a vision with them if words are unaccompanied by action. Service members know it's not just their time wasted when leaders don't follow through. Their families and loved ones also suffer when holding onto empty words.

Whether promising time off, promotions, awards, benefits, career opportunities, or anything else, leaders must back up words with action. Honoring time off is a powerful way to earn trust as a leader. Not honoring time off can be irrecoverable. I learned the Soldiers in my platoon never wanted to tell their families something hopeful if it was not guaranteed. Vacation time is no exception. Seeing the devastation in their spouses' eyes, especially their children, hurts too much. Nobody likes being let down. It was my duty to put action into words. Morale increases when promises are kept and plummets when actions don't line up. Being consistent between words and actions starts with who I am in private.

As a leader, taking action must be exemplified by how goal oriented I am in my personal life. Talking about goals helps strategize a plan but after a while, it's just hot air. Instead, when I set goals for myself, I need to immediately follow through. Small steps count. Jared taught me I should never make a habit of letting myself down with unending discussions, empty promises, or failed commitments. If I do, this will undoubtedly lead to me letting down my teammates. Now I give myself a specific length of time to talk about what my plans are and with only a few key people. Keeping accountability in mind, I do my best to make practical plans and set deadlines for myself. Leaning on trusted friends, I reach out for guidance anytime I feel stuck. And, of course, whenever I need a violent shove across the line of hesitation, I know who to call.

Thanks, Jared.

References:

Bongiorno, R., Bain, P. G., & David, B. (2014). If you're going to be a leader, at least act like it! Prejudice towards women who are tentative in leader roles. *The British journal of social psychology*, 53(2), 217–234. https://doi.org/10.1111/bjso.12032

Cooper, A. D., Warner, S. G., Rivera, A. C., Rull, R. P., Adler, A. B., Faix, D. J., Neff, R., Deagle, E. A., Caserta, R. J., LeardMann, C. A., & Millennium Cohort Study Team (2020). Mental health, physical health, and health-related behaviors of U.S. Army Special Forces. *PloS one, 15*(6),e0233560. https://doi.org/10.1371/journal.pone.0233560

Hormeño-Holgado, A. J., Nikolaidis, P. T., & Clemente-Suárez, V. J. (2019). Psychophysiological Patterns Related to Success in a Special Operation Selection Course. *Frontiers in physiology, 10*, 867. https://doi.org/10.3389/fphys.2019.00867

Khademi Mofrad, S. H., & Mehrabi, T. (2015). The role of self-efficacy and assertiveness in aggression among high-school students in Isfahan. *Journal of medicine and life, 8*(Spec Iss 4), 225–231.

Musich, S., Wang, S. S., Slindee, L., Kraemer, S., & Yeh, C. S. (2020). The impact of internal locus of control on healthcare utilization, expenditures, and health status across older adult income levels. *Geriatric nursing* (New York, N.Y.), 41(3), 274–281. https://doi.org/10.1016/j.gerinurse.2019.10.008

Smith, E. N., Young, M. D., & Crum, A. J. (2020). Stress, Mindsets, and Success in Navy SEALs Special Warfare Training. *Frontiers in psychology, 10*, 2962. https://doi.org/10.3389/fpsyg.2019.02962

Smith, N. B., Sippel, L. M., Presseau, C., Rozek, D., Mota, N., Gordon, C., Horvath, M., & Harpaz-Rotem, I. (2018). Locus of control in US combat veterans: Unique associations with posttraumatic stress disorder 5-factor model symptom clusters. *Psychiatry research*, 268, 152–156. https://doi.org/10.1016/j.psychres.2018.07.015

Wong, H. J., & Anitescu, M. (2017). The Role of Health Locus of Control in Evaluating Depression and Other Comorbidities in Patients with Chronic Pain Conditions, A Cross-Sectional Study. *Pain practice : the official journal of World Institute of Pain*, 17(1), 52–61. https://doi.org/10.1111/papr.12410

10 - TAKE THE CAPE OFF

"As men, it's important to examine how relationships with our dads influence our entire world perspective. It may be tough work, but it'll be worth it in the end."

*- **RICH** [Navy UH-60 Commander]*

Transference: transferring feelings about one person or situation onto another

Sublimation: converting unwanted angst or negative feelings into productivity

Self-Regulation: ability to slow down the nervous system and control emotions

SECTION 1: INTRODUCTION TO THE TOPIC

Bullets snapped through the air overhead as Aaron, a SEAL I met in San Diego, waited behind cover. Rounds in the air sound like the snap of a leather belt, not the whizzing noises heard in movies. Rounds pinged off the armored vehicles. More bullets were flying today than usual. The number of enemy insurgents was higher than expected, and destabilization of the country was a real issue. Iraq was a mess. ISIS was focused on disrupting the power grid. They infested buildings like termites, thanks to all the recruits who showed up.

Foreign nationals poured in through the borders to complicate things further. More targets for Aaron. Rounds kept raining down; suppressive fire at these rates can be infuriating. Minutes poured by as Aaron and his team grew more frustrated at the situation. Adrenaline coursed through his veins as anger built up, but he remained steady and calm, awaiting his window. He tried not to think about his wife and child back in the states. The thought of never seeing them again had to keep getting pushed to the edges of his mind. This wasn't the time to lose focus. He continued evaluating the EA.

How many enemies had shown up? The plan didn't entail being pinned down for this long. Time was ticking. Everyone on his team was getting pissed. They were eager to do their job and continue extracting HVTs (High-Value Targets). Each passing second added to even more frustration and their desire to kill. During direct action firefights like these, his Iraqi interpreter remained seated in the vehicle, anxiously waiting for the shooting to end so he could step out and help gather intelligence. Indigenous support is sketchy. Working with locals meant he constantly needed to watch his back. There was no telling who would suddenly turn on American forces because of a bribe. Inescapable risk. How else could he know who to grab? Aaron needed to know which doors to kick in. So far, his interpreter had been dependable and loyal. He believed in bettering his nation by relying on the US to make necessary changes.

He waited.

Tactical pauses pay off. The enemy can't shoot forever. Eventually, a window of opportunity opened. Aaron and his team collectively reengaged and with perfect coordination eliminated all targets. Fury was focused. The process was smooth. Training guided their precision, and whether aiming for headshots or center of mass, hit after hit added up. Once complete, they secured the perimeter. The rage subsided, and it was business as usual. Well, a lethal business that entails constantly living under the risk of death. Today brought relief. Aaron reflected on just how quickly a mission can take unexpected turns. His daughter's voice came to mind. He thought about his family and said a prayer of gratitude. He wondered if he would always get to come home alive. Putting the feelings away, he got back to his job. They got what they came for and headed back to base.

Political relations were beginning to complicate the job Aaron was trying to do. Local government bodies desired to regain control of their nation. Knowing who to trust was difficult. He was balancing warfighting functions and cross-cultural social pressures on a razor's edge. High-stress environment. 130-degree temperatures made life there even more hellish. One day he reached a boiling point. Someone he was working with started to lose control of their anger and ran their mouth to vent frustration at everyone around. Aaron did his best to control the situation. He spoke up to stop the situation from getting out of hand, but his warnings went unheeded. Once his wife's name was disrespected during the argument, he physically responded and left his adversary with several shattered bones. He was alarmed at his own reaction. War put a fire in him.

Returning home, his wife noticed the tension in the room. He was different. Heaviness loomed. He was easily set off and remained combative. He even worried himself. Seeing his daughter, he feared becoming a threat to her or her mother. When his wife suggested counseling, he obliged. Processing his adrenaline response in combat helped him appreciate anger's powerful role in engaging deadly enemies. Aggression and violence of action kept him alive. His team was always victorious because they focused their intense hatred for evil against the appropriate targets. In complex combat zones, they surgically picked their targets. Turning the knob down on a heightened state of excitement takes work. Some of Aaron's teammates learned the hard way.

On Saint Patrick's Day, I was at a house party with my friend Derek and a teammate of Aaron's, let's call him Jordan. Derek was a studly former offensive lineman for the Wisconsin Badgers, and although he's a civilian, he has the bearing of a military commando. This is probably why he gets along so well with military folks. Jordan was equally huge, and he was ferocious. This beach house was filled with a variety of military professionals from several branches and jobs. Jordan was home between deployments and came out to the bars with us. By closing time, the original group had separated off to different bars or house parties. Derek and I returned home around 2 am. Pizza time.

As I cut up slices in the kitchen, Jordan burst through the front door, white shirt covered in fresh red blood. Derek and I stared wide-eyed.

"Dude, are you ok?" we asked. Derek tried to examine him for wounds, but his attempts were brushed off.

"I'm fine. It's not my blood", he told us.

Again, I looked at Derek in confusion. "What happened?!" we asked.

Jordan told us that after the bars closed, a three-person gang attempted to beat up a guy who was walking alone, and Jordan stepped in to accept the challenge on his behalf. The gang initially resisted, saying they weren't interested, probably because Jordan is built like a bull. While this negotiation was happening, the would-be victim ran off down a dark street, and now, with their catch off the hook, the three readjusted focus, ready to fight Jordan. Fists flew, and all three were neutralized. Jordan came home wearing the bloody victory all over his shirt.

While this justifiable fight was a great way to help squash bullying, Jordan continued to channel high levels of aggression against any perceived threats. When set off, he'd be happy to lay waste to whoever crossed him. As an example, when he rode his motorcycle on the freeway, he split lanes to save time on commutes. If cars closed in on him and posed a risk, he'd punch side mirrors off using chains wrapped around his fists. He felt soothed whenever he could lay a small wake of destruction, but this began to complicate his life.

A woman he had dated ended their relationship due to his aggression. Anger from deployments crept back into many areas of his life, leaving him with the task of needing to slow down and figure out where to put it all. He needed to take time to understand the positive benefits of his anger in combat and the negative consequences when it operated unchecked in society.

Military careers require bouts of intensity we call "violence of action". They are intended to be short-lived. Downregulating (or lessening) such emotions at home is essential to staying balanced because family and friends are potential targets of collateral damage. A powerful tool for fighting enemies quickly becomes a terrifying destructive force that can hurt loved ones. Service members must remember to disengage from the anger and aggression that burns in them during work so they can maintain healthy relationships at home. They can either follow guidance from mentors to learn how to do so, or learn the hard way through personal conflict, lost relationships, and legal consequences.

SECTION 2: A GOOD MILITARY LEADER

Rich is a good-humored, warm-hearted Navy pilot of Germanic descent. I met him at a men's group focused on applying mentorship and spiritual guidance to help pursue personal growth. His group was composed of service members, veterans, and me as the only civilian. As a pilot in the military for over ten years, he provided great insight into applications for solid leadership. We had poignant discussions on strengthening military culture. Especially helpful was hearing feedback from veterans because it showed us all how some principles never change.

A common thread runs through all generations who serve in the military. It binds us together on a journey uniquely displaced from common society. We all share the experience of leaving home and stepping into the unknown where we are surrounded by a new family, for better or worse. The same pains are felt when suffering through horrible weather, fatigue, hunger, and endless workplace urgency. My frustrations in the military today are the same as theirs' decades ago. Even though we have never been in the same unit, job, or branch, we share the same feelings. I'm amazed at the connection we all have. It's understandable how combat experience increases this bond.

Rich created space for open dialogue and emotional processing related to life in the military. Five to ten men participated. Professionally, each path differed; careers varied. Time in service was short for some and long for others. Seniority gave credibility to those who shared advice. We listened closely to their experiences of being deployed around the world.

Personal lives also varied. Single and married men were welcome to join. Some were experiencing marital difficulties, while others were on the verge of getting engaged before deployment. While one struggled to leave his growing children to ship out overseas, another was only recently expecting. Again, seasoned members shared personal wisdom gained throughout life in the military. We discussed combat fatigue, the desire to experience war for the first time, and the trauma that combat leaves behind.

Difficult topics arose. Complexity of leadership decisions were discussed. We spoke about the relationship between decision-makers and those carrying out orders. What needs to change? What will always stay the same? Why were some military journeys harder than others? Pain points were discussed. Frustration towards peers and leaders was also a poignant topic; this was a sacred place to put everything on the table. Ideas were shared on how to reduce friction. Supporting one another, these service members shared ongoing struggles and fears. Everyone benefited from hearing the others speak. Social support is a powerful element in preserving and sharing wisdom across military generations.

America, at this time, was battling against terror being waged on several global fronts; Iraq, Afghanistan, Somalia, Yemen, the Philippines, and others. My buddies were busy. Many military members I knew were shipping back and forth on multiple deployments at a high tempo. Between deployments, some volunteered for more work overseas by augmenting various other units. Patriotic duty. Their high drive came with a heavy price. Exposure to combat yielded sights and images far too gruesome for the public. Recording live footage of missions further solidified the memory. Replaying it helped them study the enemy. It also further fueled the righteous anger underlying their deadly, destructive response. Terrorists desired to infiltrate America. Vigilance kept us safe.

Ever-increasing violence overseas only deepened the resolve of American forces. They waded into carnage. Witnessing grotesque murders of women and children plagued their minds, but it couldn't be avoided. Compounding this pain were the casualties of fellow American troops, burdening them with survivor's guilt. I was learning firsthand about the tremendous weight military service members feel and how very isolating that is. This weight was brought back home. It wore on their marriages and relationships. It's difficult to understand the nuances that permeate the lives of service members without knowing the people firsthand. Military families invariably feel the stress brought back home from deployments and training, especially what is unspoken.

Spouses sense distance. It's obvious when something is not being shared. Disconnection echoes. Withholding information about combat helps keep families safe from being exposed to trauma and also creates a quiet space where work can hopefully be externalized. Protecting them from the details of war requires a wall. The catch is that it limits the potential for processing emotions trapped in the mind and body. Our brains can't delete them. Unless another social support group exists, this can be excruciatingly isolating. Unresolved feelings have the annoying characteristic of remaining in limbo. Psychological static.

Rich encouraged us all to dig into our relationship with aggression and anger. He helped us see the good and bad impacts these emotions had on our lives. Leading us through journal prompts, he gave us context to study our tendencies. One powerful prompt was asking how we project our fathers onto our concept of God. Another was about the relationship between strength, anger, and aggression.

It was helpful for us to examine our relationships with our fathers to determine how aggression was introduced to us early in life. Was it a good thing or a bad thing? Were we trained on how to channel intense emotional states to being productive? Did we witness the destructive use of anger and aggression? How badly were we personally hurt or affected? What habits or behaviors do we act out in present-day life that have roots in our unresolved past? Are we hurting our own families today as a result? How are we working to become healthy in our anger and aggression?

Hearing responses to these questions from all the military warriors around me kept me on the edge of my seat. These were tough, battle-tested professionals with solid minds and big hearts. I loved the primal energy in the room. It was yet another piece that influenced me to join the military. Especially the part about addressing anger issues related to my father.

I hated my dad when I was young, or so I thought. We were worlds apart. He seemed to be closed off and angry all the time. He worked around the clock. Frustration with one another kept us distant. When I heard he regretted never joining the military, I knew I had to. I never wanted to be like him. His anger intensified my own, and we kept bumping heads. Thankfully I took Rich's advice and worked through my anger issues toward him. This was a long, hard path. A lot of tears were shed, and tons of sparring on the mats helped me stay sane.

Being in the Army helped me gain insight and perspective that strengthened me to engage my father with direct eye contact and fierce love. Rich's advice helped me heal our relationship. Before he died, we reconnected and bonded deeply. We both understood we butted heads not because we were so different, but because we were so similar. Beautiful moment. Nothing was left unsaid, including regrettable curse words between shouted prayers for forgiveness. I sat with him in the end. His last breath signified an honorable end to a life that helped forge me as a Soldier.

SECTION 3: PSYCHOLOGICAL APPLICATION

Rich spoke boldly about the impact that anger and aggression have on the lives of service members. He wanted us to be prepared to manage our feelings before they damaged our personal lives outside of the uniform. Anger, a powerful basic emotion, is neither good nor bad. Rather, what we do with anger determines the moral implications. One study discusses how people may overreact with anger "when a threat is very close, and escape is impossible" even if only through a misperception (Blair, 2013). Anger takes a dark turn "when it occurs at a frequency, intensity, or duration" that impairs thinking, heightens distress, or damages relationships through aggressive behavior" (Cash et al., 2018). Using this emotion correctly takes careful judgment because our brains are so complicated.

Neurologically speaking, when one feels anger or rage, behaviors will be determined by a variety of factors. Conflict style, social context, cultural framework, and signal interpretation each play a part (Williams, 2017). Our brains detect a threat and build a calculated response based on the knowledge we possess. Understanding socially acceptable behavior impacts what we decide to say or do. It's not easy keeping a clear mind when threatened. This is why training in martial arts is so powerful. Discipline instills calm. Informing the brain with objective, helpful information even while being attacked ensures an appropriate response.

Violence resulting from anger is commonly thought to be inappropriate, but there are indeed acceptable uses, especially when intended to protect against harm. Case 1: An angry child strikes a younger sibling when upset about sharing toys and must be instructed on how to use words rather than physical force. They are then coached on how to self-regulate and thereby gain new mental frameworks for relating with others. Case 2: Someone witnessing a victim being assaulted may violently strike or kill the abuser and will be vindicated of any wrongdoing because they used force to protect. In either case, social expectations are factored into the context.

Warfare is a unique situation requiring both calm restraint and violent aggression while surrounded by threats 24 hours a day for weeks or months on end. Over time, tension builds and may disrupt one's ability to self-regulate (lower one's stress levels). Devastating consequences of anger that war veterans face include: "increased rates of divorce, domestic violence, occupational instability, arrests, and incarceration (Shea et al. (2018). Studies also show a correlation between combat experience and physical aggression that increases with PTSD, traumatic brain injuries, alcohol abuse, and depression (Gallalway et al., 2012). Learning how to differentiate forms of anger and aggression is critical to warfighting preparation. Each service member deserves careful insight into how to correctly harness emotions.

Our brains can be trained to throttle our emotions. How we think plays a large role in the functionality of our brain cells. Groups of cells can be thought of as distinct, separate networks. Thoughts determine which neural networks activate. Some neural networks operate almost in opposition to one another as a means of regulating the intensity of our behaviors. For instance, one part of our brain helps inhibit reactive behaviors known as the fight or flight response while another opposing part stimulates such activation. The prefrontal cortex helps decrease the feeling of anger while the amygdala, hypothalamus, and others increase it (Blair, 2012). One part is the gas pedal, the other is the brake pedal.

Leaders must be mindful when it comes to anger because they are in a position to influence subordinates. Promoting good judgment as a leader is important. Mindfulness "improves emotion regulation" and is known to be a powerful "treatment for aggression" (Rahrig et al., 2021). This requires activation of our prefrontal cortex where we maintain complex thoughts and self-awareness. By doing this, we can help create a sense of calm even in tense environments where others are losing control. We can help pull people back into their higher minds. Mindfulness can be trained through meditation.

Meditation can be considered any mental exercise that helps us observe ongoing thoughts. It's not necessary to control or even slow down the rate of thoughts firing in the brain. Pause and reflect. Simply observing what the brain is thinking helps create a sense of calming space. No judgment about any urges we feel. We become aware of our stress levels and pain points. Engaging in meditation can eventually help slow down our brain's circuitry and override unwanted behaviors. This is how we can circumvent the fight or flight system thoughtfully.

In combative situations, mindful awareness helps one choose an appropriate level of violence with which to respond to a threat. In combat, service members must respond according to ROE (Rules of

Engagement). These rules determine whether troops can use deadly force. If deadly force is allowed, these rules determine to what extent. This means they are instructed as to how much firepower can be used. Are they allowed to use pistols, machine guns, or even higher-caliber firearms? What about explosive ordinance? Who exactly are they allowed to target? What circumstances justify taking life in a particular war zone? All these parameters are subject to constant change depending on the stage of war. Troops who are thoughtful about their behaviors in combat minimize violations of such laws. This keeps our nation in good standing on the world stage as we lead in military prowess.

I love that we train hand-to-hand combatives in the military. Martial arts training particularly uses mindfulness to throttle violence. Fighting can be paced by properly assessing an adversary's intentions. One blackbelt in Jiu-Jitsu, a bone surgeon, told me he uses a simple handshake to determine how much violence to react with. If he notices someone is becoming confrontational or threatening, say at a bar, he will shake their hand and maintain eye contact. Pressure in the hands says it all. He will instantly know how violent the situation will become. For instance, A refusal to shake hands or a crushing grip can signify incoming violence. Should the adversary decide to take an angry swing, this blackbelt knows how to shatter bones in the hand, wrist, arm, elbow, or shoulder. Alternatively, he can choose to subdue the person with a choke by pulling on their arm and taking their back. Dealer's choice.

Asking mentors to help me understand my anger and aggression was necessary because I never learned how to do that as a child. Having been on the receiving end of violent anger back then, I learned to fear it. I grew up believing these emotions are inherently bad because they lead to physical harm. While anger and aggression are effective in combat, they are destructive when misused. A prime example of misuse of aggression is domestic violence. This occurs when someone is angry about experiences outside their home and they turn that aggression against their own family. They are endangering the very thing they seek to protect above all else. This led me to repress my feelings and avoid confrontation. I didn't know when it was right to fight back in life. I had to ask Rich for help:

SECTION 4: LEADERSHIP ADVICE

> *"When you walk in through your front door, take your cape off. Don't pull rank at home. Forcefully demanding respect from family leads to instability and resentment in the home. I had to learn that before it ruined my marriage.*

Rich's humility and vulnerability make him a trusted source of counsel. He's honest about his own shortcomings and the mistakes he made as a young pilot. Recognizing how domestic disputes are caused by aggression enabled him to save his marriage. He learned how and when to use his aggression constructively, and it was not in the home.

At one point, I opened up to him about my own anger in life and my struggle to understand why I had such a negative inner dialogue. Doubt stifled my growth. Inadequacy pervaded my self-perception.

Much of my childhood anger and frustration had been left unresolved. I unknowingly lived an emotionally reactive life mired in the past. It was hard for me to understand what I found so threatening. Much of my writing in this book pertains to overcoming my own maladaptive behaviors which would have destroyed any chance to be a functional leader. So this subject is near to my heart.

Rich let me be real. Even when I cried in front of him, he never made me feel ashamed for the uncomfortable feelings and truths I brought forward. We were in his in-laws' living room with just a few men. We opened up about deep struggles. Nobody laughed at me. We were all there for each other. Many of us had experienced similar frustrations at some point in our lives. We all sought growth. It was awesome to have his support as I sat in the midst of my own brokenness to make sense of hurtful past experiences. This was invaluable to me because I knew I had found a group of men I could follow anywhere, through anything. They had my back and cared about my struggles. I knew any of these men could lead in combat because they would take care of every Soldier under their command, including mental, spiritual, and emotional health.

Simply being around them and listening to their own stories showed me how many ways I wanted to grow. Most inspiring was witnessing the humility of those returning from combat with high spirits and a hunger to keep fighting, even when losses were had. God, country, family. They were proud to fight for those they loved. It was demanding, but the reward was knowing that the future could be more secure for the next generation. War weighed heavy. It would be easy to become jaded, but they didn't want to lose their humanity. Their families still needed them to show love, especially toward their kids. They learned through men like Rich to not let anger control them. Keeping quiet and isolated would internalize the outside battle. Getting dark feelings out is a heavy process. Intentionality was necessary. Focus was especially paramount to ensure they aimed their barrels at the appropriate targets and no one else.

When returning home from deployment or training missions, they understood the importance of taking the cape off. Rank, job title, and authority were all switched off. Husbands and fathers spoke to their children with tenderness, and to their wives with honesty about their anger, fatigue, and frustrations. They knew what weight to pull out of the emotional rucksack. Burden was shared. My married buddies didn't go it alone. Social support was multilayered. I saw how their wives stepped up to support one another and also help soothe the pain their husbands felt. These women formed their own small teams that valued community and family. Oftentimes, women checked the ego of new military wives to ensure they didn't further stress their husbands who returned from combat. Powerful insights were shared. Abandonment was addressed explicitly with clear guidance.

One key tension I will share on marriage between a civilian and military service member is the concept of role expectations. A civilian spouse will become independent when the service member deploys. Everything stateside is on them. Dynamics change. They only feel down for so long. Service members may then return home realizing they are not needed. Feeling rejected they may become angry and wonder if they are unnecessary?

One military spouse told me how her husband returned from his combat tour to Afghanistan feeling frustrated that she was so independent without him. He returned to the states hoping to regain his role as a husband but felt unneeded because she had learned to adapt to life without him. Other military wives mentored her on ways to validate her husband so he wouldn't feel rejected. It was difficult for him to be in large crowds, and even the grocery store felt overwhelming. During his time in combat, he was regularly awoken by the sounds of incoming fire. She worked hard to remain aware of his heightened emotional state and ease him back into his role in her life. Women she had met through military spouse support groups guided her. These newfound sisters brought strength to her marriage. They helped her understand her husband's aggression in light of what they had previously learned about their husbands. Years later, this service member was able to reflect on how brilliant his wife's support was after war.

Some military men and women I know regrettably lost sight of their role within their families. Tensions from work-related trauma remained high as they thrashed against anyone around them. I have sat alongside service members faced with divorce or criminal charges because they struck their spouse or child. I have heard some apologize for threatening the use of a weapon brandished during a dispute. I have been told of the vast frustration felt when one is disrespected at home by those they love. Feeling invalidated can weigh heavy as a service member struggles to understand why they are treated poorly at home while respected for their positional rank at work.

Knowing exactly how to separate work life from private life seems impossible when serving in the military. Stress often follows us home. Wearing the uniform is a 24/7 profession and even while in our houses, we are always on standby. One must be ready to be called upon at any given moment. Vigilance takes energy. There is always a potential fight waiting around the corner, so learning how to switch off aggression and calm the nervous system becomes an art form. Peers affect us. When dealing with colleagues incapable of lowering their own stress levels, this becomes even more complicated.

Mindfulness provides practical steps. It's important to filter the input being poured into our conscious awareness. Who are we listening to and how is that affecting us? For the longest time, I was reflecting on critical voices from my past or negative people in my present life. I had to learn what it meant to access my emotions and deal with them appropriately instead of burying them. I'm still learning how to do this today. Eventually, I removed myself from negative influences and sought solid mentors. I learned to turn off electronic devices and journal about the habits in my life that I wanted to change, based on positive influences around me. My anger subsided and my aggression fed healthy habits, especially Jiu-Jitsu training.

Military careers are ultimately jobs, not identities. Differentiating the two is difficult because they can become so intertwined. Being comfortable with our identity outside of work is critical to staying objective. Identity beyond the uniform grounds us. How can we be present? What is the best version of a spouse, parent, or friend we can possibly be? Uniforms and rank don't help here. Understanding how to take the cape off is a dynamic that requires maturity and self-awareness. Maintaining objectivity is a shared effort in which families must provide ongoing support and encouragement. Emotions run high in military careers so personally striving to understand one's relationship with anger and aggression is key to remaining stable in times of chaos, on the outside and inside.

Thanks, Rich.

References:

Blair R. (2012). Considering anger from a cognitive neuroscience perspective. *Wiley interdisciplinary reviews. Cognitive science*, *3*(1), 65–74. https://doi.org/10.1002/wcs.154

Cash, R., Varker, T., McHugh, T., Metcalf, O., Howard, A., Lloyd, D., Costello, J., Said, D., & Forbes, D. (2018). Effectiveness of an Anger Intervention for Military Members with PTSD: A Clinical Case Series. *Military medicine*, *183*(9-10), e286–e290. https://doi.org/10.1093/milmed/usx115

Gallaway, M. S., Fink, D. S., Millikan, A. M., & Bell, M. R. (2012). Factors associated with physical aggression among US Army soldiers. *Aggressive behavior*, *38*(5), 357–367. https://doi.org/10.1002/ab.21436

Rahrig, H., Bjork, J. M., Tirado, C., Chester, D. S., Creswell, J. D., Lindsay, E. K., Penberthy, J. K., & Brown, K. W. (2021). Punishment on Pause: Preliminary Evidence That Mindfulness Training Modifies Neural Responses in a Reactive Aggression Task. *Frontiers in behavioral neuroscience*, *15*, 689373. https://doi.org/10.3389/fnbeh.2021.689373

Shea, M. T., Lambert, J., Reddy, M. K., Presseau, C., Sevin, E., & Stout, R. L. (2018). Treatment of trauma related anger in operation enduring freedom, operation Iraqi freedom, and operation New Dawn veterans: Rationale and study protocol. *Contemporary clinical trials communications*, *12*, 26–31. https://doi.org/10.1016/j.conctc.2018.08.011

Williams R. (2017). Anger as a Basic Emotion and Its Role in Personality Building and Pathological Growth: The Neuroscientific, Developmental and Clinical Perspectives. *Frontiers in psychology*, *8*, 1950. https://doi.org/10.3389/fpsyg.2017.01950

11 - AGE IS AN ASSET

"He started hollering; I had no idea what happened. Guess I accidentally broke his leg. Felt bad about it."

- ***BUDDY*** *[Navy Petty Officer First Class]*

Tacit knowledge: knowledge obtained through personal experience

Procedural knowledge: learning through instruction on skills and methods

SECTION 1: INTRODUCTION TO THE TOPIC

"You're too old to join the military, nobody wants you." My cousin's statement felt like a slap. Just a few moments ago I was pumped to tell him about my desire to sign a contract. Now my smile and excitement melted. I half chuckled in shock, paused for a moment, and then looked down at my shoes. Damn. Did I seriously think I could serve in uniform while in my 30s? How could I be so blind to consider that the military would accept me? I felt like a total idiot.

I guess I believed him because he sounded so convinced. Maybe other people could join at my age but that's because they have more value or experience than I do. As for me, I haven't done anything very risky or exciting in my life. People who join the military are probably more fit, mature, and accomplished than I am. I'm nobody special. Remaining quiet in embarrassment, I stared solemnly out the living room window.

Life up to this point lacked a real sense of adventure. I wanted more but didn't know how to go for it. Working sedentarily in a cubicle making sales calls was boring. Many entrepreneurs I admired had served in the military. Gaining leadership experience through experience in the armed forces would undoubtedly help me professionally. I wanted to experience challenging training environments and to develop my resilience. Excitement had been building around this idea the more I thought about it.

Now the words of doubt from my critic crept in and took root. It was like poison to my soul. My excitement melted. I'm feeling stuck because I can't get out of my safe, small, predictable life. Am I past the point of no return? Have I missed my chance to do something different? I'm wondering how much my age is working against me. How hindered am I by the routine ingrained in me?

At this point in life, I don't know where I fit in. Corporate jobs don't suit me. I'm never satisfied with that type of work. Even when I'm great at what I do, office life feels bland. Sometimes I wonder if I'm aging in reverse. When I was younger, I desired comfort. Fear drove me away from uncertainty. In adulthood, I feel as though I lack substance. My heart is crying out for a primal adventure into the wilderness. My brain understands business development, but it lacks knowledge about survival outside of civilization. I want to know more about life than how to send emails and network online.

With age, I'm learning more about what I like and don't like. There is a sudden pull toward the military that's tough to explain. I'm seeing how some of my strengths can carry over. Getting more physically fit has been fueling my energy levels even higher. I hate being constrained indoors. My newfound confidence at the gym is making me believe I can contribute to a military team. I feel capable of sharing weight among a group of fighters. Momentum builds in my heart until I'm slammed with negativity by someone I love.

Just like that, I crash. Critical words interrupt my positive mindset and push me back into a corner of defeat. A big part of me agrees and doubts that my being in the military is possible because of what other people say. I wonder how awkward it would feel being around a bunch of 18-year-olds during BCT. I imagine getting laughed at for being the old man. Nothing is worse than feeling isolated in a big crowd. I've had enough of feeling like an oddball much of my life and it will probably be even worse in the military.

Then I think about it again, focusing on the social misfit part. Aren't there others like me who want to get away from their homes and find a new family? What if I join and find brothers and sisters I bond with because we didn't fit in anywhere else? There must be a few others like me. Being older than them means I can help be a guide because of my life experience. Finding even one friend I bond with could be totally worth it. Without taking a risk, I will never know who is out there. All I know is that up until now something has been missing, and I want to leave everything behind to find it.

I have allowed negative people to influence my life way too long. Whenever I sit and accept self-limiting beliefs, I give my power away. Paralyzed. My growth is stifled because I don't take the risks necessary to push myself into uncharted territory. My military friends inspire me to break away from unsupportive people. They have me considering cutting ties and leaving everything I know behind so I can finally hear my own voice clearly. Who do I want to be?

I shut my eyes and imagine a stronger version of myself. Envisioning myself as a warrior pulls me away from my negative thoughts. I see myself as sturdy, committed, and bold. My ideal self doesn't stand around and let bullies have their way. He doesn't allow others to put him down or place limits on his potential. I like this version of myself. I feel an alignment, like something finally clicked into place. Then the words echo again. As suddenly as I feel strength, the harsh words from my critics come into my mind.

My own father told me I was too weak to be in the military. After one particular argument following my talks with a military recruiter I erupted. Critical words sting because they reflect my own fearful self-doubt. In rare form, I responded. I ended up cussing my dad out because of my frustration and it was a big shock to both of us. But I felt trapped for so long. At times I wished he would actually fight me so I could knock him out. It took my joining the military and leaving home for years to fix our relationship.

What if he's wrong, though? What if I'm not useless at my age? Tension built as his words echoed in my head. Why is he confident I'll fail? How could anyone know for sure? Did I want to fall into the mindset that I'm too old to change my life? Is it really my age that I struggle with, or is it disbelief? While I'm too old for most military recruiters to take me, there still is an open option. I have 30 days before I age out of eligibility to become a commissioned officer in the Army.

Finally, I put my foot down. I had enough of letting doubt keep me stuck inside my comfort zone while everyone I admired stepped out into uncertainty. Age wouldn't hold me back. I'd use my life experience to lead with a balanced perspective. I'm old enough to be my own person apart from anyone else. Screw negativity. I've had it with self-doubt. Just because someone else feels inadequate doesn't mean I have to. That is their baggage to ruck around life with, not mine. Rebelling against shame, I called my recruiter back.

"Sergeant, I'm in. Sign me up."

SECTION 2: A GOOD MILITARY LEADER

Buddy is a giant country boy from Ohio standing at 6 foot something with chiseled abs, ox-like strength, and a syrupy Southern drawl. He's got a kind face and is the human version of what a puppy with enormous paws grows to become. I don't think he realized how abnormal his strength was. Buddy snapped someone's leg in Jiu-Jitsu without even trying when the guy attempted to get aggressive, and because he's a Midwestern boy with a big heart, he felt horrible about it. I met him playing volleyball in San Diego. Strictly because of his name, I wanted to be friends. He lives up to his namesake and is a great friend to have in my corner.

We spent a lot of time on the hot beach sand playing various sports and meeting awesome people. This chapter in my life was special because it was one of the first times I experienced life without alcohol, and he was one of the first non-party friends I made. Athleticism was the foundation of everything we did, which turned me on to join the military. I wanted to meet more people like him. Whether we hiked a mountain trail or spiked the volleyball, I could always count on Buddy to be up for anything adventurous.

Our conversations deepened. We discussed our childhood, goals, struggles, and fears. I appreciated his depth and perspective on life, especially because of his experiences in the Navy. He told me about the rough parts that helped shape him into maturity. He had lost friends and coworkers in the military. Death had instilled an awareness in him that life should not be taken for granted. He understood the price of freedom and the value of enjoying the simple things in life. Seeing how he chose to grow through tough situations was a stellar example of how the military forges us into better versions of ourselves. My shallow take on life was deepening thanks to military buddies like him.

One night he invited me on a midnight hike to catch a meteor shower. A group of about 10 of us went up Cowles Mountain with his friend Steve leading. I'll never forget that moment at the summit. We all laid on our backs chit-chatting under the stars as streaks of white light cut across the blackness in stunning displays of a magical solar system. I think I was the only civilian there, and my desire to belong to the military was ever-growing. These people are great, and there are more like Buddy I need to meet. I began debating joining the Navy as I continued to study their crew.

Steve, our midnight hike guide, was an adventurous Navy Sailor who was an avid freediver and all-around explorer. He had an edge to him that indicated to me he was fearless and hungry to push limits in life. We talked about how deep he could dive on one single breath as he spearfished. Immediately, I knew this was another awesome military brother I wanted to have as a positive influence. I asked him to take me out with him on a dive, and he said he would. We planned to swim around La Jolla and snag some of the delicious fish from the water.

A couple of weeks after our night hike, I asked Buddy how Steve was doing. I wanted to see if he could take me free diving.

"Steve's gone," Buddy slowly responded. "He died a few days ago."

My brow furrowed. I was stunned. Wait, that can't be. I just saw him. He's the one full of life and adventure that mastered the ocean and was going to introduce me to the underwater world. His confident laughter conveyed his comfort in the face of exciting challenges. How could someone who is that alive be dead? I wish I could have gotten to know him better.

Steve had gone on a routine solo freedive in Mission Bay and never made it back. His body was found by a boater the morning of Tuesday, September 10,

2013. Buddy and the guys he worked with always told him to bring a swimming buddy. They didn't want him to risk a shallow water blackout. This is exactly what happened when he got tangled in his fishing line and drowned. He died doing what he loved. After his death I became aware that the military is full of exceptional young people whose adventurous spirits make them high-risk and prone to dangerous outcomes. Steve's passing fueled my appreciation for the moments I get to share with military friends between their deployments. War is dangerous enough, and their hobbies can be even more so.

Buddy remained resilient and continued to teach me about the military family he worked with every day. We continued our hikes together, and I dove deeper into the mindset of a sailor who had experienced so much life. His strength and steadfastness continued to inspire me. Soon enough I became set on joining the military as an officer. Buddy told me he believed I would be a good one. Coming from a man like him meant the world to me. Anything good about my leadership style largely has roots in guidance from him and a few other military friends in this book.

SECTION 3: PSYCHOLOGICAL APPLICATION

Leadership aptitude depends on emotional maturity and good judgment rather than the number of years of experience. Age doesn't determine how good or bad a leader will be. The biggest determining factor is how willing someone is to listen to correction and advice. Buddy wanted me to put aside my own presumptions about being in my 30s as a new military officer and instead focus on keeping a listening ear to those around me.

Everyone has an opinion. To some, older age is viewed as a marker of increased wisdom while to others it means someone is physically weak and tired. When it comes to youth, it may be viewed as a marker of ignorance and immense energy. We all know people on both ends who break all these stereotypes. Everyone is different. It's up to us to be who we want to be in life in spite of what others think.

When it comes to maturity, our individual life experiences determine how we each grow in life. While "social norms about age-appropriate behavior and developmental milestones create a timetable of developmental opportunities" not everyone develops along the same timeline (Heckhausen et al., 2010). We all mature at different rates based on what challenges we encounter and when. Adversity plays a big part. Trauma can especially inhibit growth by derailing emotional development unless active effort is applied to adapt. Post-traumatic growth is a positive outcome that results from self-awareness and an ability to find purpose through hardship (Slade et al., 2019). Growing through adversity may bring mental and emotional maturity that surpasses biological age. "Old soul" is a compliment.

Age brought along wisdom for Buddy. As a high-octane younger man full of testosterone, he made his fair share of mistakes, as we all have. At one point, his ego got the best of him when dialoguing with a senior staff member in the Navy. He made an insult that resulted in a withdrawn job opportunity that altered his career trajectory. Pain from the situation motivated him to grow. In time he saw the good and made peace with the situation. Utilizing this hard-earned wisdom, he taught me to be very cautious about how I speak to others. He told me to always consider who is in the room and how my criticism could be taken personally. The military is a small community and respect goes a long way.

Trust is foundational to any leader's success, and it's earned by treating others well. It can't be demanded because of rank, age, or positional status. One study finds that trust in leadership is enhanced when subordinates observe humility in action (Yang et al., 2019). Because of Buddy, respecting any individual I come across in the military is mandatory. Rank should never enable leaders to be disrespectful towards those they manage, especially when considering the health of the organization overall. The well-being of employees and work performance increase under humble leadership (Zhang & Song, 2020). People work harder when they are happy and will be more willing to contribute when they are proud to be part of a team. Promoting the emotional health of workers is vital to creating a job environment that inspires cohesion and achievement of shared goals.

Humility enhances leadership through these inspiring characteristics (Trinh, 2019):

- Openness to change
- Awareness of personal limitations
- Admitting mistakes
- Accepting failure
- Asking for advice
- Developing others
- Increasing performance

People will trust and follow someone they believe truly cares for them. Wholeheartedly. Putting selfish needs aside to help others is powerful because it demonstrates a willingness to meet subordinates where they are. The inverse is telling subordinates they must work their way up to their leader through various gatekeepers as a means of discouraging access. Chain of command and organizational structure is important, but shouldn't be used to discourage dialogue. Pride creates barriers. Humility is demonstrated by holding others in high esteem and giving them a voice.

Buddy wanted me to shut up and learn as a new leader. His approval meant a lot to me. Him being enlisted makes me highly protective as an officer over others in subordinate positions. He shared the pain that arrogance causes. He taught me the value of listening to subordinates for guidance and responding with openness. His advice helped many times. Leading with this knowledge kept me from adding stress to already tense situations. I strove to filter my words and watch my attitude before giving input or direction.

Having gained my total trust, Buddy enabled me to open up about personal struggles in life. Sobering up opened my eyes to many uncomfortable truths about myself. I was learning about my issues related to pride. No matter what I disclosed about myself, my mistakes and flaws were never an issue to him. He understood and valued the importance of growth. What I appreciated was his boldness in admitting how his past errors impacted his trajectory in life. He owned his mistakes and used them to shape himself into a smarter and stronger man. I loved seeing how this made him a steady, reliable asset to any team to which he belonged.

Being around him helped me pursue the same personal and professional growth in my life.

Once on a hike, I asked him to teach me about the best and worst things a military leader could do. He explained how arrogance is the worst characteristic of anyone in the military. He gave specific examples of military officers who have told enlisted counterparts they are in control and don't require anyone's help. It never ends well. Pride cuts ties. Humility, on the other hand, fosters a willingness to learn and work with others. As a future officer, I needed to learn how to trust and rely on others without attempting to control them.

Buddy also shared the importance of wanting to help serve others. Military units are communities that thrive when leaders foster a culture of connection. Humble leaders create work cultures promoting teamwork and preventing negative interactions (Chiu et al., 2020). Promoting synergy between military peers is important because we are together in the same fight. Especially when the mission gets tough, collaboration keeps morale high and minds healthy. Leaders who focus on promoting mental health and emotional well-being are strengthening the organization at the individual level. Depression, self-harm, self-medication, and suicide are all consequences of overlooking mental health. I never wanted to push anyone I led towards maladaptive behaviors if I could at all help that. Personally, I know how unproductive self-medicating, and escapism can be.

As we completed another trail hike together, I asked, "Buddy, what's the biggest thing you want me to do when I become an officer?" Thoughtfully, as always, Buddy slowly responded with his deep country voice:

SECTION 4: LEADERSHIP ADVICE

> *"Respect NCOs when you arrive at your unit, and they'll go out of their way to make you successful. They'll especially like that you are older because you'll be around their age, so you probably have an easier time understanding each other. If you treat them disrespectfully, like you know everything because you're an officer, they will stand by and watch you fail. New officers don't know anything yet."*

At 32 years old, I thought my age would be a huge liability in the military. Buddy assured me that the opposite was true because age helped me bring experience others may not yet have. As long as I remember to stay humble and avoid talking down to those younger than me, I will be fine. He was right. I never once felt age was a disadvantage. Also, some of the most mature, solid people I met in BCT were 18 years old.

One of my best friends in the military was 18 when I met him. Brent from Ohio. We still keep in touch as he attends college. He's out of the Army now and has aspirations of playing professional sports. In BCT, we spent a lot of time sparing on the concrete floors as I taught him Jiu-Jitsu. His grips are insane and he's basically a 240-lb block of muscle. Even though he's a young buck he has an old soul. The fact that we both like 90s alternative music brings us closer. We sang to each other in the showers and put on a show for dozens of other trainees.

Brent taught me that overcoming adversity in life

has a way of maturing the soul. He had experienced painful situations at home growing up. His mom fell into drug use. Brent protected her. At one point he had to fight off her drug dealer who physically attacked her. This helped restore her back to sobriety. Being a loving son, he accompanied her to 12-step meetings and supported her recovery. I love Brent like a brother and our friendship is one of the best gifts granted by the Army. Once he makes it as a pro athlete our plan is for me to be his life coach and roommate. Unless of course, I make it as an author. Then I'll be visiting him during national book tours. In either case, we are brothers for life.

Moses is another amazing friend and brother I made in BCT. We bunked together and spent a lot of time discussing our upbringings in life. We read each other letters from home and when his girlfriend mailed him chocolate, he shared it with me. He is a towering 6-foot 5-inch baby-faced young man from Africa with perfect skin and fluent French. Out of all the African nations that speak French, he has the most Parisian dialect, he tells me. Apparently, the other dialects have their own sort of twang. He told me I could only learn from him. I did.

We spent hours together in formation going over vocab words and conjugation. Soon we could tell each other private jokes, which was awesome. Anytime he saw me scowling he'd smile and say, "Hey Joseph! What's wrong buddy?" followed by some hilarious French phrases I had just learned. "Mon frère, ce mec est un clown. Reste positif!" [Brother, this guy is a clown. Stay positive!] I'd immediately burst out laughing! All smiles. He kept me sane. His maturity was years beyond anyone I met in the Army. There is a very powerful reason for this.

Adopted by relatives at a young age, he never knew his father, and his mother died giving birth to him. He told me all this with a gentle, calm voice. How terrible! I was speechless. He smiled. He always had a smile, even through the worst weather and most unbearable parts of training. His joy never wavered. When I shared my sadness about his situation, he told me never to feel bad for him. He proclaimed he was the happiest man in the world. I asked how. His response forever impacted my life. He said that losing both parents allowed him to live life as the saddest man in the world, but that would be a miserable life. Instead, he chose happiness. He made the decision to be happy despite the devastation in life. He told himself to be the happiest man in the world; he lives his mission out daily.

It was incredibly inspiring to be around young men and women like Brent and Moses. We all got along like siblings from the minute we met. Thanks to Buddy's advice, I kept an open mind to learning from anyone in the military because I knew they had some type of experience I lacked. Most of the subject matter experts I worked with during my military journey were much younger than me.

Age and life experience help develop tacit knowledge, which accrues over time. The term tacit knowledge pertains to soft skills like creativity, innovative thought, self-awareness, and emotional intelligence. They are skills one possesses without the ability to share explicitly. Personality, value systems, and beliefs feed into the tacit knowledge we each possess. Joining the military in my 30's allowed me to apply all this to the job. Having worked in numerous civilian jobs, I would help enrich the military culture with outside perspectives. One helpful skill was communicating clear expectations and boundaries to minimize emotional reactivity during times of high stress.

Example: While in the field, I let Squad Leaders know how hectic communication would be for me during our missions. I needed time alone to address our command element and adjacent units before being pulled in other directions by the platoon. They acknowledged and staggered mission tasks to give me the time I needed. Their consideration was helpful when we placed obstacles on the simulated battlefield. I needed to input dozens of 8-digit coordinates and verify the activation of each simulated minefield. At the same time, the platoon prepped for convoy movement to the next location. The Soldiers gave me space to get the data uploaded before asking for details on our upcoming movements.

Another bit of tacit knowledge was understanding how to communicate across social or cultural barriers to work effectively with a diverse community of Soldiers. The military is a melting pot of diversity, and many times is someone's first experience dealing with an outgroup.

Example: Many Soldiers I worked with came from rough neighborhoods strained with racial tension and segregation. Hearing about the violence that occurred in and around their homes was painful to hear. Sometimes, as young teens, carrying illegal firearms was necessary to travel safely. They were regularly attacked or robbed. Some had experienced being shot at while at a house party or walking down the street. This was foreign to me. I grew up in a quiet rural town, so how could I relate? Initially, it was expected that as an officer I wouldn't be able to understand.

While I found their experiences hard to grasp, I asked them how all that shaped them. Noting their strength as Soldiers, I emphasized how far they had come. What was it like going back home on leave knowing what they had left behind? My questions sparked some great talks and grew my appreciation for their service. In a small way, it validated their struggle. Having had some experience tutoring youth from troubled homes and neighborhoods, I knew to communicate without judgment. Maintaining openness with these Soldiers allowed for deeper discussions as they felt comfortable sharing the pain they endured. Ultimately, this strengthened our bonds and unit cohesion. I saw glimpses of them beyond the uniform and rank.

Procedural knowledge is information that experienced Soldiers and NCOs in the military would provide me through instruction. Like how to perform specific tasks. Soldiers helped me learn the doctrinal aspects of our craft while opening my eyes to real-world situations occurring outside the textbooks. Doctrine gives prescribed parameters to the craft of warfare, but everything changes when on the ground. NCOs wanted me to listen to the wisdom they had gained from serving over a decade in the military. I needed to keep my mouth shut and take notes while they helped me see the nuances of the job up close and personal.

One area of procedural knowledge Soldiers

educated me on was correctly assessing time to complete mission tasks.

Example: Our brief was quick. A simple map was with only basic KT (Key Terrain). I am being ordered to emplace anti-vehicle concertina wire obstacles near a hill to protect a team of scouts hiding on top. Within five hours the task is to be completed. I brief the platoon. NCOs tell me that because of the rocky terrain, high temperature, darkness, refuel location, chow time, and current manpower we'll need eight hours to finish the job. Legit discrepancies. Listening to them, I am beginning to understand how battle plans on a map miss friction points Soldiers are limited by. New officers miss this. My platoon directs me on realistic measurements to consider when calculating work hours so I can relay to higher up exactly how long we will need. The better I get at battle planning on the ground the fewer headaches we all have.

Another gap in procedural knowledge I possessed was understanding how to maintain property accountability with limited storage space and organizational resources.

Example: I signed for over $6,000,000 of government property while being accountable for every single dollar. Many of these items were routinely used and stored across multiple areas in the motor pool without distinct storage locations. As if that wasn't chaotic enough there were identical items or several variations of the same item being routinely trafficked between vehicles. One NCO pulled me aside and coached me on implementing his solution. He suggested using paint markers along with colored tape to create visual indicators used to identify toolsets. He also told me to create hand receipts identifying every individual item so I could sign the property over to the Soldiers. By doing so I incentivized the platoon to keep track of what they used. I was relieved and grateful for his advice.

Because I listened to this NCO at one point, he saved me from having to pay a $5000 statement of charges. After returning equipment to another unit working with us, I received a phone call stating that a very expensive electronic device was missing. I was expected to pay for it out of pocket. Thanks to him I explicitly asked for a complete itemized hand receipt describing every single piece of equipment in the kit given to me. Sure enough, my hand receipt showed the item was not present or ever in my possession. This meant someone else had lost it and cleared me from responsibility. What a relief.

Many other times during my military journey, Soldiers stepped in to guide me through unsettling situations. As Buddy had told me, if I respected the enlisted service members working with me, they would go above and beyond to keep me successful. Even when I felt I hadn't done enough as a leader to deserve such support, the Soldiers covered me. Having years of experience working across multiple units and overseas on combat deployments gave them a rich understanding of military systems and procedures. I listened and took notes as they coached me and shaped my knowledge. Many applications I learned in the military pertaining to personnel management were strengthened because Soldiers took the time to teach me how to lead without being a burden.

I came into the military with a breadth of life

experience. My age helped me relate to others. I still had many gaps in my military knowledge that were bridged by Soldiers who appreciated my willingness to learn. Supportive NCOs enabled me. Keeping an open mind was critical to succeeding as a leader. I was grateful to have developed strong relationships with hard-working enlisted service members well before I joined the military. I often tell people who commend me for joining that it's the troops who do all the hard work. My biggest responsibility as a leader was enabling them to accomplish the mission while listening for feedback and guidance to continually improve.

Thank you, Buddy.

References:

Chiu, C.-Y. (C.), Balkundi, P., Owens, B. P., & Tesluk, P. E. (2022). Shaping positive and negative ties to improve team effectiveness: The roles of leader humility and team helping norms. *Human Relations, 75*(3), 502–531. https://doi.org/10.1177/0018726720968135

Garske, M. (2013, September 14). Diver Found Dead in Bay Was in Navy: Officials. *NBC San Diego*. https://www.nbcsandiego.com/news/local/mission-bay-diver-identified-as-navy-service-member-stephen-wall/1959274/

Heckhausen, J., Wrosch, C., & Schulz, R. (2010). A motivational theory of life-span development. *Psychological review, 117*(1), 32–60. https://doi.org/10.1037/a0017668

Nguyen, T. T., & Jeste, D. V. (2021). Ageism: The Brain Strikes Back. *Cerebrum : the Dana forum on brain science, 2021*, cer-05-21.

Slade, M., Rennick-Egglestone, S., Blackie, L., Llewellyn-Beardsley, J., Franklin, D., Hui, A., Thornicroft, G., McGranahan, R., Pollock, K., Priebe, S., Ramsay, A., Roe, D., & Deakin, E. (2019). Post-traumatic growth in mental health recovery: qualitative study of narratives. *BMJ open, 9*(6), e029342. https://doi.org/10.1136/bmjopen-2019-029342

Training Industry. (n.d.). Declarative knowledge. In Training Industry Glossary. Retrieved July 17, 2022, from https://trainingindustry.com/glossary/declarative-knowledge/

Training Industry. (n.d.). Procedural knowledge. In Training Industry Glossary. Retrieved July 17, 2022, from https://trainingindustry.com/glossary/procedural-knowledge/

Trinh M. P. (2019). Overcoming the Shadow of Expertise: How Humility and Learning Goal Orientation Help Knowledge Leaders Become More Flexible. *Frontiers in psychology, 10*, 2505. https://doi.org/10.3389/fpsyg.2019.02505

Yang, J., Zhang, W., & Chen, X. (2019). Why Do Leaders Express Humility and How Does

This Matter: A Rational Choice Perspective. *Frontiers in psychology*, *10*, 1925. https://doi.org/10.3389/fpsyg.2019.01925

Zhang, Z., & Song, P. (2020). Multi-Level Effects of Humble Leadership on Employees' Work Well-Being: The Roles of Psychological Safety and Error Management Climate. *Frontiers in psychology*, *11*, 571840. https://doi.org/10.3389/fpsyg.2020.571840

12 - PAY ATTENTION TO PACE

"Every time you stop jogging on this trail run, I get to punch you in the face, keep up."

- ***COLE*** *[Navy SEAL Officer]*

Burnout: exhaustion, overwhelm, or fatigue caused by persistent stress

Eustress: helpful amounts of stress that promote goal achievement

Distress: heightened levels of stress that wear us down mentally or physically

SECTION 1: INTRODUCTION TO THE TOPIC

I woke up in bed with a hangover one bright, sunny Saturday. It was only a couple years after college, and I was still caught up in the wrong crowd. The weather was perfect because I lived about ten blocks from the beach. Outside my open window I could hear pub-crawlers laughing, skateboarders, and motorcycles revving up for a joy ride. Surfers were riding beach cruisers down the street to catch waves. Meanwhile I felt stuck. My heart pounded from anxiety like it always does when I wake up. Psychologists call this the cortisol awakening response. I didn't yet know how many unaddressed emotional issues writhed inside of me. Self-medicating with alcohol was all I knew to do, but it always seemed to exacerbate the symptoms. Partying doesn't resolve physical tension. Despite a pounding head and nausea, I was wired and needed to do something to get my adrenaline out. I remembered my college professor said she uses running as a means of dealing with her anxiety. Makes sense. I wanted to get my sneakers on and jog the adrenaline out. There was only one problem; I didn't know how to run.

I regularly worked out inside a gym but rarely engaged in outdoor fitness. Running was still foreign to me. As an overthinker I weighed the variables. How fast do I go, and for how long? What route should I run? Do I need to bring water with me? What do I wear? Am I fit enough to run shirtless? What's the difference between jogging and running? Is it ok to walk at all, or does that look stupid? Do I stretch before or after running? How should I stretch out? Who can I call to join me? No use. Nobody is going to pick up. All my friends are in bed nursing their hangovers. Never mind it all. I'm just going to lay here and wait for them to wake up so we could go back to another bar. I closed my eyes and pretended to rest.

At this point in life, it was hard for me to

go outside and be around people if I wasn't drinking or surrounded by a crowd of friends. Social anxiety ran my life and paralyzed me with fear. My mind was always racing with thoughts of inadequacy as I compared myself to others. I always felt behind and wished I knew how to keep up. My fear of abandonment had me constantly dreading being left behind and my codependency required me to latch onto others for identity.

SECTION 2: A GOOD MILITARY LEADER

Cole, a tall, lean Irishman from Maryland, was a Naval Academy college graduate who joined the SEAL teams as an officer. We met through his roommate who is another team guy mentioned in this book. After being inspired by a relative in the military he had a burning desire to share in patriotic duty. As a water polo athlete in high school, he decided to focus on becoming a SEAL. From that moment on, he focused on getting on the teams. He trained with precision. His top-tier college degree and elite military training created a powerhouse of American potential. To me, however, he was simply a good friend who knew how to be a nerd and debate. Cognitively, we sparred in deep philosophical arguments loaded with elements of chaos math, astrophysics, and quantum theories.

On September 11, as the Twin Towers fell in 2001, a furious passion came to life within him. It fueled his desire to bring justice to those behind the murderous destruction. "Never forget" was branded into his heart, and he would live out the ethos of a warrior dedicated to winning the Global War on Terror. Many of his childhood friends pursued lucrative business careers and encouraged him to consider joining their companies. They admired his work ethic. He had no aspiration to begin thinking about his resume in the private sector. He saw that service in the military would be the defining feature of his professional accolades. In his heart, he wanted to serve with warriors as one of them. Corporate America would always be there waiting for him. He knew that a financially stable future was always possible in the private sector. That predictable life would need to wait for a few years. First, he had to earn his trident.

He made it to the teams knowing he belonged there. It was everything he wanted and more. As a SEAL Officer, he was tasked with leading some of the most elite humans on our planet. Cole, despite the stigma associated with elite academic accolades, led with humility. I was inspired by how casually he carried himself. He was approachable and likable without any air of conceit. Never once did he draw attention to his amazing resume. Guiding my understanding of how a leader should perform alongside subordinates, he emphasized professionalism and humility. Officers should voluntarily share in any task the troops carry out, no matter how dirty or brutal. There is no room on the teams for someone who believes they are better than others.

One of my favorite memories with Cole was when we went trail running together at Cowles Mountain (a one-way distance of 1.5 miles, 900-foot ascent). We had run this route many times before, but this time I started off running past him and thereby unknowingly set our pace. Usually, Cole set our pace because he knows how to run, and I didn't. He was taking his time to train me on weekends. My bold move was about to knock me on my butt. After I ran by him, he breezily jogged to my shoulder. He gave me a brief lecture on the importance of intelligently setting and respecting a reasonable pace during long workouts. I slowly digested the information realizing how pointless my efforts were to show off speed I could never maintain. Then he calmly said that because I decided to run past him, he would hold me accountable for what I had just done.

"If at any point on this run you stop running, I will punch you in the face," he said without emotion. I audibly responded with disbelief, honestly thinking he was joking. After all, I was just a civilian, not a soldier. When he didn't recant, I stated I disagreed with his terms. He quipped that my agreement was not necessary. I sealed the deal because I ran past him, and he was always the paceman. When I stopped to protest, he turned around, faced me, and cocked his fist back.

Holy smokes, he wasn't joking! I immediately yielded and continued running with enthusiasm. For the entire run, excitement and fear fluttered in my stomach and I worried he was about to clock me in the head at any point. As soon as we hit the summit, my relief had me vomiting my guts out all over the monument. Other hikers stared in confusion as loud bursts of dry heaves interrupted their leisurely weekend walks. I never ran past the paceman again. I became a loyal K-9, never leaving the leg of his master.

I'm grateful Cole had the patience to teach me how to run longer distances. We constantly increased our run mileage and terrain difficulty. He inspired me to suck up the pain and push myself quietly. At one point, I even had to cover my foot blisters in moleskin and duct tape to keep the blood from lubricating the adhesives. He fully supported me in not quitting. On this day, we ran the "Potato Chip" trail at Mt. Woodson (one-way distance of 7.5 miles, 2130-foot ascent). We hit the summit and I am pretty sure I threw up there, too.

At some point on this run, after fatigue set in, I remember feeling intimidated by the idea of slowing down. Cole was right behind me, keeping his eye on our pace. Terrain was so steep it was like running up a giant staircase. My quads were swelling and tightening. All I could think of was to keep hammering out one heavy stomp at a time until we completed the journey. I told myself to keep going. The big picture overwhelmed me. To ease my anxiety, I broke the distance into smaller manageable pieces, rock to rock and bush to bush. No stopping until we get there, no matter how slow I have to run. Do not quit, ever! Finally, we got to the top.

One of the most profound moments for my self-confidence occurred on that trail run. After we ran back to the car, I felt relieved and surprised I had made it. I told Cole I needed to admit something to him. During most of the run, I wanted to quit and felt terrible because I was so slow. I apologized for making an elite athlete like him move so slowly up a trail he probably could blaze through in a heartbeat. Honestly, I figured he wanted to fire me as a workout partner. I braced for his judgment.

"Your pace pushed me today; good work," he said. I froze in disbelief. No way he just said what I think he said. Wait, what? What do you mean my pace pushed you? I moved like molasses up the entire mountain, my quads were tight, and everything felt stiff and slow. Again, he told me my pace was decent, and I inspired him to push himself. What a day. I just inspired an American superhero. I wanted to holler in excitement but I knew what he would say, so instead, I quietly exhaled a calm, "Hell ya, bro."

Cole is a top-shelf kind of guy, a high-class high achiever who understands the benefits of pushing oneself well beyond comprehended limits. He is also a realist who bases success on logic and common sense. His innate wisdom allows him to strike a balance between acceleration and burnout; he calls this pace. Pace creates a meaningful space where the burn rate is high without compromising the engine. Pacing myself applies universally to all aspects of my life. I contemplate this dynamic often and am continually learning how to push limits without damage. Cole gifted me a foundation on which to build continuously. Once again, a military friend opened my mind to the cross-disciplinary elements related to warfare training.

SECTION 3: PSYCHOLOGICAL APPLICATION

Our brains are built for constant recovery. Cars need oil changes, and our brain need to wash out toxic debris. Rest and deep sleep make this possible. Alcohol overuse and irregular sleeping patterns prevent deep sleep states. High-stress work environments compound the stress on our brains. Urgency used in the military to invoke a state of heightened awareness becomes harmful over time. Adrenaline is a short-lived molecule designed for temporary influence. Situations that prolong the intense response of our nervous systems cause deterioration just like a vehicle wears down with mileage. It's like revving an engine at 6000 RPM for sustained periods when normal operation is at 1000

RPM. The solution is finding a reasonable pace that throttles according to the shifting situation at hand. Bursts of intensity are fine so long as slower states occur with restfulness.

Understanding how pace prevents burnout is important for all leaders. Burnout is considered exhaustion and it applies to both individuals and organizations and is caused in part by high tempo or high-intensity workloads (Demerouti et al., 2021). Fatigue sets in when the pace of work becomes unsustainable over time (Fagerlind Stahl et al., 2018). Demanding work environments that ignore these issues will eventually begin to lose employees. Leaders can enable recovery. Adjusting the pace of work gives time to rest. Burnout can be mitigated even if stressors cannot be removed. Small adjustments help, especially in high-intensity work environments. It's important to encourage stress management. Inspiring subordinates to find methods for relief will enhance productivity.

Military training environments and deployments bring tremendous stress to the lives of service members. Leaders can help address this. Anxiety and stress create urgency and induce a rush towards action. Humans are biologically programmed to fight until achieving closure. One study found that "Health-promoting leadership accounted for less burnout," especially during deployments because leaders enabled subordinates to seek helpful solutions or outlets (Adler et al., 2017). Leaders who prioritize the well-being of others help strengthen the organization. Workers will be more engaged on the job. They will be able to focus on detail while avoiding errors. In the military, fewer mistakes translate to the preservation of precious lives.

One research study shows significant burnout rates in military medical professionals stating, "if we hope to meet the military's mounting mental health needs, it's essential that clinicians perform their duties effectively and sustainably. Reducing burnout is an essential step toward that goal" (Kok et al., 2016).

Work culture dictates how well people are cared for within a unit or department. Does leadership only want results, or do they want healthy employees? Work cultures driving towards obtaining goals at the expense of sustainable output induce burnout, unless meaningful rest cycles are programmed (Salvagioni et al., 2017). We live in a society that values accomplishments and minimizes guidance on self-care. To keep workers healthy, encourage them to rest. Promoting rest pays dividends by reducing turnover. An organization devaluing relationships will lose good talent. Losing highly trained professionals bleeds resources because large amounts of time and money that have been invested are wasted. Incentivizing employees to maintain health is an investment in the longevity of the organization.

Leaders should look out for the following signs of burnout to keep an eye on morale. Burnout occurs in three key parts: exhaustion, detachment, and a sense of ineffectiveness (Maslach & Leiter, 2016). Running at a high pace while unable to recover weakens the body. Spreading weakness creates a perception of diminishing value within an organization. Losing the heart due to fatigue is a well-known phenomenon as courage diminishes in the face of unrelenting pain. We all have an eventual breaking point, but it's our responsibility to train towards strengthening ourselves without going so far it becomes counterproductive. Even psychologists who don't take breaks to rest when providing emotional guidance to others are susceptible to burnout (McCormack et al., 2018).

Cole taught me to respect the pace and to apply it whenever I needed to stay in the game longer with a clear mind. He taught me when treading water and feeling overwhelmed; I need to slow down my strokes, take a breath, and do a mental reset back to minute zero. Calming the mind and slowing the pace promotes longevity. He told me the pace gets people through special forces selection. They remain mentally present with every step they take instead of becoming overwhelmed by the miles ahead of them. He taught me the fundamental concept of not sprinting in a marathon. Eventually, I sought to develop an awareness of breath. My pace changed to a slow, consistent rhythm. My heart rate fell and stayed within an optimal range given what was ahead.

When overwhelmed by what was ahead, I recall Cole's advice:

SECTION 4: LEADERSHIP ADVICE

> *"Steady your pace. The big picture is overwhelming and will make you rush. Get from one small goal to the next. Hit 50-meter targets before 300-meter targets. Trying to do too much at once gets people washed out."*

Combat veterans know that most issues leaders stress over are not true emergencies. When everything is urgent, nothing is. Gaining the respect of subordinates is done by correctly prioritizing work tasks. Pushing people to get things done faster than necessary gets annoying fast. Leaders must seek to remove friction points for the subject matter experts they manage. Providing reasonable deadlines is a sign of a good leader.

Soldiers who deployed to combat zones make it clear that leaders who mitigate stress to any degree improve life in the military. Anything I could do to shield them from unnecessary frustrations would be greatly appreciated. The weight that troops carry on their backs is already high, let alone added pressure from inefficient leaders. Burnout is a problem in the military because of the rushed pace of constant urgency. Leaders must regulate the intensity of deadlines. It's important to help introduce rest cycles whenever possible and streamline the workload logically to accomplish the mission.

As the officer in charge (OIC), it's my job to notify commanders that their goals will require adjusted timelines due to the reality on the ground. People see a two-dimensional representation of logistical movements in briefs using maps and slideshows. They may not accurately factor in the added dimension of real-world issues. Complicating planning factors include:

- Restrictive terrain features
    - Wadis
    - Boulders
    - Steep elevation
    - Soft sand
    - Erosion
- Uncharted obstacles
    - Anti-vehicle ditches

    - Wire obstacles
- High temperatures
    - Overheating vehicle engines
    - Exhaustion in Soldiers
    - Heat Casualties
- Communication blackout zones
    - Radio line-of-sight loss
    - Signal jamming
    - GPS Inaccuracies
    - Electronic warfare interference
    - Loss in cellular networks
- Cascading timeline adjustments
    - Circumnavigating restrictive terrain
    - Recovering disabled vehicles
    - Coordinating separation of team elements
    - Altered link-up locations
    - Water consumption & resupply
    - Fuel resupply

Everything changes once movement on the ground initiates. Contingency planning is critical. Scheduling buffer time is necessary. However, overdoing this means taking personal time from Soldiers to arrive at a mission location hours or days before any action is to take place. Sedentary Soldiers lose morale when purpose is lacking. Leaders who are able to balance pace with planning well-timed movements on the battlefield are tactical savants. They know their equipment and their troop's capabilities.

One night on a desert training exercise we conducted a routine convoy movement using NVGs (night vision goggles). On this particular night, we were wrestling with the terrain around previously unexplored territory. I noticed the soft powdery sand that kept trapping our tires became jagged rock mounds with increasing steepness. It was hard to make this out in the darkness. Night vision sounds cool, but it limits depth perception and peripheral vision. Maintaining situational awareness involves constant scanning of the horizon while readjusting the focal lens to scan for nearby threats. There are two adjustable lenses, one closest to the eye and one facing outward. Nailing a high-resolution image through perfect adjustment is a great feeling, especially with low moonlight. Of course, once the focus is precise, it applies only to a set distance. Switching from a long-distance perspective to the foreground necessitates adjusting the lens.

My driver needed me to be an extra set of eyes while he focused on reading the road up ahead. In desert terrain while using night vision optics the road can look exactly like the mounds of sand flaking on each side. Loss of visual reference points leads to sudden off-roading. Where the lead vehicle goes, the rest will follow. It was necessary to continually update everyone on the radio to ensure we stayed organized. Keeping uniform movement is tough to do when sudden surprises block the path.

Whenever a boulder or pile of barbed wire popped up, I needed to relay that quickly to avoid impact. While visually inspecting the ground around the vehicle, I simultaneously needed to monitor digital maps and manage the radio. Adjusting between night vision and a bright computer screen every few seconds for hours on end is a special kind of headache. Managing all this technological equipment is work enough. Coordinating a line of armored vehicles to make sure we don't lose each other or kill someone on the ground was a whole other problem set.

I find it difficult to stress the frustration of maneuvering a convoy of tanks and trucks with trailers attached while wearing an apparatus limiting peripheral vision. Billowing dust clouds through night vision optics are like an invisible black fog shrouding everything. Infrared signatures are masked, and it takes a while to clear if the wind isn't blowing. We had to carefully drive through the lingering blackness, ready to stop if a bumper or Soldier suddenly appeared. The last thing anyone wants is thousands of pounds of metal rammed into their vehicle. Driving over a dismounted Soldier would be worse. Responsibility is on me as a leader to set the pace of the convoy while talking to everyone involved.

Navigating moving vehicles and handling multiple channels of continual communication gets dicey. I sat beside two separate radios, plus a digital computer interface with multiple group chats involving various military units. Communication was internal to the platoon and external to my company and the units we were enabling in the fight. I was required to send up 8-digit grid coordinates, emplace obstacle dimensions, planned movements, and status on equipment. These distracted me from looking at the road to help my driver.

Multiple times I noticed we were getting rocked by the terrain, so I stopped the convoy and got out of the lead Humvee. I walked ahead and scoped out features on the ground. The convoy slowly crept behind me as I gathered information. Ground guiding happens when I feel particularly sketched out and notice the dangers that lie around us. I'll break out my headlamp, click on the red lens, and scour for a safe path. Especially if wire or ditches are present, I'll personally direct the entire platoon through. Using infrared chem lights, I'll wave each vehicle through until I know everyone passed safely.

Previously, on my first field exercise as a new platoon leader, I ended up navigating my own Humvee nose down into a ditch. It took a while to figure out how to back out of it while the rest of our convoy waited on us so we could all finally bed down for the night. Lesson learned; I won't stay seated next time we navigate through obstacles in darkness, because a leader who makes Soldiers lose precious hours of sleep loses credibility fast. Giving Soldiers their well-deserved time back is a powerful source of motivation and morale.

On this night movement I felt wary. We had a 30 km movement to our next mission location, but I found a shortcut on the map, making it a 12 km drive. The terrain would be hilly, but after running this route by the drivers, we agreed it was manageable. As platoon leader, any failures from this point forward were entirely on me. I took the gamble and notified the commanding offers above me. As we rolled along the low-trafficked territory, my nervous system wired me to stay very cautious. I tapped away on the clunky rubber keyboard to send updates and tested radio connectivity. Looking up to peer out the windshield, I saw nothing.

Mountains in the blackness of night look like starless skies to the blind eye. Terrain elevation seemed pretty mellow on the maps, but I wanted to verify. I told the driver to slow down and I leaped out of the Humvee to jog out a path ahead using the red lens on my headlamp. He kept the convoy rolling slowly behind me to save time. I darted up the sloping path we were driving in search of a culminating plateau. Panning around deeper into the enveloping blackness, I tried to make sense of the terrain. Red light makes depth perception difficult.

Then it hit me. What I thought was a slight incline was the beginning slope of a mountain. We were driving up the spine of a jagged ridgeline cut deeply into the roots of the mountain. The once wide road dwindled sharply into a narrow trail barely the width of a vehicle. We were about to park ourselves on a knife's edge. I sprint back to my Humvee, grab the radio mic and yell, “This is 1-6, All stop! All stop! Everyone stay put. Break.” I took a breath and slowed my thoughts. Chill out dummy, think. “I’m walking over to each driver. Hang tight.”

One thing I briefed my platoon when I first met them was that my number one goal was to keep everyone alive. No circumstance justified me making a decision that would kill one of my guys or gals. I would never justify a loss of life because I wanted to impress a boss. We were operating in a training capacity as part of a non-deployable unit, but the training involved potentially lethal maneuvers.

Driving by an overturned Humvee during one training even stuck with me. Just after sunset the driver hit a deep wadi and rolled over. Luckily, he survived the accident. His Humvee was practically empty, which minimized the risk of being crushed by equipment. It took a large recovery team hours to fix the situation. I took his lesson to heart. Thinking about possible death or injury still makes my skin crawl. I love the Soldiers I work with and prioritize their safety over how tactically daring I look. Perhaps I am not the best person to defer to when relating to superiors, so feel free to disagree with my attitude here.

On this night, potential risk became imminent danger. I had led our entire platoon onto a steep ridge flanked by 10-foot drop-offs. *Damn, this one's on me, and I've got to fix it,* I thought. I ran to my platoon sergeant and asked for his read on the situation. Confirming it was terrible, I immediately told my commander we were not going to make our anticipated timeline. Safety came first, and we were in rollover territory. There was nothing in my mind that would justify putting the troops in an accident in piling thousands of pounds of steel on their heads and necks. I received permission to work out the situation as safely as possible.

Hurriedly I dropped the radio mic and bolted down the convoy in the blackness. Diesel exhaust fumes filled the air as the vehicles loudly idled in wait. I walked to each driver and, shouting over the blaring engines, asked these young warriors if they felt safe pulling a dangerous maneuver off the terrain. Some said yes, and some said no. Without hesitation, if anyone said no, I had them swap out with another Soldier who believed they were able to handle the precarious maneuvers. Before I joined the military, my enlisted friends told me to never risk the life of a service member who felt unprepared.

Once we situated new drivers, the ground guiding began. The rear vehicle was first up, a troop carrier. We had all the troops dismount so that in case of a rollover, the equipment back there wouldn't crush them, not to mention the dump truck itself. A few inches at a time each vehicle backed out while reassessing the wheel-to-cliff ratio before adjusting and re-engaging. The troop carrier made it back out to flat open terrain. Next up was the dump truck carrying our hasty mine dispenser. Success again. After this, our tracked vehicles both crawled out in reverse.

Next up was the second to last vehicle, the behemoth. It's a large dump truck full of simulated anti-tank mines and very real razor-sharp concertina wire, along with a trailer hitched onto the back with even more supplies. Jackknifing the trailer results if turns aren't perfect. There is no room to spare given its size. The driver knows what he's doing, and I stand back to let him work. Ground guides flank the vehicle, shouting distances while displaying red lenses for hand gestures. We take it slow and move with precision. Pace is paramount to maintain safety. I want them to go as slow as they need, to keep everyone alive. Deadlines can wait. Nothing is more valuable than a Soldier's life.

After an hour or more, we eventually made it out. I took a deep breath and thanked God that everyone was safe. I don't have kids, but I know a little more now about what it must feel like to fear for the well-being of someone in that way. "Hey everyone," I said, my voice obviating my relief, "thank you for handling the situation so well." Cooly, they responded with a concerted, "Too easy Sir, it was nothing. We've got this." I smile at their confidence and respond, "Rog, let's go the long way around this time." We readjust our vehicle lineup and got rolling. Damn, I love these Soldiers. I wonder when they'll fire me. Later in the book, I'll share why they never do. Their answer was never what I expected.

Pacing myself has helped countless times in the military. From physical exertion during exercise to personal goal setting, I have been able to apply a long-term perspective to keep myself going especially when I wanted to quit. I managed my fitness level, avoided inflammation, and recovered from injuries. Keeping on track with online schooling, I completed my master's degree. Taking time to recover from constant stress was both challenging and rewarding. I knew when I neared my limits, although sometimes I noticed the benefit of pushing past them. Whenever I did so it was critical that I scheduled time to decompress. Avoiding alcohol, sleep deprivation, and an unhealthy diet played a big part in recovering quickly. I needed every possible chance to heal my body and mind throughout my time in uniform.

Progress didn't come easy though. Burnout did occur. I took notice of the signs in my own attitude. When it hit, I notified my leaders and did my best to manage the situation by readjusting my work environment and reducing stressors. This wasn't an easy conversation to have, but I needed to be honest because it would affect the Soldiers. They see everything.

Eventually I was able to find a new job and workplace on base more suitable for my skill sets. Burnout disappeared. I was also honest with the Soldiers about my own journey learning about pace. Many discussions occurred which allowed me to share the wisdom that helped me. Watching them apply it for their benefit was very rewarding. Several signed up for college classes, began meditating, and invested in fitness consultations at the gym to develop training programs. The only reason I was able to plug them into such resources was because of my military friends who coached me on growing past the behaviors limiting my own growth. Pace is a powerful concept and practical resource that keeps us alive and in the fight, longer. Respecting it helped me every time burnout threatened to punch me in the face.

Thank you, Cole.

References:

Adler, A. B., Adrian, A. L., Hemphill, M., Scaro, N. H., Sipos, M. L., & Thomas, J. L. (2017). Professional Stress and Burnout in U.S. Military Medical Personnel Deployed to Afghanistan. *Military medicine, 182*(3), e1669–e1676. https://doi.org/10.7205/MILMED-D-16-00154

Demerouti, E., Bakker, A. B., Peeters, M. C.W., & Breevaart, K. (2021) New directions in burnout research, *European Journal of Work and Organizational Psychology*, 30:5, 686-691, DOI: 10.1080/1359432X.2021.1979962

Fagerlind Ståhl, AC., Ståhl, C. & Smith, P. Longitudinal association between psychological demands and burnout for employees experiencing a high versus a low degree of job resources. *BMC Public Health* 18, 915 (2018). https://doi.org/10.1186/s12889-018-5778-x

Kok, B. C., Herrell, R. K., Grossman, S. H., West, J. C., & Wilk, J. E. (2016). Prevalence of Professional Burnout Among Military Mental Health Service Providers. *Psychiatric services (Washington, D.C.), 67*(1), 137–140. https://doi.org/10.1176/appi.ps.201400430

Maslach, C., & Leiter, M. P. (2016). Understanding the burnout experience: recent research and its implications for psychiatry. *World psychiatry : official journal of the World Psychiatric Association (WPA), 15*(2), 103–111. https://doi.org/10.1002/wps.20311

McCormack, H. M., MacIntyre, T. E., O'Shea, D., Herring, M. P., & Campbell, M. J. (2018). The Prevalence and Cause(s) of Burnout Among Applied Psychologists: A Systematic Review. *Frontiers in psychology, 9*, 1897. https://doi.org/10.3389/fpsyg.2018.01897

Salvagioni, D., Melanda, F. N., Mesas, A. E., González, A. D., Gabani, F. L., & Andrade, S. M. (2017). Physical, psychological and occupational consequences of job burnout: A systematic review of prospective studies. *PloS one, 12*(10), e0185781. https://doi.org/10.1371/journal.pone.0185781

13 - YOU'RE WELCOME HERE

"Dude, I think I just broke my rib wakeboarding. My deployment starts this week, and I really don't want to get it x-rayed. Can you ask your physical therapist buddy for advice?"

- ***MATT*** *[Navy UH-60 Pilot/Instructor]*

Acceptance: receiving approval from a social group

Belonging: believing one has the right to exist within a social group

Self-acceptance: non-judgmental view of oneself despite flaws

SECTION 1: INTRODUCTION TO THE TOPIC

Snow softly drifted down outside, blanketing the icy streets in Saint Robert, Missouri. It seemed that a few weeks ago during the fall season we were constantly waking up to the sound of tornado sirens during a torrential downpour. Winter seemed to have stopped all this and now the cold ice was welcomed. I was far from the coastline and beaches I love by hundreds of miles. To make up for this, my apartment was decorated with surfing photos while the tv live-streamed footage of the beach. To combat seasonal affective disorder, I did my research. This involved having bright interior lighting and a pineapple or coconut scent on the diffuser. Stepping into my apartment felt like walking into a beach resort. Clearly, I was in denial about being in the Army stationed in the middle of nowhere.

Pining for my life back in California would make for a lonely existence if I didn't find some close friends, especially since I didn't have roommates. Active-duty military officers can collect BAH to pay for rent off base, while National Guard and Reservists remain on base, sharing hotel rooms. I found my apartment in Missouri and signed the lease remotely online while still in Georgia finishing OCS at Fort Benning. I didn't know who I wanted to live with because I was so accustomed to living alone before I joined the military. Also, we get no time to ourselves in training, so I felt it was wisest to have a place I could go to be by myself and recharge. This meant I would have to put in quite a bit of effort to organize a social life outside of work. Then I met Joe, who helped me cope with the distance from home.

Joe is a hilarious Midwesterner with a thick head of brown hair, strong hands, and a warm soul. He gives great hugs. If you don't have a buddy who bearhugs you so long that you get a full inhale and exhale, you're missing something. Working in construction developed his solid work ethic. Salt of the earth. He had the perfect sense of humor anytime stupid things happened in training. Spot on. Whenever I wanted to freak out, I would scan the room for him, see his square-jawed smile, and immediately grin my anger away. If Joe was staying positive, I would get my attitude back in check and follow behind him.

Joe was a new Army officer who had previously been enlisted in the National Guard. While enlisted, he had multiple combat deployments, including to Iraq, where he survived triple-digit temps constructing roads and laying foundations. He loved being a Soldier. We met in engineer school just as I was becoming overwhelmed with the constant ruckus of having dozens of peers around without any reprieve. I was drawn to his steady, calm demeanor and his ability to make light of tough situations. He and I were similar in age and mindset. We instantly became friends. Having a similar taste in music made for some great jam sessions when he came over to play guitar. Despite all the job stress around us, I felt right at home whenever he came around.

Friends like Joe created incredible highlights in my military journey. Whenever I felt lonely, I reached out and was reminded of the connections there. He pulled me out of my head, especially because he knew exactly how to not talk about work. We could talk about music or hobbies that gave us even brief moments of decompression from work. He always had a construction project back home or a classic truck renovation to talk about. Amazing skill. His deployment experiences seasoned his perspective and sense of values. His calm, relaxing demeanor soothed my overwhelmed brain. People like Joe always encourage me to slow down and enjoy the present moment without being overwhelmed by friction points and clashing egos around me.

I could also count on him to push me when necessary. One graduation requirement for EBOLC is a 12-mile ruck. Completing it in under three hours opens the door for the Sapper Leadership Course. We started around midnight. There was a lot of uphill terrain. Even with a fast uphill pace, we stayed with each other the entire time, along with our friend AJ. These two were faster than me and I fell behind by a few meters, but I was on their heels. They pulled me through some of the worst pain I have ever felt. My feet were screaming, and my quads burned but these two were great company and made it a fun time. We barked positive comments to each other through the pitch-black woods: "Let's go boys", "C'mon!", "We got this." I remember seeing them slightly ahead of me while wondering if I could keep up.

Do I even belong in this group? When will they run off because I'm so slow? With their encouragement, I made sure to keep sticking to them. Yes, I belonged. Towards the end, we all picked up our trot to a full-out run. It was excruciating. Joe and AJ bolted ahead, and I did my best to keep up. I remember seeing the headlights of the cadre's vehicle, doubting I made the cut.

"2:59," my instructor said sternly, "you barely made it. Now hurry up and weigh your ruck."

I stared with wide eyes, my face dripping sweat. We weighed our rucks to verify the appropriate weight and I hugged the boys for inspiring me. This feeling was what I joined the military for, and it stayed with me all day. I drove home with tense legs and prepared for a full day of engineering classes. Floating in a hot, pre-dawn salt bath after this ruck felt great.

Joe is a brother to me. My friendship with him is one of my most treasured prizes for joining the military. Meeting people like him and AJ is the best part of the journey. But before I went into the military, I feared I wouldn't fit in or find close brothers. Hesitation made the fear grow. Then Matt came along. He was a Navy friend who helped reassure me I would definitely find a sense of belonging in the military, no matter how out of place I might feel.

SECTION 2: A GOOD MILITARY LEADER

Matt is a boyish-looking East coaster with blonde curly hair, blue eyes, and a chiseled frame. Surfing is one of his favorite pastimes when he's not zipping around in a helicopter. Being from Maryland did little to keep him from being a perfect fit in Southern California. Flip flops, boardshorts, done. As a homeschooled youth, he missed out on a lot of the pop culture references that influenced his peer group, giving him an endearing sense of innocence. Sports helped him socialize throughout his youth, so he wasn't terribly awkward. He and I met at a men's group at church, and as cautious as I was about making new friends, I decided to probe him a little.

I was transitioning from the post-college party scene and now many of my friends were getting into legal trouble, including arrests for multiple DUIs, bar fights, drug trafficking, and more. To keep myself out of trouble, I was the designated driver and slammed energy drinks all night. This meant my nights entailed shuttling friends to bars, clubs, and house parties while navigating the chaos as private security, especially for the ladies. I was a cabby. Partying had once been fun, but now the scene was exhausting.

I kept watch over several close female friends during our nights out, partying into the morning hours. They told me about some scary moments in the past that put me on edge and made me very protective of them. A few had experienced being drugged by predatory men at night clubs and some had even been sexually assaulted. But they still wanted to go out and party with friends. Being sober made me reliable. This was when the trouble started picking up.

It was common to get calls after midnight asking to pick someone up who had woken up confused at a random house with no clothes on. Combining different drugs impaired their bodies. Other friends, whom I initially trusted, would get in my car with cocaine or MDMA without telling me. Driving downtown one night, the friend I was driving told me to stop my car as he jumped out and bolted around the corner. I sat there idling in the street completely confused. He jumped back within minutes.

I was irritated. "What the hell was that about?" I asked.

"Nothing. Just had to get something from my friend."

Later he told me he had purchased a bag of white powder. I was pissed. If we got pulled over, I could've been implicated in some serious criminal activity.

I noticed the downward spiral in my friends' behavior. It seemed they were on stimulants at night, depressants in the morning, or alcohol in the afternoons. Never sober. I put up with their illegal behavior because I wanted to feel welcomed, but I hated the drug-induced impairment. Summers were especially wild. International students, businessmen, and DJs were regularly in town mixing with my inner circle. I remember standing in the bathroom one night at a downtown restaurant watching my friends snort powder together with the door wide open. We acted like we ran the town. Stupid.

The manager ran over scolding us because he didn't want customers to see this. He said to just hurry up as he closed the door on us. Later that night several in the group were arrested for getting into fistfights outside of a club. I tried to intervene and rush a few to my car but nobody would listen, so I had to stand by and watch while the cops put handcuffs on them. One guy was getting arrested as his girlfriend screamed at the officers. Next, she was on the ground getting pepper sprayed for resisting arrest and was charged with hitting a police officer. It was nuts. I walked back to my car feeling I failed them because I wanted to take them home before all the drama.

Party scenes get hectic fast. Drugs have a way of fueling madness that crosses boundaries. Celebrities, musicians, and professional athletes were commonly involved as well. The downtown afterparty scene was getting wildly out of hand, and I realized how empty I felt inside. I wanted to associate with the cool crowd but also noticed my growing discomfort.

Here's what really crossed the line for me. That same summer someone brought dozens of ecstasy pills on a party bus that the police found when they raided it. One pill ended up in a man's drink without his consent, and it was his first time he had ever taken an illegal drug. He went home early from the bars to sleep but couldn't. His heart began racing and he soon received a text saying the party crowd was waiting for him to come back out. They drugged him to ensure he'd keep hanging out instead of sleeping. I offered to come over, stay up with him and keep an eye on him, urging him to stay away from those guys. He refused any help and decided to go back out to the clubs. This convinced me to distance myself from the group for good. I wanted a family to fit in, but this wasn't it. I wondered what other peer group could help me feel like I belonged, only without all the bad decisions.

I moved out of my place, found a neighbor to take me in, and headed to a church men's group in search of new friends and mentors. I decided to try meeting friends who carried a sense of purpose beyond self-gratification. Introducing Matt.

When I met Matt and found out he was in the military, I told him about my life of sin and hedonism. I told him outright it probably made me someone he would not want to associate with. He seemed like a clean-cut, good church person who didn't want to get muddied by someone else's filth. Pleasure-seeking led me down a path of bad choices and dark places in a world medicated with distractions. For the first time ever, I poured all this out. Tearfully. I disclosed my past trauma to him, including physical abuse as a child and sexual abuse after that. Anger and pain had a grip on me. Numbing the wounds was all I knew how to do. This pulled me away from the light and into a horrible fog of despair. Expecting him to respond with disgust, I projected my fear of rejection onto him.

Contrary to the shame and judgment I felt inside

my own soul, Matt admired my raw honesty and said it increased his respect for me. Wow. Not expected. If he could stomach my confessions, there was nothing left for me to hide. We instantly became close friends who were able to share deeply about the hardest parts of life. From that second, he always made me feel welcome in his home and helped me feel welcomed into the military as well.

As a civilian, I perceived the military as a class of strait-laced squares who looked down on others. I believed they joined the military out of self-righteousness and a need to exert authority. Over time I learned that almost everyone who joins the military has experienced a dark chapter in their life just as heavy as my own. Personal struggles may vary, but facing adversity certainly builds character. Many Soldiers I know have big hearts and a desire to avoid bad influences which otherwise could destroy their lives. Even the ones who haven't stumbled through a cascade of poor decisions like I did at least know what it means to be a reliable support. They offer a shoulder to lean on. Difficult situations don't scare them. Matt is a man of strong character and was one of the first service members to help me appreciate acceptance by the military.

I felt more and more welcomed by my friends who helped me face my personal issues and keep on a good path.

SECTION 3: PSYCHOLOGICAL APPLICATION

Most military service members are well acquainted with adversity. One study of 162 Soldiers found 83 percent experienced adverse childhood experiences early in life, including domestic violence, drug abuse, physical abuse, psychological abuse, and more (Applewhite et al., 2016). Many joined the military to escape horrific living situations at home. Without appropriately receiving adequate care for such trauma, they often suffer more than others when experiencing combat-induced trauma. Despite such compounding damage, they seek community and purpose by putting on the uniform.

Continuing the trend of a tough backstory, another study found, "men with military service had twice the odds of reporting forced sex before the age of 18 years" among various other traumatic childhood experiences (Blosnich et al., 2014). Military service members report more trauma in childhood than civilians for both the enlisted and officer communities (Lamson et al., 2020). Pain is prevalent. Again, this research points to the military service being a means of overcoming personal adversity for many who have suffered at home.

Because people with a history of childhood abuse tend to join the military, this correlates with increased suicide rates especially induced by combat experience (Nock et al, 2013). It's important to appreciate the significance of such findings because it helps highlight the importance of therapeutic intervention to keep service members healthy, especially during combat. Troops deserve to receive all the support they can. Our military force will be stronger overall when individuals are strengthened.

Another study "linked childhood abuse and neglect to an individual's decision to join the military in an effort to escape their family of origin, further linking child abuse and neglect to adult homelessness among this veteran sample" (Montgomery et al., 2013). Many other studies make similar connections between service in the armed forces and adversity. This adds weight to the importance of encouraging self-care and healing to ensure organizational readiness. We join to train ourselves for combat. We're open to being reshaped. Potential for self-development is high and exciting outcomes are possible if addressed appropriately. The military offers an opportunity to build powerfully effective citizens who will contribute to our nation's ongoing success. Active-duty service members can be strengthened before becoming veterans who will retain resiliency skills. This is why optimal leadership is so important.

Military careers provide structure, discipline, and mentorship. Service can be a wise investment. Leadership skills can be developed, especially when inner potential is uncovered through hardship. Good leaders understand this process and help build others up by offering necessary tools. They demonstrate how we can harness our resilience. I sought several role models to emulate as they walked these paths alongside me. I was invited to grow under their guidance continuing what had been started even before I joined.

Matt was a Navy Officer who opened my mind and heart to believe that the ugliest parts of my life would never label me as unwelcome in the military. For so long, I feared the scars I carried. What they said about me. Ego defensiveness was incredibly exhausting, and I longed to finally be authentic. Acceptance meant everything. His compassion and support helped me heal from my past and gave me a lifelong brother.

Friendship with Matt gave me the confidence to finally sign my contract and ship out. His advice forever changed my life and motivated me to serve:

SECTION 4: LEADERSHIP ADVICE

> *"Your honesty about your struggles makes me appreciate friendship with you even more. Military life involves a lot of tradition while portraying a strong, professional image, but it's always encouraging to be around someone who's transparent and real."*

This advice helped me maintain a sentiment of vulnerability and compassion while in uniform. I was able to be part of group discussions in which Soldiers were encouraged to express themselves in light of mental health struggles ravaging our entire planet during the pandemic. We quickly moved from current psychological struggles resulting from lockdowns to preexisting abuses in life. I will never forget the amount of pain and tears being expressed that day. Many of the stories were heart-wrenching to hear. The courage it took to share such things made me proud to be part of the military family. Being open about my own past in front of over a dozen Soldiers was easy to do because they bravely disclosed their own stories.

Vulnerability in the military is a complicated concept. Of course, there are times we must be stern and resolute whenever a difficult training or mission is at hand. When tensions are high due to lethal risk, it's understandable that voices will be raised and curses shouted. Add in hunger, sleep deprivation, darkness, inclement weather, miscommunication, inconsistent intelligence reports, and malfunctioning equipment to aggravate the situation.

However, this doesn't ever need to take away from the humanity we share. It's never necessary to feed off the weakness of others or inflict control based on their past trauma. Rather it's much more powerful to speak hope into dark situations and inspire inner greatness to come forth. It's much more beneficial to an organization when individuals are taught they can accomplish difficult tasks in spite of any perceived weaknesses.

While there's a time to break people down to build them back up, it's never good to keep people broken as a means of control. Leaders in the military have the responsibility of guiding subordinates toward any resources they need to strengthen themselves. These can include access to chaplains, mentorship programs, or professional services like psychotherapy, anger management, marital counseling, parenting classes, financial advisors, addiction recovery groups, and so much more.

Matt stood out as a powerful resource in our men's group because of his military professionalism. He mentored me towards a sense of freedom and levity after I had endured years of emotional repression. As I said, my prior lifestyle was exhausting. My energy levels constantly drained as I attempted to maintain a superficial sense of control. Inside I was spiraling. Escaping pain was the motivating force pushing me down a path of numbing out or distracting myself with drama. I needed help sitting in that pain and working through the hard stuff.

Matt's welcoming spirit helped convince me to join the military. Friends like him eased my fear of social stigma or coming from a life of bad decisions. Acceptance of mistakes was key. Lessening my fear of the past helped me clean up my act and participate in a healthy social group. Trust was being built. Relearning how to interact with a healthy peer group takes time, and I am still learning how to be honest about needing help. The military taught me how to be authentic as a leader and seek out guidance while pursuing self-enriching behaviors and goals. I wanted to be someone who championed aggressive growth in others.

I'd like to encourage anyone scared about joining the military in light of past mistakes or failures to consider the fact that the majority of military service members have endured hardship, adversity, and trauma. Suffering unites us. Joining such an organization creates a sense of community even among those who choose never to disclose past issues. In BCT I was honored to hear about the devastating pasts of multiple peers who confided in me. Their honesty helped me feel welcomed and, in turn, I was able to share more about myself. Knowing I wasn't the only person with deep wounds gave me a sense of gratitude and relatability. No one in the military would ever drive me away because I was too dirty, broken, or unlovable.

Putting on the uniform helped me realize the importance of sharing a common mission and purpose. Past issues, damage, and hang-ups are, for the moment, not relevant. Seeing Soldiers around me wearing the same uniform I had on was a symbol of solidarity. We each have a purpose in our work meant to enable one another as a single-family unit. Each member is valuable, even though each story is different. Some of us are more wounded than others, yet most of us carry some scars within us. No one is at risk of rejection because they experienced a version of hell not wished on enemies. Instead, vulnerability is a brave act that increases solidarity and commitment to helping one another.

In the military, all are welcome.

Thanks, Matt.

References:

Applewhite, L., Arincorayan, D., & Adams, B. (2016). Exploring the Prevalence of Adverse Childhood Experiences in Soldiers Seeking Behavioral Health Care During a Combat Deployment. *Military medicine, 181*(10), 1275–1280. https://doi.org/10.7205/MILMED-D-15-00460

Blosnich JR, Dichter ME, Cerulli C, Batten SV, Bossarte RM. Disparities in Adverse Childhood Experiences Among Individuals With a History of Military Service. *JAMA Psychiatry.* 2014;71(9):1041–1048. doi:10.1001/jamapsychiatry.2014.724

Lamson, A., PhD, Natalie Richardson, MS, Erin Cobb, PhD, The Health and Readiness of Service Members: ACEs to PACEs, *Military Medicine*, Volume 185, Issue Supplement_1, January-February 2020, Pages 348–354, https://doi.org/10.1093/milmed/usz197

Nock MK, Deming CA, Fullerton CS, Gilman SE, Goldenberg M, Kessler RC, McCarroll JE, McLaughlin KA, Peterson C, Schoenbaum M, Stanley B, Ursano RJ. Suicide among soldiers: a review of psychosocial risk and protective factors. Psychiatry. 2013 Summer;76(2):97-125. doi: 10.1521/psyc.2013.76.2.97. PMID: 23631542; PMCID: PMC4060831.

Sher L. (2017). Commentary: Adverse Childhood Experiences and Risk for Suicidal Behavior in Male Iraq and Afghanistan Veterans Seeking PTSD Treatment. *Frontiers in public health, 5*, 72. https://doi.org/10.3389/fpubh.2017.00072

14 - PEOPLE OVER POLITICS

"It was pouring rain as I drove passed a young man walking alone on base so I gave him a ride. Because he happened to be a student, somebody reprimanded me for helping him. I believe I made the right call as an NCO taking care of people."
- ***LLOYD*** *[Air Force Engineer]*

Altruism: caring for others through selfless behavior

Politics: power dynamics within a group that enable authority and policies

SECTION 1: INTRODUCTION TO THE TOPIC

While in Basic Training, the officer candidates were occasionally separated from enlisted Soldiers for a series of discussions on leadership responsibilities ahead of us. One time, we were each asked why we wanted to become officers. One candidate in the group stood up. Boisterous as usual, he bellowed out an arrogant response.

"I want the accolades that come with being an officer."

Oh boy. Annoyed, I closed my eyes and let out a slow sigh.

This same person at one point tried to demand non-officer candidates clean up his area in the barracks. I assumed he was either royalty or had grown up with a maid, judging from his demeanor. He told his bunkmate to sweep. No argument. Then he went back to organizing his own belongings. A few people looked over, angry about what they had just seen. Knowing this was going to be my classmate for several months really bothered me. Red flag already. If he started off this conceited, what was going to happen when he ranked up? I spoke up and let him know he was a grown adult who could clean up his own messes. Others chimed in. He eventually got the point. Watching him walk to the garbage can and deposit his trash felt like a win for the military and society.

Later on in the training program he again defaulted to this original behavior. Correction is a process. Again, we spoke up. The other candidates and I had to continually remind him to stop demanding that people obey him so he could win recognition. When things didn't go his way, it was never on him. He felt blameless. Everyone else messed up. Dealing with him was a constant process.

To be clear, no award from military BCT affects anyone's military career downstream. The point is to graduate and simply move on to job-specific training. Even still, this officer candidate was hell-bent on creating a perfect image while still barely out the gate. I felt horrible for anyone he would oversee in the future. He would have the power to ruin the lives of Soldiers both professionally and personally. He could overwork them. The tension he created in the workplace could follow his subordinates home. They'll ruminate on the stress he invokes to control them. Mental health is at stake. Their marriages could suffer. Their children will notice the disconnection. It will harm Soldier readiness in the military overall.

We need our warriors to be strong mentally, emotionally, and physically. Leaders must enable this. Otherwise, they contribute to declining morale. Hopefully, he will learn to mellow out and treat people of all ranks respectfully. Within all professional organizations, some individuals strategically plan ways to use others for their glory. When it comes to warfare, that is a dangerous game to play.

SECTION 2: A GOOD MILITARY LEADER

Before shipping out to my first duty station, I met my friend Lloyd at a cozy cafe where he and his wife had represented half of my total audience for open mic night. At 6 feet tall, this cornfed Airman with broad shoulders, sandy blond hair, and a huge smile is hard to miss. The other couple in the audience were friends of mine from Army Engineering school. Between songs, I conversed with my listeners and asked what they wanted to hear. Seeing everyone smiling put me at ease and kept me going. The mashups continued as I fumbled my way through chords I could barely play while trying to remember song lyrics. Thankfully, I can freestyle pretty well. After an hour of singsongs, we all had a good laugh and hung out until closing time.

Lloyd knows how to enjoy himself while bringing a sense of humor into everything he does. His personality contrasted against the stern Army environment I was saturated in every day. I needed a friend like him since I was living in Missouri for the first time and had no existing social network. There's a special warmth of familiarity within military life when making genuine connections in completely unfamiliar places. Getting away from rigid training environments to decompress is important and tough to do in isolation. He's also a great friend because he's an avid hunter who keeps a freezer stocked with delicious deer meat. *Yum.*

As a hunter, blood and guts don't bother him. He showed me his small arsenal of guns and hunting equipment. I learned interesting facts about crossbows and the various bladed arrows available. His arrows make a bloody mess. When he hunts, he aims to get the animal to bleed out quickly by severing arteries and inducing hemorrhage shock. This is why many of his arrows have blades that expand upon impact with the animal. When bleeding profusely from traumatic wounds, blood pressure drops steeply. As compensation for low blood pressure, the animal's body will increase its heart rate to compensate for low blood pressure. This forces the body to bleed out even faster. We learned this in BCT.

In trauma care, getting a tourniquet on a severed artery during the first few seconds of the golden hour is vital. The golden hour is the first 60 minutes following a traumatic injury, a critical time during which patients must receive lifesaving medical intervention to help determine their chances of survival. Otherwise, unconsciousness results when blood flow and oxygen to the brain diminish. Fade out. On the hunt, that's precisely when Lloyd traces the blood trail to his prized and newfound source of meat.

On his combat deployments, Lloyd relied on his situational awareness to avoid becoming a casualty whenever Iraqi insurgents attacked his base. He repaired damaged airfields to enable aircraft access, occasionally under indirect fire. He had to be aware of his surroundings day and night if the enemy decided to engage him and his team with mortars.

Using ice, the enemy time delayed a mortar round in the tube. They aimed for his base, placed ice in the tube, put the round in, and left the area. Once the ice melted, the round would drop down and launch at the intended target. Mortars inbound. Lloyd needed to react quickly and seek cover. Red tracers by the hundreds appeared above. C-RAM (Counter-Rocket, Artillery Mortar) weapon systems would suddenly activate with red tracers streaming into the sky as they begin rapid firing ropes of explosive rounds to intercept incoming mortars. *Bwahhhhhhhhmmmm! BOOM!* A few times the mortars made it past the defensive systems and impacted the base. One time he saw a projectile intercepted by the C-RAM break up into several pieces, each with its own small explosive impact a hundred or so meters from his position.

Shortly after mortars began to land, Special Operations units combined from various military units would quickly spin up aircraft and seek to neutralize the enemy. What a relief. Seeing those service members prepare for battle always provided a sense of confidence to the ones they protected.

This relationship demonstrated the importance of collaborative warfighting functions. Lloyd felt the impact of losing such powerful support assets when mission updates required them to detach. He continued working with the remaining Airman in his AO (Area of Operations) and looked forward to future joint operations.

On a later deployment in the Middle East, he was tested in his ability to put aside personal differences and refrain from playing politics. Lloyd worked in an environment involving military personnel from various nations. There, he learned a firsthand lesson about establishing working relationships, regardless of conflict and despite the games that others want to play. One person was particularly hard to get along with because he kept trying to get away with taking shortcuts on the job while making himself look a lot better than his peers. He brought friction to the workplace daily due to his arrogant conduct. He didn't communicate clearly. Information he needed to provide to Lloyd was often sporadic or missing entirely. It was selfish behavior. He worried more about looking good to supervisors than contributing to peers. Over time this behavior began to create animosity in the workplace. It needed to be addressed.

Lloyd was forced to endure that friction and desired to maintain productivity on the job. Refusing to play politics and stir up trouble, he had limited options. Observing daily disrespectful attitudes at work, especially on deployments, can escalate already heightened tensions. A fight was certainly brewing. He could either allow a violent confrontation or find a personal compromise. Something needed to give.

Carrying all that stress only created misery that lasted around the clock. Even when the workday ends, the mind continually ruminates on such tensions. Rest is precious on deployments. Lloyd grew tired of being tired. Being wise, he decided to make peace with differences and focused on accomplishing the mission.

He directly confronted his colleague but with respect. He emphasized his desire to keep a healthy working relationship. He admitted they would never see eye to eye. In any case, he wanted to get along. This changed everything. His colleague responded with appreciation and acknowledged the importance of aligning efforts. Lloyd was relieved. His enemy had become a friend. They decided to help each other and dialogue respectfully despite their differences. Bonds between them strengthened. In time this once antagonistic relationship became a professionally sound partnership.

Lloyd wasn't always on top of life, he faced some deep struggles earlier on. He had previously allowed pain from relationships and hardship to impair his judgment. Suffering caused him to disconnect from himself and others. His foundation felt unstable. Military structure and discipline provided him with a framework to rebuild. It provided community. People who genuinely cared about him and who believed in his potential let him know they had his back. He leaned on them and decided to invest in his future by taking on more responsibility. He became dependable. Lloyd has grown during his time in the Air Force from overcoming personal struggles to challenging himself to pursue goals beyond what he thought was possible. He faced the ugly parts of his life and realized the decision to change was within him. Change would not come easy. He accepted the hard work needed and focused on developing stronger values. Mentors arose and helped.

Good people from within and outside the military supported him to help him overcome the difficult parts of life. Their faith in him taught him to value other individuals and to love people despite their humanity. He learned to have fun without drinking and eventually trained to run multiple marathons and two ultra-marathons, completing 50 and 75 mile runs in single days. Remaining positive through tough situations, he used his strength to encourage those around him. He knows what it's like to be discarded and conversely what it's like to have someone give a helping hand and pull him up, so he pays it forward.

SECTION 3: PSYCHOLOGICAL APPLICATION

Why forgo self-promotion when others are totally fine throwing anyone else under the bus? Depends on who you ask. Lloyd inspired me to approach life in the military with a focus on caring for others, regardless of politics, personality conflicts, or job stress. He encouraged me to help others, even if it meant letting them outshine me. In his mind, there was ample opportunity for success if we were supportive within our work community. Being good to others will ultimately lead to peace of mind and future opportunities to excel. Staying grounded with personal integrity, despite work politics, helps avoid being pulled into negativity. Mission accomplishment can rest upon reconciling differences with others while accepting discomfort. No matter what happens in the office or on the battlefield, stay focused on caring for others.

Politics in the workplace have been known to cause adverse outcomes, including "stress, burnout, turnover intentions, job satisfaction, and organizational commitment" (Landells & Albrecht, 2019). However, contrary to the negative publicity, the researchers believe a positive aspect of politics includes employee engagement. However, the degree to which this outweighs negative variables is up for discussion. Trust is built when politics serve to strengthen working relationships through meaningful policy implementation. Politics do not have to involve power plays or corruption. They can serve to represent change on behalf of the common good.

Politics solely for personal gain damage morale. Using social influence within an organization to invoke helpful changes turns politics into a resource subordinate directly benefit from. An example would be using influence to obtain resources needed by Soldiers. Stress reduction is pursued, not consolidation of power. It sends a clear message that leaders care about those they lead. Subordinates want to know their "vulnerability will not be exploited and that they will not be harmed" (Tomazevic & Aristovnik, 2019). People want to know that leaders care.

Power inherently creates politics. As with any large organization, the military infrastructure is composed of subsets organized according to complex, overlapping managerial matrices. It's structurally dense. In war, this helps absorb the impact of sudden losses in personnel. People die, the machine keeps moving. To accomplish this, several redundancies exist. This means one person may technically have several bosses, and each boss has a different area of jurisdiction.

When multiple armed force branches cooperate on a single base, further compounding management complexity. Learning to navigate this type of environment takes political savvy and high levels of sociability. It's critical to manage up and down the chain of command. Communication helps minimize wasted efforts. It's important to establish strategic relationships. Again, leveraging relationships strictly to gain power is wrong. When this becomes self-serving, it negatively impacts the work environment by creating destructive competitive tension.

We don't have to be held down by this bureaucracy. Even large organizations can create subgroups with friendly work cultures. Leaders enable this. Small departments and teams can choose to emphasize personable working relationships. Even in high-stress work environments, morale is preserved when individuals are cared for. Small gestures of kindness help. Communicating with dignity and respect goes a long way. In organizational cultures involving collaborative professional teams, "highest team functioning scores were achieved by teams with a more personal and dynamic organizational culture rather than those that were more bureaucratic and formal" (Korner et al. (2015). Stuffy people are exhausting. Really wordy psychology explanations are too, so I apologize for doing that.

Leaders who treat subordinates well nurture positive attitudes and collaborative teamwork. Deferring to rank for control leads to a loss of credibility in leadership ability. Leaders who are adaptive and focus on maintaining a positive work environment inspire team cohesion to accomplish shared goals successfully (Kozlowski, 2017).

Politics are a part of every organization. Cliques are everywhere. There is no way to remove political leverage wherever social influence exists. To a large extent, employers rely on this biological dynamic within human nature. Filtering for optimal leaders strengthens the organization. These influences become all the more powerful whenever leaders compete with each other. Again, organizations encourage this. Leaders are understandably driven to exemplify their abilities by continually increasing authority and influence. Some might want to look good because it means they are helping the organization, while others seek the ego boost. It's important to differentiate between stewarding one's profession and seeking self-promotion.

In a publication called *Lying to Ourselves: Dishonesty in the Army Profession*, the authors find that military leaders are prone to misconstruing information as a means of falsely satisfying job requirements to ensure career success (Wong & Gerras, 2015). By doing so, they fail to nurture the organization and instead lie to protect their positional status. Anyone honest about their inability to meet an impossible deadline will be flagged for inferior performance while dishonest peers move up. It's understood that "workplace politics can make new work environments stressful…and can lead to burnout quickly if they are not navigated successfully" (Hecht et al., 2021). Ignoring situations like these will lead to the loss of strong talent and the retention of weak leaders.

Leaders with integrity influence the workplace

by reducing uncertainty, fostering trust among subordinates, and encouraging employees to increase the degree of support they have for one another (Choi et al., 2020). They demonstrate consistent behavior and good judgment. Subordinates have an accurate compass guiding them. Expectations are consistent. Contrast this with a leader who displays behavior, not in line with their words. This will create a work culture in which subordinates begin to emulate this process. Teammates will counterproductively pull support from one another. The organization will suffer under such leadership.

Influence is an asset. Teams need guides who can leverage available resources. While learning the necessity of maneuvering social structures within one's organization is wise, this should not be an all-consuming focus. Otherwise, this will lead to a desire to gain social influence through misrepresenting facts about oneself and others. Self-image is valuable within an organization, but artificial facades will mislead people and hurt morale. Subordinates feel the effects of authenticity in their leaders. Trust in leadership eases stress. Challenges are welcomed with high spirits.

Being a good leader and being a successful leader are two different things. Politics in the workplace can progress careers, but if this ever involves taking favors to create unfair advantages, it will lead to dishonest gain. Ideally, organizations don't incentivize rewards based strictly on political influence. How is that influence helping others? Are subordinates feeling support? Is their voice being heard at the top? Measurable results that directly benefit subordinates ought to be emphasized. It doesn't matter how influential someone is if they don't strive to enhance the workplace and systems around them.

Leaders must push organizations forward so each worker benefits from progress. Above all, it's important to measure a leader's accomplishment by their care, support, and development of others. People are the most important asset of any organization. Leaders who demonstrate this in their work strengthen the organization by promoting peer cohesion. Such professionals are best suited for promotion.

Once I completed Engineer BOLC, I was due to move to my first real job in the military. Meeting with Lloyd to say farewell, I asked him how I could keep focused on what matters most:

SECTION 4: LEADERSHIP ADVICE

> *"Never let politics discourage you from being a genuinely good person. The military is a people business built on relationships. Treat others well and avoid getting caught up in power games."*

Politics aren't all bad. Not every politically savvy leader wants to spotlight their own resume and eclipse the needs of subordinates. Some choose to enable others especially by offering increased authority to lower positions. One-way conversations become respectful dialogue. Using political influence to help the voiceless speak up is great. The work environment shifts from being hyper focused on competition to seeking straightforward solutions. Common sense prevails. Authority is seen as a responsibility to serve rather than be served.

Rank creates distance. This makes alignment

difficult. Military leaders who remember to step back into the shoes of those they lead offer tremendous strength to their units. Soldiers seeing a general in the field get fired up. They feel heard. Such leaders make it clear they care. Morale increases. They ensure the direction in which they are moving improves the lives of the men and women on the ground. They listen. Feedback is critical to verify meaningful progress. It's important to ask for honest dialogue regarding pain points throughout an organization, especially at the lowest levels. Individuals working in these areas are prone to vulnerability via retribution and must be protected when speaking up.

Politics can be used destructively by power-hungry individuals to obtain awards, promotions, and accolades at the direct expense of helping others. A universal issue within all human organizations involves the manipulation of social influence for selfish gain. Money and power are powerful motivating factors to overlook compassion and connection. Using authority to create barriers through policy and bureaucratic bottlenecks may protect those in charge. With such barriers comes greater distance and separation from those doing the hard work. This distance helps minimize feedback and discourages hope for change.

In the military, I saw generals speak with privates and offer a listening ear. I got pumped. They sought to create policies to provide resources to subordinates while holding leaders accountable for enabling access. Sincerity felt real. Leaders like this create a buzz of energy throughout the ranks. It's not just words. Change is demonstrated. It's important to let Soldiers know what changes are coming and when they will occur. Many plans may be long-term, but the troops want to know how they are being cared for now. Even small gestures can go a long way. Sudden beneficial changes in the military are not always easy for leaders to execute, but it's powerful when they do.

I have learned a tremendously helpful truth as a military officer. What happens behind closed doors in confidential meetings is always felt by the Soldiers. Subordinates pick up on tension, conflicts, and unresolved issues. Politics do not go unnoticed. There is no pulling the wool over the eyes of those who support the base of the organization. As much as leaders may attempt to present information to the contrary, the truth comes out in the daily lives of those on the ground. Careful attention must be paid to investing in and supporting those doing the hard work.

Leadership is messy. No perfect answers exist, just varying degrees of alignment with organizational goals. Someone is always going to have something negative to say. The most difficult part of managing influence as a leader involves the mosaic of opinions and perspectives of those who compose the unit being led. In the military, this can range from a team of three to a corps of thousands. Division will exist, and no singular solution will be universally agreed upon. Decisions must still be made. Leaders must attempt to hit multiple moving targets using information that is delayed through various communication channels and potentially biased in its presentation. Taking the hit for mistakes is part of the job. Being resolute is necessary. With or without all the information, solutions must be provided. Finding an internal sense of calm in the middle of the storm helps leaders serve as pillars for others.

Getting the warm fuzzies on military leadership decisions is a rare joy because change moves slowly. Soldiers, in the meantime, carry the weight while waiting for relief to come. Talking to them helps me understand how best to help. Creating an open dialogue is the only solution to prevent cutting out voices from the discussion. Using political influence to create meaningful policies for the men and women on the ground makes for great leadership. The men and women accomplishing the mission on the ground (or up in the air) matter most.

Thanks, Lloyd.

References:

Choi, Y., Yoon, D. J., & Kim, D. (2020). Leader Behavioral Integrity and Employee In-Role Performance: The Roles of Coworker Support and Job Autonomy. *International journal of environmental research and public health, 17*(12), 4303. https://doi.org/10.3390/ijerph17124303

Hecht, K. N., Bolton, S. M., Adelman, M., Bell, C. M., McElray, K. L., Hancock, B. S., & Adams, A. L. (2021). Navigating the roadmap of workplace politics: Advice for new practitioners. *American journal of health-system pharmacy : AJHP : official journal of the American Society of Health-System Pharmacists, 78*(2), 89–92. https://doi.org/10.1093/ajhp/zxaa332

Körner, M., Wirtz, M. A., Bengel, J., & Göritz, A. S. (2015). Relationship of organizational culture, teamwork and job satisfaction in interprofessional teams. *BMC health services research, 15*, 243. https://doi.org/10.1186/s12913-015-0888-y

Kozlowski S. (2018). Enhancing the Effectiveness of Work Groups and Teams: A Reflection. *Perspectives on psychological science : a journal of the Association for Psychological Science, 13*(2), 205–212. https://doi.org/10.1177/1745691617697078

Landells, E. M., & Albrecht, S. L. (2019). Perceived Organizational Politics, Engagement, and Stress: The Mediating Influence of Meaningful Work. *Frontiers in psychology, 10*, 1612. https://doi.org/10.3389/fpsyg.2019.01612

Tomaževič, N., & Aristovnik, A. (2019). Factors of Trust in Immediate Leaders: An Empirical Study in Police Service Environment. *International journal of environmental research and public health, 16*(14), 2525. https://doi.org/10.3390/ijerph16142525

Wong, L., Gerras, S. J., Army War College, U. S. S. S. I. & Army War College, U. S. P. (2015) Lying to ourselves: dishonesty in the Army profession. [Web.] Retrieved from the Library of Congress, https://lccn.loc.gov/2015490010.

15 - FAMILY FAR FROM HOME

"Being docked in Alaska when it's 20 below freezing outside is rough. Luckily, I'm part of a tight-knit unit and we motivate each other to get off the ship and go on fun adventures."
- ***ERIC*** *[Coast Guard Chief Petty Officer]*

Affiliation: being connected in identity with a particular group or individual

Secure Attachment: social bonds that provide a sense of stable identity

Shared-Environment: where influences affect multiple community members

SECTION 1: INTRODUCTION TO THE TOPIC

Austin, a formerly enlisted Marine, is a good friend of mine who lives in Arkansas working as a first responder. He told me about his multiple tours in Afghanistan and other Middle Eastern nations and said they were some of the most cherished memories he has. There he learned what is most important in life. Warzones, he said, put everything into perspective. War is not something he wishes for anyone to experience, but he did value the relationships he had with everyone around him. The biggest concern was caring for the safety and lives of others willing to die for the cause of freedom. This was his family away from home.

Whenever I called him to vent frustration at having to deal with mundane tasks in the military, he reminded me that there is a difference between a peacetime military and a military engaging in war. Americans from all different walks volunteered to serve after 9/11, and this added a unique strength to our military force. Austin met good men and women with genuine convictions and faith in our nation's ideals. Their pride in our country fueled an excitement to confront evil around the world with determination and strength. Through their shared service, he learned what it meant to fight alongside an American family in foreign lands. A connection like this meant he was never alone, even in the darkest situations.

Back home in the states, his wife and kids felt the weight of his absence when he is away on missions or training, but they understood he was alongside a group of like-minded peers. Sometimes he had to remind them that just because he was in the military didn't mean he was happy about the situations he or the people around him were in. Just as with our civilian family members, we can't choose who we serve with in uniform. At certain points, the only thing we can do is make the best of tough situations and try to focus on the commonality we do have. Otherwise, minimizing contact with anyone who compounds stress is the best way to avoid altercations and keep from wasting precious energy. At the end of the day, the most important thing to focus on is keeping everyone safe.

Outside of the military, Austin noticed there wasn't the strong bond or connection with those you work with like there is in the military, especially when considering combat deployment. The only thing closest to it was belonging to a close-knit community such as the fire or police department, SWAT teams, EMTs, paramedics, or other first responders. He strives to deepen his current career by pursuing expert roles within elite communities working to keep our nation safe. Even now, he faces death regularly and must operate to save as many lives as possible without allowing despair to pull him down. Twelve men he knew in combat have succumbed to suicide because they lost connection outside of the service. He loved each of these brothers. He carries their memory and honors them as best he can by living out a purpose he knows they would be proud of. Applying what he learned in combat, he can stay calm in the chaos and is a solid brother to lean on.

SECTION 2: A GOOD MILITARY LEADER

Eric was an Irish-Italian All-American with contrasting features; jet-black hair and light skin. The day we met, he was flying his new drone on Silver Strand Beach. Waves were only a few feet high and perfectly shaped with a smooth, glassy texture. I decided to try out the $20 epoxy surfboard I had just purchased at the thrift store. Nobody else was on the beach, so I had a great time being a complete newbie without face planting onto other surfers' waves. After inhaling my fair share of saltwater, I decided to stumble back to my car and dry in the sun.

I asked Eric if he had snagged any cool footage of me in the ocean, which he hadn't. Instead of filming the waves, he was focused on using his drone's follow feature and was busy walking around the parking lot as it kept locked on his signature. He had a few weeks before his upcoming deployment and wanted to enjoy the beaches of Southern California as much as possible. I asked him questions about his branch to see how vastly different it was from the Army. Despite the difference, the fact that he served in the military created an instant air of familiarity that was common with all my other military friends.

Being from Boston, he was far from home. On the west coast, he experienced a brand-new climate and culture. He fit in well because he liked nature and had an aptitude for hiking and meeting new people. His demeanor was serious and calm, yet he was passionate about making friends, especially within his unit. The military provided social connections. Instant community. He saw the Coast Guard as a close-knit family and was excited to deploy worldwide to meet new people and expand this network. I was inspired by his courage to leave behind everything he knew and forgo the comforts which for so long confined my own life.

Deeply patriotic in his values, Eric emphasized his pride in policing waters around other nation-states to protect the American service members of our other branches. His part was meaningful. He viewed himself as a member of the military family entrusted with deterring attacks from the seas. When stateside he worked on seizing narcotics being trafficked up the coastlines. Domestically and abroad, he kept America safe. Working with the Navy brought him a stronger sense of comradery. Miles of ocean separating vessels across the globe doesn't prevent our government ecosystem from functioning as a cohesive unit. His conviction was compelling and gave me a taste of belonging to a mission greater than myself. There is honor in the desire to help keep others safe, and I wanted to be a part of that.

SECTION 3: PSYCHOLOGICAL APPLICATION

Humans are social by design. We have a need to belong that is tied to a deeply biological drive. This concept, known as social motivation, forms in infancy when we experience a need for belonging. One study reports that "children seek to affiliate with others and to form long-lasting bonds with their group members" and "when children are deprived of a sense of belonging, it has negative consequences for their well-being" (Over, 2016). Adulthood involves a continuation of these patterns. This serves to guide our career aspirations as we seek professional purpose alongside others. Military careers fulfill this need to belong. Eric joined the Coast Guard to fulfill such a desire.

Social connection is a common reason people join the military. We want somewhere to belong. Community. As a family unit, we support one another to accomplish shared goals. Mission success relies on our relationships with one another. Researchers state that "a greater sense of community may translate into a higher likelihood of people mobilizing participatory processes for the solution of their problems" (Michalski et al., 2020). We work better alongside others because of the shared connection. Relationship bonds strengthen our job performance. We are also happier. The authors also find that "community Belonging, and engagement contributes to quality of life which results in a greater sense of identity and confidence, opposing anonymity and loneliness" (Michalski et al., 2020). It's important to stay connected, especially in times of hardship.

Unit cohesion helps provide troops with a sense of connection. Such connection involves comradery between members within a military unit and with their leadership. It saves lives. "Higher levels of unit cohesion are associated with lower risk of developing PTSD among Soldiers exposed to combat." (Nevarez et al., 2017). By ensuring our service members feel supported we can set them up for mental health and resilience before any future conflicts arise. Not only does this increase troop readiness overall, but it also preventatively treats PTSD and helps minimize post combat suicide. Leaders who earn the trust of subordinates help strengthen the organization by contributing to higher unit cohesion. A strong military family leads to robust warfighting power.

Eric demonstrated the value of finding purpose in connection through one's military mission. He saw his job as a means of building connections. Fulfillment of purpose increases when viewing the impact we have on supported units, even when geographically displaced. In the military, we count on each other to be reliable when support is needed. Regardless of the uniforms we put on, there is a singular mission that supersedes every individual unit. I longed to know how this felt and asked Eric for some context:

SECTION 4: LEADERSHIP ADVICE

> *"The unit you deploy or train with is all you have at times. You can easily get confined to really small areas. It's important to be close to each other while keeping egos in check to keep from wearing each other out."*

I learned quickly that life in the military minimizes or removes privacy altogether. Boundaries are removed to ensure constant collaboration. Basic training involved living in a single bay with over 80 trainees. We knew exactly who snored at night, who had terrible hygiene, and who was prone to getting in fist fights with others. Proximity helped to keep us from feeling alone. We always had each other for better or worse. While there was no place for privacy, we also had no ability to isolate ourselves. I still keep in touch with friends from this chapter in my military journey.

In the field, a sense of privacy is altogether obliterated. Without bathrooms or buildings, we had to conduct hygiene in full view of others. Even evacuating our bladder or bowel needed to occur in completely open spaces when training in the desert. Oftentimes when I could sneak away to hide behind a rock for personal time, I could hear a drone buzzing overhead and I knew it had the capability of zooming right in on me. When nature calls, especially after a fresh cup of morning coffee, all concern goes out the window. At night there was at least the cover of darkness.

This made for perfect opportunities to walk away from the rest of the platoon and strip down for a canteen shower under starlight and storm clouds. Again, the drones could see everything with night vision, but good hygiene in the desert is priceless.

Being constantly surrounded by others has its pros and cons. While social connection makes the military a great place to be, it can become taxing due to an endless barrage of updates and mission details. Personally, I struggled. Soldiers knew I was being pulled in several different directions at once. I needed to find time to break from comms (communication channels) and take a breather. Quiet times were rare. And priceless. It was critical for me to let Soldiers know what was expected of me by the chain of command so they grasped the situation. Their need-to-know updates were important to address. Realistically, however, when I was constantly receiving bits and pieces of information regarding ongoing mission changes, I needed to ensure I wasn't passing along bad information.

At some point, I learned to let situations develop before firing off upcoming orders. It became clear any directions we received were sure to change mid-execution. Mission start times, link-up locations, chow delivery schedule, fuel points, and basically everything else would change. We had to adapt. This pressured me to minimize the stress induced by uncertainty. Tough role. Communicating my own needs to the Soldiers helped keep me in a good place. I let them know when I needed space and when I anticipated I'd be able to give them actionable information. They understood. However, anytime they were painfully curious about updates I was happy to share partial information so long as they understood it wasn't very meaningful without further guidance. They appreciated the fact that I was willing to entertain their curiosity as it proved I was in no way attempting to leverage information to keep myself elevated as a leader with all the answers. We were in the thick of it together.

Families need to talk; it keeps them together. Military families are the same way. Communication is key to managing working relationships. As a leader, it was especially critical that I strive to remain open with my peers, superiors, and subordinates. Just as with family, it's necessary to nurture relationships with honest dialogue. Avoidance leads to distance and a breakdown in connection. I personally experienced this with relatives and learned that anytime someone feels unable to express themselves authentically, they will eventually choose to leave a relationship.

Soldiers want to feel connected by sharing information. It kept us close. As a platoon leader, I found myself training in the field with a dozen channels of communication. This strained my cognitive resources and left me feeling completely drained when it came to interpersonal dialogue. At first, I never thought to explain to the Soldiers in my platoon just how many directions my attention was being pulled. Eventually, I realized the vast number of resources I was pouring into managing these channels. Once I did, I began to share with everyone how taxing it was so they would give me the space I needed to sit in silence and recharge.

Here's a breakdown of my constant communication channels:

1. Radio comms internally with platoon vehicle convoy
2. Radio comms on company net
3. Radio comms on battalion net
4. JBC-P* chat group with Company
5. JBC-P* chat group with Battalion
6. JBC-P* chat group with Company we are attached to
7. Smartphone chat app with Company
8. Smartphone chat app with sister platoons
9. Smartphone chat app with platoon internal
10. Smartphone chat app with Maintenance platoon
11. Smartphone chat app with Company we are attached to
12. Text message with Commander
13. Text message with Platoon Sergeant
14. Text message with 2nd Platoon
15. Text message with 3rd Platoon
16. Text message with 4th Platoon
17. Text message with XO (Executive Officer)
18. Text message with attached Maintenance Soldier

*(Join Battle Command Platform)

Talk about a family plan. Needless to say, my head was constantly spinning with continual sit-reps (situation reports), inquiries, commands, RFI's (requests for information), status updates, grid coordinates, prospective missions, and more. Imagine 20-hour days glued to multiple screens sending copious amounts of redundant information on multiple parallel channels. Often, the information treated with utmost urgency would become completely irrelevant within minutes. This was all meant to simulate warfare but at an increased tempo to ensure we were prepared for the worst. While this training strengthens the military, it simultaneously wears down the mind.

Just like when dealing with our families of

origin, taking breaks is key to reducing stress. Rest is important. Being exhausted from logistical issues alone compounds the risk of accidents. Driving in darkness by night vision complicates movements through rough terrain. This is why it's necessary to slow things down when asking Soldiers to drive huge vehicles up and down steep hills with cliff faces flanking the ridgelines. When simulation artillery rounds are tossed to mimic incoming indirect fire while negotiating tight turns throughout a mountain of boulders, the stress just piles up. Writing this now makes me need a long inhale and exhale while I reflect on all the chaos.

I learned the art of taking deep breaths and tactical pauses. Juggling dozens of conversations with various leaders all at once and managing movements on the ground can be a headache. When I first became a platoon leader, the Soldiers had a good laugh seeing me struggle to figure out what to do next as I rushed through a cascade of solutions. Meeting the commander's intent was paramount, but there are multiple ways to do so. Common sense solutions are best. From the beginning, I knew to at least check in with the NCOs to ask for advice. They always knew what to do, and I maintained a high level of agreeableness to enable their autonomy. My job was to coordinate information and allow Soldiers to own their lanes. They always succeeded, despite the odds.

Just like our families of origin are rife with tensions, so too are many relationships in the military. Personalities clash. Tempers flare up. We can't choose who we work with, so it's important to know when to seek confrontation and when to be agreeable. Very simple problem sets can get overcomplicated when people make demands and become forceful. Keeping credibility as a leader is based on mutual respect between colleagues and peers. Stress and anxiety management help us stay in emotional control instead of being reactive. Martial arts instill this principle. I sought personal guidance in gaining mastery over my knee-jerk reactivity to discomfort. Finding mentors helped. Going back to lessons I learned on the mats, it's key to share the type of training I received.

My mat-mentor, (another) Eric, is a double black belt, one in Jiu-Jitsu and one in Judo. He is 6'3" and weighs around 250 pounds, all muscle. His hand grip alone could break bone. On the mats, he crushes my diaphragm while teaching me to control my anxiety by calming my breath. I learned when to fight his grips and when to surrender to maintain breath control while I awaited an opportunity to escape. Overall, he wanted me to know how to refrain from both panic and overt aggression so I could calmly execute appropriate actions that would aid my tactical response to his aggression. This carried over into the Army countless times. It helped me be less of a headache for others to put up with during hard times.

Every family has issues. Not everybody is going to get along. Military work environments force us to stick together throughout the entirety of the mission regardless of differences. Because we work so closely together, whatever one person is dealing with will be felt by everybody else. Tension is shared. Fights can result if that energy is not channeled appropriately. Repression does nothing other than amplify an eventual outburst. Instead, it's important to put that aggression to positive use. Leaders must demonstrate how exactly to handle work stress and put it to use so that others can emulate healthy behaviors.

Family is never perfect, and dysfunction is a universal aspect of any social community. Humans are emotional beings with constant fluctuations in temperament. Intentionally training our minds can help bring control. Regardless of the behavior of others, it's important to maintain self-awareness. Navigating a minefield of emotions in others is foundational for any trained fighter, in the military or on the mats. Leaders must go out of their way to help minimize the distress others feel. Knowing when to induce stress for training purposes is key to ensuring that it won't remain high perpetually.

Joining the military offered me a new family to rely on when I was far from home and in a new city or state. I needed them to keep me going. There was always at least one person in my unit who I could deeply connect with and oftentimes, there were several. My Navy friend Micah calls a sudden, deep connection or conversation a "D&M". Deep and meaningful. These are awesome bonding scenarios in which a total stranger suddenly feels like family. Army life was full of this. From peers in training to Soldiers I led, family was all around me. Knowing that I was supported inspired me to continue bettering myself for their sake. The stronger and smarter I became, the less they had to carry my weight. When I needed strength, I could rely on them to help me see things through.

Family relationships are messy, and so was my time being a military trainee, a student, and leader. Adversity can bring about growth if honest self-reflection is applied. I'm grateful to those who put up with my ignorance and who guided me toward success on this journey. While far from home, the military instantly became family, providing me with some awesome relationships I will have for the rest of my life.

Thanks, Eric.

On War Stories from Veterans...

I'd like to write an observation on being part of an active-duty military family with combat veterans. They want to share wisdom with brand-new leaders. Giving them a listening ear with an open mind is a sign of respect they deeply deserve. Being mentored by them is priceless because the lessons these warriors learned in combat are devastatingly heavy and must be retained.

When I spoke with them, I prepared myself for raw feelings to come up and tried not to be shocked when it got messy. War was hell for them then and it still is today. It would be wrong to judge them for mistakes made in the heat of battle because it's never as clean as history says.

After they finish sharing about the past is when it really takes a toll on them. When they lay down in bed, they'll be reliving the worst parts because they were willing to reopen that door. Sometimes sounds and sights spark up lucid dreams and when that happens it's physically exhausting. Even just a several-minute conversation about war can result in days of exhaustion. That's how much emotion their brains have stored up within those memories. It's considerate to check in on them after the heavy conversations to validate the price they are still paying.

References:

Over H. (2016). The origins of belonging: social motivation in infants and young children. *Philosophical transactions of the Royal Society of London. Series B, Biological sciences,*

371(1686), 20150072. https://doi.org/10.1098/rstb.2015.0072

Michalski, C. A., Diemert, L. M., Helliwell, J. F., Goel, V., & Rosella, L. C. (2020). Relationship between sense of community belonging and self-rated health across life stages. *SSM - population health*, *12*, 100676. https://doi.org/10.1016/j.ssmph.2020.100676

Nevarez, M. D., Yee, H. M., & Waldinger, R. J. (2017). Friendship in War: Camaraderie and Prevention of Posttraumatic Stress Disorder Prevention. *Journal of traumatic stress*, *30*(5), 512–520. https://doi.org/10.1002/jts.22224

16 - RELATIONSHIP MANAGEMENT

"Check this picture out, bet you can't find where I'm hiding."
- ***LEE*** *[Navy SEAL Sniper]*

Secure Base: emotional security and confidence founded on early relationships

Social Support: care and assistance provided by relationships with community

SECTION 1: INTRODUCTION TO THE TOPIC

"How does one million dollars in shares, plus five hundred thousand cash over a five-year exclusive contract sound?" Rick, a startup CEO, asked me with a direct gaze. I struggled to keep up. "If you get the business side up and running and we perform, you'll secure your share in equity. That's fair, right?" Damn, he knows to get any verbal yes early on in negotiations to increase his leverage.

Business Negotiation 101 is coming at me fast. I squirm in my seat, attempting to run the math in my head.

I'm sitting with the two founders of a stealth startup in San Diego. They build genetic-based machine learning algorithms. Cutting-edge computer technology harnesses cloud-based computing to align gene sequences and identify mutations. Vast data sets are analyzed to determine medical treatments involving inherited diseases. If we find genes that are screwed up, we will know what proteins are creating problems. I love this field of science because it helps doctors forecast disease onset even decades out. We can help people plan holistic lifestyle adjustments to combat disease symptoms. We can reverse-engineer viral vectors like HIV to infect DNA with functioning genes. Solutions are endless, and we are just starting to explore this new frontier.

This CEO knows I have the industry relationships to expand his vision. I proved my value by setting up several executive-level business talks, and I did so for free. My mentor, George, a Navy veteran from my hometown, told me to stop doing free labor for everyone. He said I was seeking male approval from business executives because I didn't get any from my dad earlier in life. I choked up on the phone when he said those words. But he was right. It explained all the drunken debauchery of my college days seeking validation from everyone around me.

"Focus up," I told myself. These businessmen are staring at me as I contemplate the marriage proposal. Do I let go of my own company to fold into theirs? Do I hit abort on venturing out on my own to secure a W-2 paycheck? Could I pioneer solo and thrive on 1099-

based freelance work? Will foraging in the wilderness of business entrepreneurialism overwhelm me? What would Teddy Roosevelt do?

"I need to think about it," I timidly responded. My heart is racing. I'm new to discussions about stock options. They both softly clear their throats and sip their coffee in subtle frustration. "Ok, but we'd like you to make a decision very soon so we can move forward and get going." I thanked them for breakfast and grabbed my backpack. Still confused about all the math, I started to make my way out of the restaurant. Something didn't feel right. How could I focus on quantifying my personal value while my gut is telling me to start sprinting?

George can always read between the lines, so I give him a call. In the Navy, he saved all his cash and worked hard to invest. He's a simple man who grew up with learning disabilities. After serving in the Navy, he learned how to put his 22-inch biceps to work. One time a business executive mocked him behind closed doors, and he grabbed the man by his collar, telling him never to do that again. Message received, do not ever mess with George.

I called him and shouted, "They offered me 1.5 million! I should say yes, right?" He responded calmly and reminded me, "Right now, they've only offered you $0 because the company isn't worth anything yet. You must be careful about assuming you'll get any of that money." I was shocked by this faceful of cold water, but I knew to listen. George loves me like a son, and he's very successful. His words are gold to me.

"Danny, according to their terms, your equity vests after five years. You lose everything if they let you go a day before that mark. Even if the equity takes off, they cannot guarantee that you wouldn't be screwed out of it. You need better contract terms because if you go exclusive with them, they own all your relationships. Relationships in business are everything. You worked hard for a decade making connections. Stop giving away your value for free."

George knows how passionate I am about connecting with others. I love networking and building relationships. My business took off because I could genuinely connect with high-power scientists in genetic research. I enjoyed getting to know them personally, which led to meaningful transactions. Now I was about to give all that away to two men who could turn around the minute I handed it over and fire me. I needed explicit guarantees of protection in an uncertain world. Business negotiations make my stomach curl.

"You left corporate America to explore your potential. You want to go on an adventure. Don't sell yourself short already. You don't need them. Go pursue what scares you," George kindly said.

His words hit home. I didn't want to work with these men. Not because they were bad people or anything like that, but because I wanted a different working relationship. Depth. My heart told me I wanted to find a group of men more like myself. I wanted a deeper love for work, something based on commitment outside of money. My life lacked that. Corporate gigs were too transactional. I rarely felt a true connection with others there. Only a few managers I came across truly inspired me. I wanted to be in a professional world requiring commitment because of the dangers involved.

Something that involved fear. A global impact. I wanted to expand my network to encompass people from all around the United States and the world. Travel had to be involved. And there was something deeper than all the rest. I wanted brothers and sisters.

It wasn't corporate business that interested me anymore, even as I made my six-figure income. It was predictable. Happy hours with executive leaders carried an air of desperation as employees competed for attention or relevance. People wanted to work the room. I wanted to get out. I wanted to suffer more and bleed to earn a victory. There was another community out in the world for me; the military was the family I wanted. I craved more awesome relationships like the ones I had with these friends you're reading about. They were my trusted inner circle. Breaking the monotony of my safe, predictable life. The service members who guided me on leadership principles put a fire in me. Veterans like George inspired me to challenge myself, face my fears, and lean into fear. I knew right then I needed to walk away from business, money, and sales.

Everything inside of me said to engage the military. Picking up the phone, I called an Army recruiter in San Diego. He answered the call and agreed to have me come in. We scheduled a meeting time as I let the two founders know I'd be rejecting their kind offer. They were shocked, and honestly, I was too. My journey would take me to face the unknown of the military. My stomach settled down, and I felt aligned. I was eager to see what relationships lay ahead of me once I wore the uniform.

SECTION 2: A GOOD MILITARY LEADER

Corporate life was slowly losing its magic. I felt lonely. A business executive in my industry invited me to a potluck dinner. His modern three-story house in Bay Ho, San Diego, is tucked away on a hillside overlooking Mission Bay with floor-to-ceiling glass windows. The giant windows were matched with an enormous ceiling fan and a 120-inch flatscreen TV visible from the highway. While there, I met Lee and his girlfriend.

Lee is a soft-spoken country boy with a short, stocky build, light brown hair, and exquisite posture. I figured he was in the military based on his tactical ripstop pants. The flip-flops made me assume he was a team guy. He told me he was a brand-new baby sniper on the SEAL teams. I looked at him in disbelief. I'm pretty sure my jaw dropped as I reflected on this celebrity moment. Starstruck, I poured on the praise and told him he was already one of the coolest people I had ever met.

He smiled and shyly responded it wasn't that big of a deal. Yes, there were great parts to the job, like grabbing as much ammunition as he wanted to go shooting on weekends because, technically, it was competency training. Night skydives, underwater demolition, and tactical room clearing (CQC) added to the awe. His training with cutting-edge imaging technology and access to various sniper scopes kept me leaning in with a grin.

This guy is a superhero from the movies, I thought. Then he flexed on me a little. He pulled up his phone with a photo of the forest and told me to find him. I scoured the image for several minutes, but all I could see were trees and bushes. Searching up and down, there was no sign of human beings, so I gave up. He pointed his finger at a perfect black ring hidden among the trees in the foreground. It was the suppressor on the barrel of his rifle. Wearing a ghillie suit, he camouflaged perfectly into the enveloping foliage. Even in a photo, he could land a bullseye between my eyes.

Despite all this military badassery, he stated that the best part of his day is spending time with the woman he loved. "We do cool stuff for work during training, but I look forward to coming home to my girl and being around her family." I was dumbfounded because I pictured a sniper wanting to spend his whole day around weapons and tactical equipment. Our government gave him the authority to develop his lethal abilities beyond almost anyone on the entire planet. Regardless of all the flash, he was humble and considered authentic relationships foundational to true joy.

He wasn't the first team guy to draw an apparent distinction between work and personal life. While their community is much closer and more intimate than conventional armed forces communities, they still have private lives. They are human beings who tire of being around coworkers night and day. Even though they are a tight-knit family at work, they also need people outside of work to enjoy life with regularly.

All service members need social support outside of work. We want fresh perspectives from people different than us. When someone in the military goes to a civilian gym to avoid working out on base, that's their way of drawing a line between work and time off. Whenever a service member packs their vehicle up on

Thursday night so they can speed off base after Friday release formation to see friends out of town, it's another sign. Even the coolest jobs in the military don't bring complete fulfillment. We all need people in our lives that bring us pleasure outside of work. Relationships like these give us purpose and value beyond our careers.

SECTION 3: PSYCHOLOGICAL APPLICATION

Lee successfully became an elite operator within Navy Special Operations, yet he never lost sight of his need for intimate community outside the military. Work was separate from personal life. Common interests with others enriched his friend circle. He took breaks from training. Deep recharge. The SoF Teams became his family, but he still sought further variety. He invited his teammates to join him as he socialized with outsiders. His perspective at work stayed fresh because he built so many extracurricular friendships. Being selective, he bonded with trusted friends outside of the Navy. They were always willing to entertain him and his coworkers for a day of outdoor recreation or a night out. This was a source of strength, fueling him to excel throughout training and deployments.

While a civilian, I viewed military friends as my support group outside of the corporate gig. Military service members helped me recharge because I didn't have to focus on work metrics. Conversations were novel. Their jobs were unique. Plus, they had the drive to stay physically fit. We bonded through shared primal energy chasing down our fears and pursuing fun adventures. They were easy to get along with. No pretense. We didn't have time to waste when pursuing enjoyment because they always had another deployment around the corner. We lived in the moment.

When not deployed there was an emphasis on investing in fun, rewarding friendships. Healthy relationships are restorative. They help the mind and body heal from stress. This is especially critical for those working in high-stress environments. Social support is tied to mental recovery. Even PTSD is minimized. Researchers state that "higher levels of post-deployment support were associated with lower levels of post-deployment PTSD severity" (Han et al., 2014). Finding support means connecting with individuals who don't suffer the same stress. Avoid aggravation. Sharing the same complaints repeatedly among peers gets overwhelming. It's critical to socialize with people outside one's own military unit. Having outside friendships allows for genuine conversation and leisurely activities untainted by work.

Researchers discuss how "social support, particularly from family and nonmilitary-connected peers, can bolster healthy intimate partner relationships and, in turn, improve the well-being of military service members who are deployed" (Cederbaum et al., 2017). Hanging out with friends who remind us of our inherent value outside of uniform facilitates decompression. Many times this is overlooked, resulting in destructive acting out behaviors through which service members seek to mitigate repressed anxiety. A few examples pertained to increased alcohol consumption and aggressive violence. The body needs to expel energy which only amplifies whenever it's repressed. Finding friends who help get the stress off of our chests is necessary for good health.

Not only are non-work relationships good for stress relief, but they also lead to a plethora of benefits if they are enriching and fulfilling. "Happy individuals tend to have larger social rewards, better work outcomes, greater coping abilities, better immune systems, to be more cooperative, prosocial, charitable, and to live longer than individuals who are not happy" (Siedlecki et al., 2014). It's simple to imagine how important this is for those in difficult working environments. Exhaustion from training requires a place of healing and peace.

Cardiovascular health has been found to clearly benefit from emotional and social support, signifying the relationship between our emotions and physical bodies (Williams et al., 2013). Others explain the protective effects good social support has in preventing mental illness while also fueling our brains to maintain high levels of resilience due to diminished cortisol levels (Ozbay et al., 2007). Maintaining healthy social connections helps heal and prevent damage to our brains. Oxytocin increases when social connections strengthen, which further benefits the body. In a very biological sense, it's critical to human health that positive social connection is maintained.

In light of this, it makes sense that Lee put so much value on the relationships he had. I assumed he would have been satisfied strictly socializing with his peer group, especially because his job was so exclusive. Instead, he corrected my thinking by telling me:

SECTION 4: LEADERSHIP ADVICE

> *"We need people from both inside and outside of work who make us happy. A job can't be our entire life or source of fulfillment. Relationships make us human."*

It's important to invest in recovery time between military training exercises. We have a motto that explains the intensity of the job, "Train like you fight." Life in the military regularly involves long, arduous days in miserable conditions with little sleep or personal space. We want the field to be as close to deployment as possible. Stress is needed to develop preparedness for battle because war is hell. Decision points during times of confusion can quickly become overwhelming and service members must be able to handle sudden intensity with little rest.

When heightened stress continues for weeks or months at a time, the body suffers significantly. The brain is also exhausted from cognitive overload. Mental fatigue results from managing several incessant communication channels while mission planning, assessing threats, and monitoring logistics. Recovering from such long-term stress involves self-care techniques that recharge both body and mind.

To recover from said stress, social support and relationships help. Relationships outside the military are critical to finding the social support needed to rest and recover. Being selective about who we spend time with during personal time helps ensure our well-being. Little is left in the tank when we get home, so much of our energy is spent on the job. Time off is valuable and must be managed strategically to avoid lingering fatigue and burnout. Positive influences induce a sense of calm, allowing rest to repair damage caused by stress. If we are surrounded by negative people who continue to chip away at our energy, our stress worsens.

People process feelings about work stress by venting frustrations. In the military, we complain. We armchair quarterback every decision. Everyone shares how they would personally lead the situation if they were in charge. We scrutinize details. This can quickly lead to an echo chamber effect where negativity is all that is discussed. Cathartic release is understandable, but there becomes a point when incessant complaining amplifies the problem. When released from duty day, it's important to disengage with anyone who only wishes to focus on what has been happening at work. Taking a break from thinking about work is healthy. Rest is critical to keep the mind and body recharged before the next wave of stress hits. I have seen what happens when peers in the military meet after work to hang out, only to continue discussing the job.

Take, for instance, our frequent field training exercises. We spend weeks living in the barren desert. Everyone returns to base dirty, hot, and sweaty. Body odor fills the air. Fatigued bodies are crusty with grease and sand. Salt crystals sting in our clogged pores. Conex boxes are open as the equipment gets put away. Vehicles get refueled, washed, and put back online. Trash is carried off to the dumpsters. We stand around in blistering heat waiting for the accountability of all personnel, weapons, and sensitive items (radios, NVGS, cryptological keys). The pavement is so hot it burns our feet through the soles of our boots. Hours pass by while we wait around. Finally, the accountability report is complete. We are green across the board. The sun is setting as we get released to go home and finally shower.

Warm water washes off dirt and sand that circles the drain. It feels like a rebirth as soap removes the past several days of grime. After a few minutes, the phone starts to ping with text messages. There is a get-together with coworkers eager to get a buzz on. As festive as this may sound, it comes with a price.

Coworkers in the military have a knack for talking only about the military. Drinking alcohol only removes inhibition to increase the volume with which stress is released into the air. How exactly can we decompress from the job if we stand around talking about every detail that bothers us? On nights like these, I relax alone at home, work out at the gym, or I pack my car and drive for hours to get away from the base and see non-work friends. In any case, I have a strict policy on not discussing work.

Relationships with positive friends and mentors nurtured my well-being throughout all difficult aspects of the Army. Socializing with friends far removed from my military life was critical to self-care. Intentionally seeking out people I looked up to based on emotional stability and joyful spirits inspired my own growth. Church groups have been a great source for me to find responsible, mature influences. Training in Jiu-Jitsu granted me another family that helps me channel my frustration physically while developing self-control.

When I cannot travel to see these friends in person, I am sure to pick up the phone for regular talks. During BCT, letter writing kept me connected to this community.

Self-care was a new discovery I made through healthy relationships shortly before I joined the military. My friends taught me methods to ensure I helped my body recover during high levels of stress. Physical release through exercise is a great way to actively work stress hormones out of the body. Stretching and salt baths are some phenomenal passive techniques as well. Aromatherapy is clutch; I suggest lavender before bed. At sunset, candlelight helps ease the brain, triggering the release of melatonin around sleep time. Listening to low-volume music and soothing instrumentals brings stillness to thoughts. Journaling allows mental processing to offload cognitive burdens from the brain. Audiobooks help too. Many more techniques are involved, and I have my social support to thank for this.

Earlier in life I had no idea how to rest, so I would get drunk instead. Numerous negative consequences occur when alcohol consumption is substituted for a healthy physical release. Hangovers, dehydration, malnutrition, disrupted sleep rhythms, and various physical side effects result. Heightened nervous systems require higher volumes of alcohol. Stress makes us drink. When distracted by negative feelings, it takes that much more alcohol to feel good. This same concept applies to drug use, prescription or illicit.

Alcohol is known as a social lubricant. It eases people and they open up. When intoxicated around coworkers, chances are the inhibitions drop and negative comments fly. Professional critiques pour down like a waterfall. Venting eats away free time. So much for relaxing. Worse than a hangover, mentally, there is the horrible effect of knowing that during time off from work, the only topic discussed was work. Decompression failed. This is a huge letdown when the entire goal of the evening was originally to remove oneself from job stressors.

I encourage anyone in the military to intentionally develop a healthy social support group outside of work whenever possible. Invite coworkers who don't talk shop. Strict enforcement. Have a codeword to shout every time someone mentions anything work-related. Meet new people. Explore life outside of the predictable routine. It's much easier to relax this way. There are no discussions about the chain of command or the many improvements that should be made. No one is egging others on to share gossip about a peer nobody likes. There's no need to compare resumes or posture over who will get the better title. Instead, a genuine sense of connection eases the mind into relaxation. For now, the work mind is switched completely off to recharge so Monday can be met with a full tank.

Thanks, Lee.

References:

Cederbaum, J. A., Wilcox, S. L., Sullivan, K., Lucas, C., & Schuyler, A. (2017). The Influence of Social Support on Dyadic Functioning and Mental Health Among Military Personnel During Postdeployment Reintegration. *Public health reports (Washington, D.C. : 1974), 132*(1), 85–92. https://doi.org/10.1177/0033354916679984

Han, S. C., Castro, F., Lee, L. O., Charney, M. E., Marx, B. P., Brailey, K., Proctor, S. P., & Vasterling, J. J. (2014). Military unit support, postdeployment social support, and PTSD symptoms among active duty and National Guard soldiers deployed to Iraq. *Journal of anxiety disorders, 28*(5), 446–453. https://doi.org/10.1016/j.janxdis.2014.04.004

Ozbay F, Johnson DC, Dimoulas E, Morgan CA, Charney D, Southwick S. Social support and resilience to stress: from neurobiology to clinical practice. Psychiatry (Edgmont). 2007 May;4(5):35-40. PMID: 20806028; PMCID: PMC2921311.

Siedlecki, K. L., Salthouse, T. A., Oishi, S., & Jeswani, S. (2014). The Relationship Between Social Support and Subjective Well-Being Across Age. *Social indicators research*, *117*(2), 561–576. https://doi.org/10.1007/s11205-013-0361-4

White-Williams, C., Grady, K. L., Myers, S., Naftel, D. C., Wang, E., Bourge, R. C., & Rybarczyk, B. (2013). The relationships among satisfaction with social support, quality of life, and survival 5 to 10 years after heart transplantation. *The Journal of cardiovascular nursing*, *28*(5), 407–416. https://doi.org/10.1097/JCN.0b013e3182532672

17 - GARRISON, FIELD, & YOU

"Hey, do you wanna read stories to each other before bed?"
- ***JAS*** *[USMC Artillery Officer]*

Distress tolerance: engaging in healthy coping skills during times of duress

Self-Control: the ability to control impulses of desire or emotions

Social Influence: influencing the behavior of others due to one's social status

SECTION 1: INTRODUCTION TO THE TOPIC

It was another broiling hot day out in the desert as our platoon convoy made its way through jagged rocks and rough terrain. We had a grid coordinate to get to, and no clear avenue of approach. The satellite imagery shows washed-out paths, but it fails to signify how steep the gradients are. Everything looks flat in the picture. Sunlight directly perpendicular to the Earth's surface doesn't create shadows and prevents imagery from conveying terrain features. We won't know what it looks like until we get there. It was common to suddenly drive up to a steep climb or drop-off that we didn't expect and needed to maneuver through or around. At some point there was a wall in front of us as we crawled vertically up dirt and rock mounds to try to make a path. Tracked vehicles overheat and frequently need to stop moving to cool off. They'll blow gaskets and spray coolant if we push them too hard. Comms are spotty, so we rely on maintaining visuals on the dust kicked off from each vehicle.

Once we finally get to our grid, we are exhausted, dehydrated, and hungry. We space out the vehicles and Soldiers dismount to eat chow under the shade of the wheel wells. I make contact in our link-up with another unit and chat with their platoon leader. We walk around to sight in the obstacle emplacement. The platoon leader says he wants one or two kilometers of triple standard concertina wire obstacles laid out within six hours. One of the NCOs listening in looks at me with a scowl and shakes his head as he walks away. Given the rocky terrain and heat index, it will take several times longer to complete the task than anticipated. This other platoon leader's expectation is wildly unrealistic given the equipment, manpower, and resources we brought out.

I bring the situation back to the squad leaders being that our current platoon sergeant is collocated with headquarters for the time being. "No way, Sir, he's crazy," one sergeant tells me. "Look at the rocks and hills around us. It doesn't make sense anyway because the road is way over here and funnels right here perfectly for the assault. They need 200 meters tops." He's lowballing me on that 200, but overall, he's spot on. I trust him as the SME (Subject Matter Expert). I need to bring this up the chain of command to adjust the mission parameters for the Soldiers or there's a good chance my convoy will abandon me in the desert.

Comms are down, of course, so I take it upon myself to make the call. I signal for the other officer and we meet halfway. "We can bang out 400 meters for you, but we have to get started now. The sun is setting, and the battle kicks off at 2100." The other Lieutenant pans around the desert and remains silent. Finally, he responds by asking for one kilometer. "Look, we can maybe get you 500 meters, but that's it, and even then, it's overkill." After a few more back-and-forth rounds of this, we finally settled around 450 meters and got the job started.

As I inspect the construction progress, I notice the Soldiers are chuckling while passing glances at me. I nod to them and ask what I did. An NCO loudly states in front of the entire platoon, "Hey Sir, keep doing what you just did right there. Don't let people take advantage of us because they don't understand the terrain like we do. We'll get the mission done with a fraction of what they want." I shake his hand in agreement as the others give a hearty, "Hell ya, Sir."

I realize these Soldiers are solid. They know how to load and move the convoy, build obstacles, and get everyone fed and hydrated. I need to alleviate the pressure that's constantly put on them. Listening to the NCOs helps me learn where my value as a leader lies. I need their help to lead effectively in garrison (meaning on base back at the office) and out here in the field.

SECTION 2: A GOOD MILITARY LEADER

Jas, a Marine Corps artillery officer, is a handsomely clean-cut, red-haired South Carolinian with exquisite taste in poetry and scotch. He is the son of a doctor who raised him to be a scholar with an impeccable style. I based a lot of my fashion sense on what I learned by going through his closet rummaging for pants and shirts to borrow. He literally dressed me because I had forgotten what adults should look like at cocktail parties. The southern dress style has a great way of working in pastel shirts with earth-tone pants.

He also taught me the importance of rich literature and poetry. With a knack for reciting monologues, Jas can be found suddenly standing atop a chair or table at a party to enrapture his audience with speeches in full character. He boldly speaks in verse without hesitation until his crescendo is met with applause. Then a toast is made as he beams.

I met Jas a couple of years after I sobered up from my crazy party life post-college. Back then, I used to drink excessive volumes of alcohol almost daily. On my 25th birthday, I remember seeing that it was about noon and was surprised I hadn't yet blacked out. I looked around at my friends and wished I was doing something better with my life. The parties were getting old and celebrating myself felt empty. That day I told myself I was ending my relationship with alcohol.

My friend circle immediately changed. I found a roommate who was in the Navy and trusted he would help keep me on a good path. Jas was a friend of his from the Naval Academy and crashed over one night.

I came home to find him on my couch, and we had a deep conversation about the meaning of life. From that moment, we became good friends and later roommates. D&M (Deep and Meaningful).

There was a library room in Jas' house with expensive bottles of Scotch. I was used to drinking wine in red cups and vodka from plastic bottles. Jas' bottles hovered around the triple-digit mark per bottle. One night as we discussed literature, military history, and leadership, we moved on to the topic of scotch.

Jas taught me to appreciate the aromatics, break the surface tension with a single drop of water, and slowly pour the beverage over a smooth ball of ice to ensure it doesn't bruise. We sipped tiny amounts of the gold liquid. He walked me through the pallet of taste on my tongue. He taught me how to slowly enjoy a single drink, avoid getting drunk, and dive into a meaningful talk with a brother. Later he walked me through packing a corn cob pipe that was cleaned out with honey and further expanded my knowledge of good tobacco. He loved taking his pipe out to the field to smoke with his marines.

His library was full of history books and military weaponry, including an old battle saber and dummy 105mm Howitzer artillery shell. We closed the glass doors and secluded ourselves together from the hubbub of the world around us. Here we had philosophical discussions about the impact of leadership during war. Reading historical accounts of courage during battle was astoundingly inspirational.

We spoke in depth about military leadership with examples of both the good and bad. He shared personal knowledge on how best to treat one's subordinates and lead with humility. In his study room, I learned a good many things. It was here that a Marine officer taught me how to lead based on his own experience and through historical accounts. He also taught me the value of self-control and openness to coachability as a military officer.

SECTION 3: PSYCHOLOGICAL APPLICATION

Self-control is a characteristic all leaders must possess. Knowing how to manage ourselves gives us the ability to guide others. This also enables us to accept criticism without attempting to run away from challenges. Often when I struggle with self-control, it's based on my desire to either avoid discomfort or seek immediate gratification. Both conditions make for a poor leader. Developing one's capacity for stress tolerance helps manage anxiety and withstand negative emotional states (Overstreet et al., 2018). Practice is key. Quick decisions must be made during difficult situations. Leaders who can keep a clear mind when facing challenges will evaluate the best options. In the military this saves lives.

I wanted to clear my own mind and rebuild a solid foundation. New boundaries were required. Intentionally leaving behind negative social influences that kept me stuck in immaturity was critical to my growth. My friend circle thrived on instant gratification. I needed to develop self-control and remove distractions. I cut ties. Researchers explain how "manipulating our surroundings to advantage is, in fact, a highly effective form of self-control" (Duckworth et al., 2017). Physical changes in the brain occur, especially during adolescence, when we experience new social influences (Telzer et al., 2019). It's important to be very selective about who we choose to be in our lives.

As I walked away from bad influences, I needed to discover peers and mentors who could continue to develop me. Sobriety helped. It's fitting that most of these folks were serving in the military. This paved the road to my eventual service. Gaining such relationships helped me observe healthy leadership dynamics at a very personal level. Self-control led to self-mastery as I gained insight into controlling impulses. As a leader, this helped me keep an open mind to the reality on the ground without giving into my knee-jerk emotional reactions. Easier said than done. I checked myself constantly and Soldiers let me know each time I screwed up.

Jas instilled the importance of being a leader who doesn't compound stress. Self-control. Using scotch as an example, he taught me to slow down and appreciate fine details. Control emotions. I no longer desired to use alcohol as a means of coping or escape. I became more present every time Jas and I hung out. My relationship with him helped decouple my association between alcohol and self-medication. Thoughtfulness minimized impulsivity. My self-awareness increased along with my desire for growth. Little did I know how beneficial this would be as a military leader who strove to pursue healthy, intelligent outlets to address workplace stress.

I watched Jas closely. Researchers investigate the effects of social influences impressed upon the brain when peers observe each other undertaking new behaviors (Ciranka & van den Bos, 2019). He demonstrated healthy behaviors, and I admired the way he was able to walk his own path without feeling the need to conform or seek approval. As a military officer, he knew what it meant to be under constant scrutiny. Military leaders live in a fishbowl, meaning we are constantly being observed by everyone around us, especially when we don't even know it. Again, self-control is critical. Credibility can be lost with one poor decision or emotional reaction.

Coachability helps. It helped me keep an open mind to growing past my current limits. The military offers countless people to learn from. Just as Jas taught me how to slow down and appreciate the finer things in life, he informed me that experienced service members, especially the NCOs, would provide mentorship in the military. As I desired to become a fellow military officer, I reflected on what it meant to seek guidance while on the job. I never wanted to make others suffer because of my immaturity. This opened my mind to being coached by the subject matter experts I met.

Before I shipped out for Basic Training, I asked Jas how I could be a well-rounded leader that minimized frustrations for the staff supporting me. He shared some wisdom that a gunnery sergeant gave him:

SECTION 4: LEADERSHIP ADVICE

> *"An officer is at most only strong at two or three things: garrison life, the field, or being a good person. I don't care which of the first two you are but always be a good person. Your NCOs will make sure to help you with the other two."*

New officers are blank slates. At least, this is how everyone else perceives us. We come to our new units with academic knowledge gained from military training, but that has more to do with technical aspects of our job, not leadership guidance. In engineering school, we were told that leadership training would start on the job, not in the classroom. Truth. I would need to keep an open mind to the criticism more experienced service members had provided me. Respect went a long way to grant me access to the knowledge possessed by others. I made it a point to speak to a private the same way I spoke to a general. Everyone I spoke with was treated as a professional adult. Some people hate this, but it kept me from having to manage several versions of myself.

On base, paperwork is the thing to master. Leaders put the "office" in officer. From taking a vacation to running a shooting range, there are multiple layers of permission required. Red tape means that approval must be sought from several leaders through a variety of government forms to ensure the bosses give permission for whatever is being requested. Every punctuation mark counts. Sometimes even a comma or period in the wrong place can delay the process by several days or weeks. Some forms required a period after my middle initial while others didn't. Rejection of the form communicated something was off and I had to start all over. The learning curve is steep. Insight from anyone who knows the process helps. Advice saves time.

I needed help. NCOs are key to enabling a new officer to manage office policies. I sought guidance instead of wasting time recreating the wheel. Friendliness built bridges. Soldiers appreciate it when a leader pushes to get them approved for whatever it is they want. There is no way I would be able to draw up the appropriate documents and fill them out with the required information unless someone walked me through each step of the painstaking process. Next is the review. Proofreading and signing documents correctly is a group effort. Had I spent time in isolation attempting to hammer through all this alone it would have communicated that I didn't want help from anyone. I'd drown in government forms. Any help was more than appreciated. Jas's advice was spot on.

The field gets gnarly. Fast. It's high stress around the clock when you're always on standby for last-minute missions requiring convoy movements across rough terrain. Commanders demand responses anytime they call. The enemy's decisions impact our plans which are ever-changing. Battlefields evolve unpredictably. Always be ready. Sleep involved me cuddling up next to a radio, rifle, and night vision goggles. When orders came to move, I had to wipe the exhaustion away and get everyone moving. I also needed to ensure nobody got hurt. Mistakes fall on leaders. Safety comes first because deadly consequences can quickly arise from poor, hasty decisions. Driving in darkness at night next to cliffs and wadis is hellish.

Stay calm. As stated previously, self-control is key to keeping a level head. Leaning on the platoon sergeant and squad leaders eased the burden. Clutch allies. They knew I wanted help. Anytime I asked for it they delivered. Solid, dependable, and hardworking Soldiers make a leader's job easy. My stress melted when they got hands-on with the issues ahead. Whether we needed to build hasty obstacles, prepare for enemy contact, or offensively engage targets they knew exactly what to do. Combat experience is golden. Seeing Soldiers who have been in war zones leading their peers is such a rad feeling. They earned it. How could I possibly micromanage an experienced, battle-tested Soldier? Make way. I observed and took notes.

Being coachable means inviting in knowledgeable experience from Soldiers who've been around. Minimizing their stress is appreciated. I always asked them what they needed and where I could help as a new officer. Often, this involved briefing the commander that we were adjusting to unexpected situations on the ground. We would meet the intent with modifications. Getting yelled at was my job. Theirs was handling the situation according to real-world issues that were impeding progress.

When they weren't breaking their backs pounding pickets into the ground or throwing razor wire around, I needed to help them get rest. I told them what needed to be done in full detail to minimize surprises. Soldiers love certainty. I gave as much as I could based on briefs I attended. This way they know how much work is ahead and when rest is coming. Also, they could figure out how to break up work hours to avoid operating at the peak heat index of the day. Should they have any requests, rebuttals, or concerns, I would get on the comms to address that. Basically, I wanted to remove friction points and trim the workload to exactly what was necessary to win the fight.

In the field, we also had a lot of downtime. Hours on end pulling security. Waiting on enemies. Card games and handheld video games helped. One of my biggest focuses was getting Soldiers to engage with the education center and library. I wanted them to further their academic careers, thereby strengthening the military while setting themselves up for professional success on the outside. Many credible universities have online platforms accessible in the field through hotspot data. These institutions work closely with the military educational department to provide financial aid and tuition assistance. I wanted others to experience the benefit of reading and studying during downtime in military training. This keeps many people I know on a good path.

I knew that I was limited in my experience with engagement area development, so I gladly asked the NCOs to guide me. My perspective was limited. Still a fetus. These Soldiers are the subject matter experts, and I trusted their direction when it came to tactical emplacements of obstacles. Reading terrain is tricky. Multiple variations of utilizing natural chokepoints are possible. Logic grows when the puzzle is shared. My platoon knew I wanted to learn. They saw my deficits and knew that I was open to being coached. They'd fist bump me with a "We got you, Sir." If I had closed my mind to them, this would translate to unnecessary work and loss of resources like building materials, ammunition, fuel, water, and troop morale. To keep myself from being stranded alone in a desert, I listened and applied what the experienced professionals were advising.

I'm lucky. Military mentors changed my life. Arrogance in my younger years impaired me and I still wrestle with it. Much of my life involved being trapped in ignorance because I was too scared to ask for help. I don't like conveying positive aspects of my leadership experience without honest details related to being insecure. Had I joined the military without guidance from friends like Jas, I would have hurt Soldiers. My pride would have led to painful situations where they were trapped between a hard situation and a difficult boss. Value of a leader depends on stress minimization. Antagonizing a hard-working Soldier is bad enough, let alone one who has been to war and carries unimaginable burdens they rarely share with anyone. Chokes me up.

As Jas said, military leaders need help with several aspects of the field and in garrison. I learned the most valuable thing I could do was remove weight from the back of subordinates. Care for the troops and get their voices heard, no matter how inconvenient to the missions. Managing upwards in the organization is not easy due to the many layers of leadership. However, this is the only way to push back on work volumes while explaining how we will meet the intent with more efficient parameters.

During my platoon leadership time, I missed several months of field training time due to a neck injury aggravated by a car accident. But the Soldiers were prepared. As a leader, I sought to manage with as little influence as possible. My focus was on relaying clear information about end results while allowing everyone under my supervision to come up with solutions. Delegation helped keep the team strong. My absence didn't hinder the platoon's success because they knew how to handle the templated obstacles and convoy movements.

Earlier in this book, I wrote about the Soldiers' responses when I asked how much they thought I had been letting them down as a leader without a tactical resume. They insisted that the only thing they wanted from me was continued respectful treatment. The missions we ran were repetitive and fairly consistent. For me to try and make myself relevant would become burdensome to them. I would serve them best as a leader who fought to enable their autonomy and ensure they had clear directions from above.

I learned much from the people I worked with in light of their combat deployments and decades of military experience. They taught me how to manage my equipment, set up my gear, and provide relevant information in the field. In garrison, they taught me to speak up when I could to ensure that I minimized unnecessary workloads and stress. Above all this, they taught me the importance of staying true to myself and the wisdom these many service members provided me. When I became stressed or overwhelmed, they reminded me to slow down and focus on treating others with kindness and respect. I often believed I was failing others and organizations because I wanted to do more to help actively.

"Sir, all we care about is how you treat us. We know how to do our job. Just keep fighting for what we need, and we'll keep you looking good to the higher-ups."

Thanks, Jas.

References:

Ciranka, S., & van den Bos, W. (2019). Social Influence in Adolescent Decision-Making: A Formal Framework. *Frontiers in psychology, 10,* 1915. https://doi.org/10.3389/fpsyg.2019.01915

Overstreet, C., Brown, E., Berenz, E. C., Brown, R. C., Hawn, S., McDonald, S., Pickett, T., Danielson, C. K., Thomas, S., & Amstadter, A. (2018). Anxiety Sensitivity and Distress Tolerance Typologies and Relations to Posttraumatic Stress Disorder: A Cluster Analytic Approach. *Military psychology : the official journal of the Division of Military Psychology, American Psychological Association, 30*(6), 547–556. https://doi.org/10.1080/08995605.2018.1521682

Telzer, E. H., van Hoorn, J., Rogers, C. R., & Do, K. T. (2018). Social Influence on Positive Youth Development: A Developmental Neuroscience Perspective. *Advances in child development and behavior, 54*, 215–258. https://doi.org/10.1016/bs.acdb.2017.10.003

18 - DON'T FEAR TYRANTS

"Next time he tells you an officer shouldn't talk to privates in the platoon ask him: In war, are the troops more willing to follow a leader they like, or one they hate?"

- ***JAY*** *[Navy SEAL Officer]*

Competence: the ability to accomplish certain tasks

Humility: viewing oneself as equal among others without a prideful display of strength or accomplishment

SECTION 1: INTRODUCTION TO THE TOPIC

Two young and beautiful Iraqi girls, my cousins on my mother's side, were on a bus heading north out of Baghdad in June 2014. They were on their way to Mosul, after which they would head to Turkey. This was not a vacation, but rather a final effort to escape ISIS. They are Christian minorities, and therefore prime targets for terrorists to use as an example of their evil abilities.

Their mother and father had received financial help from relatives in the United States to help cover the cost of their daughters' journey. After much resistance and a tearful goodbye, the daughters were urged onto the bus by their parents, who didn't join them.

The elderly father's health declined with age, and he had no energy to try and outrun young, vicious terrorists. ISIS lusted for the blood of anyone resisting to bow. He could not bear to slow his family down and risk being caught. They were weak prey to a rabid lion. A quick death would be merciful. If caught, the atrocities ISIS would commit on his wife and daughters were unbearable to imagine. He knew they would surely keep him alive to watch. His loyal wife would not leave his side despite his wishes. Accepting death as inevitable, they were comforted by the thought of their kids growing up in a safer country.

The girls wept from their windows and waved goodbye for what they knew would be the last time. The bus's engine rumbled as it started up, and the doors were closed. Their escape from Iraq began.

On the way to Mosul, a stationary pickup truck carrying a load of red bricks and coal came into view on the dusty roadside. Next to the truck was a sign still too far away to make out. Children kicked soccer balls in a dirt field by the parked vehicle. Nothing seemed out of the ordinary. Continuing down the road, suddenly, the driver screamed and slammed on the brakes and came to an immediate halt. Passengers shuddered at the stop. Looking out the window, they were struck with a senseless sight. Slowly they began to realize that what initially seemed like a normal day had become a nightmare.

The bus was stopped ahead of the pickup truck, but close enough to see that its load was severed human heads decapitated at the neck with rough saw blades, the fresh blood blackened by the blistering sun and dirt. The ball the children kicked around in the dirt was not a soccer ball. It was a human head. The sign read, "Keep coming this way. ISIS is waiting." The bus immediately turned around and returned to Baghdad where the girls rejoined their parents to await their doom. ISIS then took Mosul. The plague would be coming to Baghdad to take over the capital.

Certain that death was coming for them, the family said prayers to prepare. An older woman in the family reminded them to never fear death at the hands of evil men. She said that even if their bodies were raped and burned alive, their souls were eternally protected by God. For generations, they kept courage in a dark and evil world, choosing never to fear a tyrant.

SECTION 2: A GOOD MILITARY LEADER

I met Jay for the first time in Jiu-Jitsu class. His solid build gives the impression he's made from concrete and rebar. His voice is coarse, and his steely eyes burn with intensity. He is a retired Navy SEAL who fought in many battles, some of which were located in the Iraqi villages my parents grew up in. He and his men fought against and killed enemies terrorizing the local populace. Iraqi Christian minorities, my family line, were some of the most vulnerable targets of destruction by these terrorists. With Jewish-sounding last names, we are easily identifiable. ISIS would often murder people in the streets based on the spelling of our names on driver's licenses.

After becoming aware of Jay's prior missions in Iraq, I wanted to thank him on behalf of my parents and family for his and his team's tremendous sacrifices. My parents often told us how blessed we were to be living in the USA, growing up without knowing the traumas they had suffered as children. Part of me wondered if this would be inappropriate or presumptuous, but I felt compelled to show gratitude. Knowing that American service members were willing to die to protect people they owed nothing to was inspiring to say the least. I wanted to tell him that despite any criticism he may get from society regarding the atrocities of war, he had the moral support of the people indigenous to the region he fought in.

As I approached from across the gym floor, he immediately noticed my trajectory and turned to face me. Nothing takes him by surprise. I'm convinced he can see behind him somehow. I wondered how many gym protocols I was breaking to approach a black belt. At this point, my heart was pounding, and my hands were clammy with sweat. Was it wise to tell him my family is from Iraq? Was reminding a combat veteran of his war in the middle of Jiu-Jitsu the first impression I wanted to make? He continued to gaze at my approach. His eyes pointed like lasers directly into mine. Bearing no expression, he had the face and disposition of a stoic.

"Hi Jay," I sheepishly said from afar. His gaze lasered into me, tracking my approach, and my hands grew sweatier by the second. We shook hands, and I was immediately aware of the power in his grip. He wasn't exactly as tall as I imagined, but he was twice as wide.

I was terrified and still am sort of. "Jay, I just wanted to say thank you. My family is from Iraq, and you fought to keep our people safe. That means a lot because it wasn't your mess to begin with, but you stepped into that darkness. There is an evil there that preceded Saddam, and he wielded it to torment my people into submission. Thank you for what your men suffered there."

It all came pouring out, and I said more than I had planned. He took this in, and I braced for his response. He smiled and then asked what villages my family grew up in. We talked for a few minutes, and I shared some stories about their lives growing up in Iraq as ethnic minorities. One hilarious story involved my shy grandpa getting routinely flashed by a woman in his village who sought to rebel against the authorities who had been forcing her to wear burdensome coverings. He thought it was hilarious. He then motioned for his friend on the mats to come over.

Introducing me to his buddy, Jay told him about my family's villages. They fought there alongside each other. It was amazing to meet two warriors of this caliber. I repeated the story about my grandpa. I also thanked his friend for everything they did to free the oppressed. Ever since that day, my respect for Jay has only increased. His confidence fires me up to push myself. His humility and his heart are genuine beyond what I anticipated.

He asked me if I wanted to spar for a round, and I accepted. Pretty sure that was one of the most awkward matches of my life. Partly because mid-spar I was geeking out over the fact that he is SOF, and partly because I was terrified he'd have a flashback as he looked at my face and would see an Iraqi man trying to fight him. Despite me, he maintained total control of the situation. After our roll, he had me pair up with his SEAL buddy for the remainder of class lessons. He was super cool and told me not to be nervous about screwing up, because he was learning too.

A few months after this day I began my application to the Army. A year later I shipped out for basic training. This meeting with Jay had a profound impact on my desire to serve. Putting on a uniform made me proud because it helped me connect with war heroes. I never deployed to Iraq, but I have worked with many who fought there. By the time I shipped out for BCT, the battle against ISIS had wound down. All the effective work by the United States and its allies helped eliminate the evil terrorists. Our tactical prowess is unmatched, and Special Operations units are the razor edge of the military blade.

As a new officer, I was guided by several NCOs based on their own battlefield experiences similar to Jay's. Learning from any service member who had fought in past wars was a tremendous gift. They are all heroes in my eyes, despite the way they downplay their sacrifice. The confidence they exuded during times of distress helped me know and believe our nation will overcome any evil adversary we face. Our service members battle with heart, and though war takes a toll, the human spirit in America's military is galvanized by fire. These men and women fear no tyrant.

SECTION 3: PSYCHOLOGICAL APPLICATION

Military leadership relies on exuding confidence in the face of tyrannical evil. Take a confident stance.

Actions follow beliefs so it's important to believe we have what it takes to make a difference. What we think about ourselves dictates our actions. Being confident in our minds translates to heightened physical performance. Researchers find our brains rely on beliefs about ourselves "to guide behavior" (Ott et al., 2019).

Posture changes as our thoughts tell the brain how to activate the nervous system through chemical signatures impacting body positioning, eye contact, and vocal intonation. We straighten our backs and pull our shoulders back. Chin up as we face adversity. Lacking confidence results in the opposite as we collapse in posture and lose heart. Our thought life plays a foundational part in determining how we live, and as leaders it's important to exude confidence, especially to inspire others. Adversaries count on their ability to divide and conquer, but staying united in confidence combats this.

Leaders, especially in the military, must be cautious about maintaining positive thoughts to ensure we inspire courage in others. Avoiding despair is one part of this; boldly empowering our team through our continued support enables actual progress toward accomplishing goals. Just like when Jay encourages us on the mats to train and fight because he wants us to know how to stand up against violent adversaries. When our bodies ache and we keep getting submitted it's important to believe in ourselves and not quit. We look to him as a reference point because his toughness inspires us.

Confidence is best when it's not only demonstrated by a single leader but also shared across the entire unit. Subordinates pay great attention to observable actions in leaders to judge their ability and attitude. They emulate those in charge. Even down to personality characteristics and behaviors. Being aware of this is powerful because it helps inspire changes. Being approachable as a leader makes these awesome characteristics even more attainable. People want to learn from mentors who guide them. It's a great sign when leaders build confidence in subordinates while humbly remembering "to stay grounded in reality...as their success grows" (Kerfoot, 2010).

Jay does exactly this. He carries himself in a manner that motivates others to build confidence while remaining grounded and relatable. He doesn't allow rank to isolate him. He is hands-on with the development of others. We see his physical toughness on the mats as he pushes maximum technique in Jiu-Jitsu. Ego controlled. He'll bleed and keep going, inspiring us to push ourselves. We suffer towards developing stronger skills because that is what our coaches and leaders do.

While confidence may be physically displayed, there's certainly much to be said about psychological steadiness when led by someone who exudes calm and control. Jay commands attention by challenging how we think about our own limitations. We listen closely to the advice he gives because it makes us step beyond our comfort zone. He asks us what we are willing to sacrifice to pursue growth. In his own life, he shows that he can live without the comforts most take for granted and he has no interest in using success to live an easy life. He works hard and consistently trains. His own willingness to endure pain communicates the mental meaning of being in charge. Psychological stability is admirable because it provides a strong standard to pursue. He is not intimidated by suffering, and this emboldens us.

He also meets us wherever we are without making us feel inadequate. He wants us to grow from our current state regardless of how far ahead or behind we are compared to others. There is no room for pride to play a part because he wants us to check our egos at the door. At the gym, we notice how he treats others courteously and strives to exemplify similar attitudes of humility. Confidence grants him the ability to be present and fully engaged. The other coaches do the same. The culture at the gym tells us that the ones with the most power don't need to beat others over the head with it. While it can be weaponized to protect and provide safety, there is a specific trigger. Behaviorally, we feel what it means to be fearless because we see it demonstrated in someone we admire.

Superb leaders balance humility and confidence while maintaining self-awareness to control ego (Kerr, 2007). Jay mastered this through countless lessons learned as a Navy SEAL who moved from the enlisted ranks to becoming an officer. His robust experience fostered tremendous personal growth and situational awareness. Increased responsibility on the job built confidence, self-esteem, and competency. Self-esteem and confidence reduce fear and anxiety (Byrne, 2000). This is a great way for leaders to build up confidence in others thereby enabling them to maintain calm control during chaos.

Confident leaders patiently allow calculated risks. Assertive behavior is rewarded, though honest self-assessment is required. Processes must be reviewed in detail to find areas needing improvement. In the military, we call these AARs (After Action Review). We must make clear statements about observed failures and successes. There's also a requirement to state constructive criticism that will improve the process in future attempts. Leaders who nurture growth ensure this process is thorough and offers real self-reflection. Often it can be a quick box to check, but that defeats its purpose. It takes a leader with a robust ego to absorb responsibility for failure.

Fear is healthy. It operates to keep us safe. It becomes unhealthy when we lose the ability to self-regulate and lash out emotionally, such as with passive aggression or anger because of frustration (Cavaness et al., 2020). Bullies and tyrants who do this are weak people. The panic they create is contagious. Facing our fears builds up courage and resilience (Taylor & Wilson, 2019). Confident leaders demonstrate self-mastery and compartmentalization of fear. They control emotions during distress and positively influence the temperament of those around them (Stedham & Skaar, 2019). Calm is contagious.

Leaders must inspire subordinates to win. Win hearts and minds. Believing in one's ability to succeed is the basis for confident performance (Bailey, 2019). Effective leaders show the path towards success. It's a path they took. Offering advice, confident leaders share their mindset on overpowering fear. Their scars teach lessons. Guidance they provide helps others to minimize unhelpful behaviors resulting from uncontrolled impulses, like fear and passivity (Doci et al., 2015). They teach what it takes to defeat the enemy, bully, or tyrant who is hurting others. Jay lives this out.

At one point in the Army, I feared having to face a leader with the potential to be a powerful adversary. He was the highest-ranking official I had ever engaged. I wanted to speak up about friction points we all wanted addressed. Soldiers needed policy changes at the highest level, yet many times people don't want to speak up. Fear created painful silence. I wanted was to leave the Army better than I found it, even if in the smallest of ways. I sent up a suggestion through an online comment system complete with my name and phone number. Most comments are anonymous, rarely does anyone sign their name.

My phone rang. It was a call from the top of the chain telling me to get ready. Everything was about to change for me. Orders came to prepare a detailed brief. No way. What if I screwed up? I had an option to backpedal out of the situation by deferring to miscommunication. I could also provide ambiguous or vague details. Or, risking my career, I could share objective information. I wavered in confidence for several days until Jay told me:

SECTION 4: LEADERSHIP ADVICE

> *"Speak up for the men and women you lead when you know you need to. Don't worry whether a leader above you is a tyrant. If what you have to say is true, boldly say it. Be sure to bring solutions for each problem."*

Following Jay's advice put me on a path I will forever be grateful for finding. The leader engaging me was not a tyrant. He genuinely cared for the lowest ranking service members, who often felt voiceless. He understood the importance of valuing mental health. If I allowed fear to stop me from speaking up, I'd regret it. I found I could share the Soldiers' concerns and inspire them to speak up.

I asked for continued input from the Soldiers I led. Gathering information painted a clear picture. We took emotions out of the situation. Through due diligence and engagement with subordinates, I could clearly depict what was impacting morale without placing blame on any individual(s). We need to examine the "why" for certain taskings. Many policies were built on previous existing frameworks leading to stagnation. We needed to prune down. Other policies were rendered unnecessary after lockdowns. Redundancies were slowing down processes and overwhelming Soldiers.

Paperwork for certain approval processes could take weeks or months when they ought to be completed in a few days. Soldiers love it when they see a longstanding need addressed by a leader. Hand walking a memo to a superior for a signature of approval is necessary but can become exhausting and unscalable for entire companies of Soldiers. Granting approval power to lower positions removes such restrictions. Soldiers immediately feel they are no longer a burden to the chain of command. Because of this, morale spikes immediately.

When addressing our command team, I pointed out organizational deficiencies that leaders could quickly address at various unit levels. Jay coached me to provide a solution for every problem. Bull's eye. Pairing multiple solutions with each problem made this both respectful and practical. Again, I kept focus on problem sets, not people. Had I mentioned any specific leaders by name, it might have suggested I was attempting to start a personal vendetta. I could quickly make enemies by leveling personal attacks. However, by maintaining a focus on loosening restrictive systemic procedures in the military, I could potentially create collaborative group discussions with various leaders. Each leader involved could see where they could contribute. Trim the fat. With valuable data from Soldier feedback, we could work on streamlining or removing policies that hindered them.

Learning to speak up and provide solutions helped me work on strengthening the organization. It was important not to just vent complaints. How could I help? Where could we improve? What could be done better? I focused on enabling individuals, not enforcing rigid systems. Soldiers who are disciplined and dependable need to feel supported in pursuing their goals. Drive increases morale. The military is strongest when individual service members are at their best physically and mentally. The unit will deteriorate whenever there is a loss in morale, purpose, or job satisfaction.

My leadership style involves maintaining sensitivity towards those doing the work. Hearing their perspectives firsthand helps me enable those above me to lead with objective data points, not assumptions. Distance from subordinates resulting from increased rank creates a loss in direct communication. Leaders who pay attention to the sentiment of those on the ground help correct deviations from healthy organizational goals. No matter how inconvenient the truth is, objective information is key to keeping the organization's body healthy.

Speaking up takes courage. Standing for what's right can be especially dangerous when challenging a potential tyrant. Professionally, it's scary to face someone who can dismantle careers. Scarier still to face enemies who violently destroy lives. In war, troops stand against tyrants who dismantle human bodies as a show of force. Knowing that Soldiers had confidently battled through such deadly horrors, how could I justify my fear of professional destruction? Their courage in facing real tyrants gave me the confidence to take a comparatively minute risk.

Furthermore, silence is contagious. When individuals remain quiet due to fear of reprisal, the situation worsens for the organization and the world. Weakness spreads. It keeps spreading. Leaders can step up at any rank or level to make a change. Risky, but powerful. There comes a time when threats and perceived threats must be faced with courage, no matter the consequences. Tyrants be damned.

Fear is not absent in such situations but rather simultaneously exists alongside courage. It'll never feel comfortable, nor should it. Take advice from other leaders who have proven their own ability to face and overcome powerful enemies because they know what it takes to win. When they tell you to make a path for others, lunge headfirst. It could be career-ending or even deadly to take a bold stance, but that is the mark of a true leader. Confidence helps warriors make aggressive attempts to engage in challenging situations. Bold changes require audacity.

Tyrant or not, fear no one. Fight for what is right.

Thanks, Jay.

References:

Bailey R. R. (2017). Goal Setting and Action Planning for Health Behavior Change. *American journal of lifestyle medicine*, *13*(6), 615–618. https://doi.org/10.1177/1559827617729634

Byrne B. Relationships between anxiety, fear, self-esteem, and coping strategies in adolescence. Adolescence. 2000 Spring;35(137):201-15. PMID: 10841307.

Cavaness, K., Picchioni, A., & Fleshman, J. W. (2020). Linking Emotional Intelligence to Successful Health Care Leadership: The *Big Five* Model of Personality. *Clinics in colon and rectal surgery*, *33*(4), 195–203. https://doi.org/10.1055/s-0040-1709435

Dóci, E., Stouten, J., & Hofmans, J. (2015). The cognitive-behavioral system of leadership: cognitive antecedents of active and passive leadership behaviors. *Frontiers in psychology*, *6*, 1344. https://doi.org/10.3389/fpsyg.2015.01344

Kerfoot K. M. (2010). Leaders, self-confidence, and hubris: what's the difference?. *Nursing economic$*, *28*(5), 350–349.

Kerr J. Confidence and humility: our challenge to develop both during residency. Can Fam Physician. 2007 Apr;53(4):704-7. PMID: 17872723; PMCID: PMC1952607

Ott, T., Masset, P., & Kepecs, A. (2018). The Neurobiology of Confidence: From Beliefs to Neurons. *Cold Spring Harbor symposia on quantitative biology*, *83*, 9–16. https://doi.org/10.1101/sqb.2018.83.038794

Stedham, Y., & Skaar, T. B. (2019). Mindfulness, Trust, and Leader Effectiveness: A Conceptual Framework. *Frontiers in psychology*, *10*, 1588. https://doi.org/10.3389/fpsyg.2019.01588

Taylor, J., & Wilson, J. C. (2019). Using our understanding of time to increase self-efficacy towards goal achievement. *Heliyon*, *5*(8), e02116. https://doi.org/10.1016/j.heliyon.2019.e02116

ABOUT THE AUTHOR

Daniel Zia Joseph

After over ten years building a career in the biotechnology industry, he decided to join the military. Inspired by mentors who served in various military branches, he witnessed the value of gaining such experience.

While serving as an Engineer Officer in the United States Army he received a Master of Science in Psychology with an Emphasis in Industrial and Organizational Psychology.

Currently residing in San Diego, he plans to further his education and maintains a desire to provide leadership guidance to strengthen our armed forces. He can be reached through social media and his website:

combatpsych.com

Manufactured by Amazon.ca
Bolton, ON

34118470R00208